PRAISE FOR M. WILLIAM PHELPS

Sleep in Heavenly Peace

"An exceptional book by an exceptional true-crime writer. Page by page, Phelps skillfully probes the disturbed mind of a mother guilty of the ultimate betrayal."

—Kathryn Casey, author of *She Wanted It All*

Every Move You Make

"An insightful and fast-paced examination of the inner workings of a good cop and his bad informant culminating in an unforgettable truth-is-stranger-than-fiction-climax."

—Michael M. Baden, M.D., Host of HBO's *Autopsy*

"M. William Phelps is the rising star of the nonfiction crime genre, and his true tales of murderers and mayhem are scary-as-hell thrill rides into the dark heart of the inhuman condition."

—Douglas Clegg, author of *Nightmare House*

Lethal Guardian

"An intense roller coaster of a crime story. Phelps's book *Lethal Guardian* is at once complex, with a plethora of twists and turns worthy of any great detective mystery, and yet so well laid-out, so crisply written with such detail to character and place that it reads more like a novel than your standard nonfiction crime book."

—*New York Times* bestselling author Steve Jackson

Perfect Poison

"*Perfect Poison* is a horrific tale of nurse Kristen Gilbert's insatiable desire to kill the most helpless of victims—her own patients. A stunner from beginning to end, Phelps renders the story expertly, with flawless research and an explosive narrative."

—*New York Times* bestselling author Gregg Olsen

"M. William Phelps's *Perfect Poison* is true crime at its best—compelling, gripping, an edge-of-the-seat thriller."

—Harvey Rachlin, author of *The Making of a Cop*

"A compelling account of terror that only comes when the author dedicates himself to unmasking the psychopath with facts, insight and the other proven methods of journalistic leg work."

—Lowell Cauffiel, bestselling author of *House of Secrets*

"A bloodcurdling page-turner and a meticulously researched study of the inner recesses of the mind of a psychopathic narcissist."

—Sam Vaknin, author of *Malignant Self Love, Narcissism Revisited*

Also by M. William Phelps

Perfect Poison
Lethal Guardian
Every Move You Make

SLEEP IN HEAVENLY PEACE

M. WILLIAM PHELPS

PINNACLE BOOKS
KensingtonPublishing Corp.

http://www.kensingtonbooks.com

Some names have been changed to protect the privacy of individuals connected to this story.

PINNACLE BOOKS are published by

Kensington Publishing Corp.
850 Third Avenue
New York, NY 10022

Copyright © 2006 by M. William Phelps

All Kensington Titles, Imprints, and Distributed Lines are available at special quantity discounts for bulk purchases for sales promotions, premiums, fund-raising, and educational or institutional use. Special book excerpts or customized printings can also be created to fit specific needs. For details, write or phone the office of the Kensington special sales manager: Kensington Publishing Corp., 850 Third Avenue, New York, NY 10022, attn: Special Sales Department, Phone: 1-800-221-2647.

Pinnacle and the P logo Reg. U.S. Pat. & TM Off.

First Printing: January 2006

10 9 8 7 6 5 4

Printed in the United States of America

For Regina,
the most wonderful,
caring, and loving
mother God could ever bless
upon a child

AUTHOR'S NOTE

ACCORDING TO THE U.S. Department of Justice, between 1976 and 2002, nine thousand children under the age of five were killed by a parent.

Nine thousand—an incredible number—and it translates into nearly one child per day killed not by a stranger or a pedophile or a random act, but by his or her *parent*.

Taking it one step further, females commit only 13 percent of all violent crimes in this country. Yet, of those nine thousand children killed by a parent, mothers were responsible 50 percent of the time.

Why do so many mothers murder their children? Why is it that a child in this country under the age of five is more likely to be murdered by his or her parent than anyone else? What is it that causes nearly one woman a day in the United States—who has spent nine months carrying a child, bonding with it, nurturing it, feeling it move and kick inside her womb—to kill that same child after it is born?

Susan Smith? Mary Beth Tinning? Andrea Yates? Marilyn Lemak? Dr. Ruth Kuncel, a clinical psychologist, said Lemak "acted like a nurse as she performed what she considered a 'healing process,'" sedating and then smothering her three children: Nicholas, seven, Emily, six, and Thomas, three. These names have become synonymous with mothers who murder their children. My God, Andrea Yates allegedly chased one of her children around the house before drowning him in the bathtub.

Enter into this discussion a woman named Dianne Odell, a fifty-one-year-old Rome, Pennsylvania, mother of eight. Odell is articulate. Intelligent. She speaks like a highly educated woman and presents herself as a caring, loving mother. She's raised eight healthy, living children. Looking at her, you might be inclined to think of a Sunday-school teacher, or a long-lost aunt who pinches your cheek before Christmas dinner and tells you how cute you are. Thus, when you stare into Odell's eyes, you certainly don't see the reflection of a baby killer and multiple murderer.

It is rare that an author has the opportunity to speak with a convicted murderer and interview her for the purpose of writing a book based on those conversations. The only way I would have been able to write this book, I decided early on, as I began to look into the story, was if Dianne Odell agreed to talk to me.

After a letter and a meeting she did.

The reason I wanted to speak to Odell centered around the victims in this story: newborn babies. Victims are often overlooked during trials and in the media coverage of any murder case. I want my readers to get to know the people who have been viciously taken away from their loved ones. The books I write are not, simply, true-crime books; they are nonfiction accounts of people, murder being only one aspect of a much larger dynamic.

When I met Odell at Bedford Hills Correctional Facility for Women in Bedford Hills, New York, during the summer of 2004, one of the first things I said as we sat down was "I am not here to judge you. I am here to tell your story."

Among other things, Odell was accused of carrying around the decomposed and mummified remains of three dead children (in boxes) from state to state for nearly twenty-five years. I was entirely curious as to why a woman—the mother of these children—would do this.

From day one, Odell has maintained her innocence—that someone else murdered her children. I may not have agreed with her or even believed her, but I promised I'd tell her story. "I will stay objective. I will listen to you and try to report what you tell me."

Odell, I think, felt someone was going to give her a chance to speak, which is, she told me, all she has ever wanted. She asked me for money (it happens with every book; inevitably, someone—sometimes two or three people—asks for money in exchange for interviews), not for her, but her "family." In 1977, the New York state legislature passed a law "prohibiting criminals from using their notoriety for profit." Aptly titled the "Son of Sam" law, it provides that a convicted murderer cannot be paid for his or her story. Many try to get around this by asking journalists to "donate" money to their families. It is, I guess, a noble request—in some strange, criminal way—also something I have *never* done and will *never* do. In my view, money poisons information.

As Odell and I spoke, we talked about children, of course, about her youth, parental abuse, spousal abuse, and other dysfunctions plaguing many American families. Oddly enough, as we sat at a table in the prison visiting room and spoke, a very loud and violent thunderstorm rolled in. It got so dark outside—I was there in the afternoon—it felt as if it were the middle of the night. As the lightning and thunder crashed and banged and the rain pelted the tin roof above, the lights flickered on and off.

Within a few minutes, I found myself sitting in a cavern-like dark, cafeteria-style room with about fifty or so female inmates, one guard, and no lights. I couldn't see my hands in front of my face.

For a minute, we sat there in silence and waited for the generator to kick on. That day would become a metaphor for my continued talks with Odell. Over the course of listening to Odell's stories, I realized this book, in many ways, is about blacking out and trying to recall lost memories—memories that I am convinced are shrouded in a veil of evil.

Throughout the past year or so, I have corresponded with Odell through letters and phone calls. I have well over twenty hours of interviews on audiotape. I must say, much of Odell's story cannot be backed up by secondary sources. In certain places, I have tried, without success, to track down people and get a second or third version. In many instances it just couldn't be done. Either the people involved had died, records didn't exist, or those individuals who could back up Odell's claims would not speak to me, for whatever reason.

I decided to open the book with Odell telling her own story. At times, she is quoted in these passages. Other times, however, as the narrative flows without quotations and I tell Odell's story for her (as she told it to me), it is *still* Odell speaking. I have simply taken what she has said and put it into an easy-to-read format. I have added nothing to those passages except background information and regional town and state research. It is all fact—but based on Odell's version of the events.

In addition to Odell's story, I have related the truth as we know it: the Sullivan County, New York, District Attorney's Office version of what happened. To write those passages, I used a multitude of documents, trial transcripts, police reports, medical reports, and dozens of interviews with many of the individuals involved. I've inserted this additional layer of factual information into the narrative to offer you, the reader, the *entire* story as I have uncovered it.

Lastly, any name in the book where *italics* appear on first use represents a pseudonym. For whatever reason, that person wishes to remain anonymous. In some instances, I have decided to change the name to protect the identity of said person.

As when a woman with child in the ninth month bringeth forth her son, with two or three hours of her birth great pains compass her womb, which pains, when the child cometh forth, they slack not a moment.

—II Esdras 16:38 (Apocrypha), the Holy Bible, King James Version

My mother was the most beautiful woman I ever saw. All I am I owe to my mother. I attribute all my success in life to the moral, intellectual and physical education I received from her.

—George Washington

CHAPTER 1

1

IN THE EARLY 1960s, the Molina family lived in a three-story house on Ninety-fifth Avenue in Jamaica, Queens, New York, near Brooklyn, Coney Island, and JFK Airport. Bright lights, big city. Neighborhoods made up of what seemed like a thousand and one different cultures. It was a time in New York when a ride on a graffiti-free subway cost twenty cents and racial riots were part of the fabric of everyday life. Shea Stadium, an iconic structure by its own merit and home to Major League Baseball's New York Mets, was built back then. In 1964, some 51 million people flocked to Flushing Meadows Park to visit the World's Fair, where today the only hint of a fair is the massive steel globe sitting at the base of a wide open green blemished with homeless, drug dealers, crackheads, trash, and abandoned vehicles.

The '60s were a time of great social change in America. Martin Luther King gave his famous "I have a dream" speech in Washington, DC, and was fighting furiously to get blacks registered to vote. Around the same time, well-known Black Muslim leader Malcolm X was assassinated. America, one could say, was at a turning point: two worlds colliding, people fighting for an identity.

None of what was going on in the world mattered much to little eleven-year-old Dianne Molina while living on Ninety-fifth Avenue, however—a house, incidentally, Dianne would later refer to as a "prison." What Dianne focused on, even then, she said later, was survival.

It was near Easter, Dianne remembered. A time of year when it was "still cold enough to wear a jacket." Her father had come home from work drunk. He had been celebrating, she claimed, yet rarely needed a reason to drink.

"I don't ever remember a happy holiday. He always came in drunk and ruined it."

One night, while sitting at the table and eating, Dianne's father, John Molina, a mechanic by trade, said, "If anyone rings the doorbell, you be sure, Dianne, to answer it." He obviously didn't want to be bothered while he was eating. John would laugh, Dianne recalled, a certain grunt whenever he gave her an order. She had learned to fear that laugh and everything else about him. John was born in Santiago, Chile, in 1900. "His eyes were green to silver." He had a temper. According to John, or at least the story Dianne Molina said he would tell the kids, he was "sold into slavery at the age of nine." From there, things just got worse until he moved to America.

There were bedrooms on the first, second, and third floor of the Molina home. Dianne was the youngest. Two of her brothers lived in the home with their wives: one on the second story, the other in the attic. There were problems between Dianne's brothers and father, she said, but she didn't know exactly what had caused such acrimony.

The front door was at the end of a long and narrow

corridor downstairs. At night, her father kept most of the lights turned off in the house. Perhaps there was a flickering television coming out of the living room and lighting up the other rooms, like a strobe light, but other than that the house was always theater dark. Much in line, Dianne insisted, with the secrets it held.

She sat that night, waiting, anticipating. *He wouldn't tell me something unless there was a reason behind it,* she thought. *"If anyone rings the doorbell, you be sure, Dianne, to answer it."* That's what John Molina had told his daughter. And that's what John expected her to do.

Dianne would later hear that sentence over and over again. She had to remember—because disobeying her dad wasn't an option. Yet, what ended up being behind the door that night was a horror, Dianne remembered, she could never have imagined.

2

Fifty-eight-year-old Thomas Bright was born and raised in Safford, Arizona. When he reached the eleventh grade in the early '60s, Bright decided he wanted to serve his country. So he enlisted in the army and became one of Uncle Sam's coveted paratroopers.

"I made thirty-eight jumps," Bright recalled humbly. "I was stationed in Panama."

When he got out of the army, Bright moved to Illinois, where his half brother lived, and found a job in manufacturing.

After bouncing around the country, getting married and divorced, Bright finally settled down where his roots were, in Safford, with his second wife, Molly. To Bright, like a lot of people in Safford, getting up every morning in such a beautiful part of the country was like staring into God's eyes. The mountains. Trees. The land. Pure bliss.

Located in Graham County, which also includes the towns of Thatcher and Pima, a visitor's guide to the region boasts of its "green valleys and open spaces." Indeed, much of the county is made up of desert land, mountains, and talcum-dry terrain. On average, the high temperature is 80.9 degrees, while the low comes in at around forty-seven. Based on a thirty-year average, as little as 1.3 inches of snow, hail, and sleet fall annually.

Not a bad place to live.

For Thomas Bright, living in Safford had always been a solemn, simple way of life: hot weather, long, straight roadways, maybe a stop at a friend's house once in a while to chat it up. Getting on in years, Bright never saw himself at the center of one of the biggest stories ever to encroach upon Safford—a story so bizarre, mothers and fathers, sisters and brothers, PTA members and churchgoers alike, would be talking about it for years to come.

3

Little Dianne Molina's father told her to answer the door if the bell rang. He was eating (and drinking) and didn't want to be disturbed.

When the doorbell finally rang some time later on that night, Dianne jumped up off the couch and began walking toward the corridor. It was dark going down that hallway, she remembered years later. But she knew there was a light switch at the end. All she had to do was make it there and the darkness would disappear with the flick of a switch.

Her father was still sitting at the dining-room table, one room away, eating and drinking, watching her out of the corner of his eye.

At the end of the hallway now, with her left hand on

the doorknob, Dianne reached with her free hand and turned on the light.

No sooner had the hallway lit up when Dianne saw a man waiting on the doorstep. He was tall. Heavyset. An adult for sure. She couldn't tell who he was because he had a black stocking over his head covering his face.

Looking at him, Dianne screamed . . . then she ran.

"He chased me down the hall," she recalled, "and I turned a corner to hide and he followed me. Then he backed me into a corner of the room."

Like a boxer caught between the ropes, she had nowhere to go.

"Do you want to live, little girl?" she claimed the man said, staring at her through the mesh of the black stocking covering his face.

Then he took a switchblade knife out of his pocket and snapped it open. As soon as she saw the stainless steel of the blade glaring in the light, Dianne held her hands over her face and once again started to scream as loud as she could.

As he twisted the blade in front of her face . . . "Daddy?"

No answer.

"Daddy?"

Nothing.

As far as she could tell, John was still sitting at the dining-room table.

She was sure he could hear her.

4

One of Thomas Bright's favorite after-work and weekend activities was sitting on his front porch, or walking the lot near the Thunderbird Mobile Home Park, where he lived, watching the birds. It was meditative for Bright to sit and gawk at what amounted to over three hundred species of birds inhabiting Graham County and much of Arizona. With the Mexican border one hundred miles south, "many migratory birds from Central and South America," the Graham County Chamber of Commerce says, swoop into the region and offer residents like Bright a wide spectrum of species to observe.

With his binoculars, Bright would sit for hours waiting, watching.

A cement- and dump-truck-driver, Bright was living happily during May 2003 at the Thunderbird Mobile Home Park, going to work every day and returning home to spend time with his wife and watch the birds—this calming ebb and flow of life seemed to fit Bright well at this stage in his life. He had quit drinking alcohol some time ago because, he said, "it's done taught me a lesson after I got busted a second time." He added, "Safford itself is made up of about [thirty-five thousand] people. Compared to towns back east, it's not very big."

Bright speaks with a patent Western drawl. His voice is low-pitched, relaxed, composed. He wears a tightly cropped beard, neatly trimmed. The directness he exudes is admirable. Thomas Bright doesn't mince words. He tells it like it is and, for the most part, speaks confidently.

Molly, Bright's wife, had suggested he go to an auction that a local self-storage facility was having.

"Molly's boy got in trouble . . . and he lived in the same trailer park we are," Bright recalled. "We helped him get a trailer and he was livin' down on a lot in the same park."

That trailer, Bright said, needed to be furnished. Around the same time, Smith Storage, a self-storage facility near the center of town, had announced it was going to auction off the contents of about fifty units whose renters had been delinquent on payments.

Some people had rented units, stocked them with personal items, but for whatever reason failed to keep current on payments. Part of the contract renters signed read that should the bill not be paid, the contents would become the storage-facility owner's property. Auctions were held at various times to make restitution for delinquent payments. Collectors, mostly, flocked to the auctions with the hope of buying relics and antiques people had forgotten about.

One man's junk is another man's . . .

Bright had never been to an auction. It just wasn't something he had ever put any thought into, he said, and didn't much interest him.

Early Saturday morning, May 10, 2003, Bright got into his truck and drove to his good friend Tom Summers' house. When he got there, he asked Tom if he was interested in going to Smith Storage to attend the auction with him. It would be fun, Bright said. Two friends hanging around on a beautiful spring Saturday morning.

"Sure," Tom Summers said, "but I don't have any money."

The bidding was supposed to start somewhere around 9:00 A.M. It was pushing 8:45 now.

"Let's get it goin,' then," Bright said. "We runnin' late."

Bright and Summers arrived shortly after nine o'clock, but got lucky; the bidding hadn't started. There were about one hundred people anxiously waiting, scurrying around the site, Bright remembered. There were about one hundred units, many of which were small, five feet by eight feet. Bright was hoping to purchase some items for his stepson's trailer and maybe—just maybe—hit a cache of collectibles or antiques for himself.

The first thing Bright had to do was find the auctioneer's table and register. By that time, the auctioneer was in the middle of explaining how the bidding was going to work.

As potential bidders walked in front of each unit, sizing up the contents, Bright and Summers speculated about what Bright might end up with at the end of the day. Laughing, Bright said, "Maybe we'll hit a treasure, Tom . . . somethin' somebody dun forgotten about."

Tom Summers shrugged his shoulders and laughed. "Yeah, sure!" he said in jest.

As the bidding go under way, Bright was outbid on a unit he'd decided earlier might be worth his money. He had noticed a bed, refrigerator, and some other items that could potentially help out his stepson. With Bright, most of what he did in life centered on other people. Sure, he might end up with an old lamp or box of baseball cards worth a few bucks, but his main objective was to help out his stepson.

Being outbid wasn't the end of the world. There were plenty of units available. When the auctioneer got to unit number six, Bright recalled, "That unit looked like there had been parts of a bed in it."

An old friend of Bright's, who also happened to be at the auction, apparently had the same idea, because he started bidding against Bright as soon as the unit went up for sale. For a while, the bidding went back and forth. When it got to $75, however, Bright won.

"And there I was," he recalled, a chuckle in his voice, "with a seventy-five-dollar bid. And I really didn't think I wanted it."

Regardless of Bright's ambivalence, it was a purchase, he was about to learn, he would never forget— and a purchase that would have nearly every news organization in Arizona looking to talk to him about.

5

When her father didn't rush into the room to save her from the man with the stocking over his face, holding a switchblade knife in front of her, little Dianne screamed again.

"Daddy . . . ?"

The man was waving the switchblade back and forth, Dianne recalled, like he was going to do something with it. She was terrified.

"I had been raped by my half brother," Dianne claimed later, "when I was six." It was a safe bet the thought of the man in the black stocking violating her had crossed Dianne's mind as she sat crouched into the corner of her living room in a fetal position wondering where the hell her father was.

After Dianne screamed again, the man, who was holding her down now, said, "Looks like you're on your own, little girl."

Dianne started struggling to break free. But she couldn't move; he had placed his hand around her throat. He was laughing.

She recognized that laugh: the voice, its affect and inflections.

She begged, "*Don't, please, don't . . .*"

He let go. Backed away. Stood up. Then took off the stocking and started laughing louder as Dianne sat trying to figure out what was going on.

As the man walked away, Dianne could see her father, who had poked his head around the corner of the opposite room. He had stood there and watched it all. Her father and the man, Dianne said, were now both laughing at her.

When the man turned to show his face, Dianne couldn't believe it was her older half brother. He had since walked over to their father, who then patted his son on the back as if he had just hit a home run.

"Good job, son!"

Years later, after telling the story, Dianne said, "I realized that day I had always been invisible, but after that I would always have to *be* invisible . . . or I'd be dead."

She cried herself to sleep that night, and every night she had to spend in the Molina house afterward. *Maybe tomorrow will be better,* she'd tell herself under covers, as if it were some sort of prayer.

"Little did I know that tomorrow and all the tomorrows after that would never be all right."

Indeed, in the coming weeks, months, and years, Dianne's life at home, according to her, would become a litany of incredible, almost unbelievable episodes of abuse and emotional torture.

6

After the bidding concluded, those who had purchased units at the Smith Storage auction had to pay off their debts and, with locks, secure the units they had purchased. Bright had purchased another unit to go along with number six, but he didn't have any locks. So he ended up driving to his brother's house in town, picking him up, and then heading home to get a few locks.

Within a few hours, Bright was back at home with the contents of the two units he had purchased, scurrying through the boxes to see what he had. Yet, inside the next forty-eight hours, Thomas Bright's simple life of driving a cement truck and bird-watching would take an inconceivable, horrific turn.

CHAPTER 2

1

THOMAS BRIGHT LET the boxes he had purchased at auction sit in his stepson's trailer at Thunderbird Mobile Home Park in Safford for a few days while he decided what to do with everything. There were dozens of boxes. Upon a quick look, Bright didn't see a treasure trove, or cache of antiques, as he might have hoped. What much of it amounted to was nothing but papers and film and old pairs of panties and letters: some unknown person's life packed away in boxes and sold to the highest bidder.

"The unit I took the boxes from," Bright recalled, "was pretty dusty. It turned out, I thought, ain't nobody had been in it for years."

Bright's stepson's trailer had a rather large carport protruding over a good portion of the front of the trailer. Bright figured it was as good a place as any to store half the boxes, while "a dozen or so," he added, "we put in the livin' room" inside the trailer.

On Sunday evening, May 11, Bright returned to the trailer to begin digging through the boxes. Immediately he uncovered a keyboard for what appeared to be an old computer, and hoped to find the hard drive and perhaps even a printer. It wasn't a bag of gold coins, but better than nothing.

After a night of searching, all Bright could come up with was an out-of-date Nintendo game set.

As usual, he went to work Monday morning, May 12, and didn't think twice about the boxes. While talking to a friend, however, the boxes came up.

"If you got anythin' good," Bright's friend said, "I'll buy it from ya."

"All right. I'll go home today and check it out and bring whatever I have with me to work in the mornin.'"

On Monday night, after dinner, Bright and his grandson walked over to the trailer where the boxes were and began searching through them one last time to see if there was anything of value.

"That monitor and that other thang," Bright told his grandson, "is in the livin' room. Why don't you go and look at it. I'll go through some of the boxes on the porch."

"Sounds good."

Bright walked onto the porch and picked a box at random. "It was about two foot by two foot."

Bright could tell the rather nondescript box was old. Inside, he found a few wrinkled, worn, and musty blankets. One was yellow, one red. Surprisingly, underneath the blankets, there was another box. Smaller in size.

Ah . . . , Bright thought. *This must be my treasure.*

He laughed.

Pulling the tiny box out of the larger box, Bright noticed a white plastic bag inside the smaller box.

What the hell is going on here?

"As I opened it," Bright recalled, "I smelled an old musty odor. There was some brown, dried stuff in thar, too."

I hope this ain't what I think it is, Bright thought.

With that, Bright immediately considered the notion that an animal had somehow crawled inside the box and, like a lobster caught in a wire trap, couldn't get out.

"I had already gone through some boxes that had some old groceries in them and some of the cans of food had broken open."

Still, this little white bag, Bright insisted, didn't have the same odor.

"It was more of an earthy, musty smell."

Bright put the bag down for a moment and noticed a second white bag, same size. When he opened it, the smell overtook him. It was stronger. Much more potent.

What the hell?

Looking farther down into the main box, Bright spied a third bag. After opening it and looking inside— there it was again: that same raunchy, earthy odor— Bright realized his simple life was about to change.

2

For Dianne Molina, living at home with her mother and father and brothers became a test of her emotional and physical will, she later said. Since the episode with her brother wielding a knife and threatening her under the orders of her dad, life inside the home became a constant state of fear and submission.

Dianne's mother, born Mabel Myrtle Smith in Brooklyn, 1915, was a peanut of a woman at four feet eleven inches. Mabel had wavy, curly gray-and-black hair, frayed at the ends like rope. Her nose was stubby, as if someone had pushed it in and it never recovered. Mabel's own birth, she would tell Dianne, had been unusual and strange. According to Mabel, she was born in a funeral parlor. Mabel had been brought into this world where human life normally ended.

Mabel's life with John Molina, after they married in

the '30s and set up a home in Jamaica, Queens, centered around Mabel currying favor and never questioning John's strong-arm tactics with the kids. "My mother," Dianne said later, "no matter what my father did, my mother was right there on his side."

Mabel would wear what Dianne later called "housedresses" and slippers around the home and keep herself rather dumpy and plain-Jane. The only time she'd ever get dressed up, where she "put things around her neck and hung things from her ears," was when she went out on a job interview or over to see her sister.

While Mabel cooked his meals and made sure he had plenty of booze hanging around, John spent his days working on cars.

"He had handshake deals," Dianne said, "with car dealerships in the area. And when they got a car that needed to be repaired, so they could resell it, they called my father and my father fixed it."

Dianne was rail thin as a young girl, she claimed. So skinny, she said, her bones were visible through her skin—rather noticeably, like a concentration camp prisoner. It wasn't that she had been starved, but as a girl heading into her teens she developed tonsillitis that hadn't been taken care of and it made her severely ill, which led to drastic weight loss. Doctors insisted she be hospitalized, but, she said, her parents "refused to let the doctor do anything medical." It wasn't until a neighbor, a year or so after she became ill, gave her "some sort of vitamin" that she started to gain weight and feel better.

Yet, similarly, she said dealing with a medical condition, which was certainly treatable but wasn't being taken care of, was a blessing compared to the abuse her dad was perpetrating against her.

"My life kind of went like that on a weekly basis," Dianne said. "My father would think it was funny to lock me down in the basement and shut off all of the lights and then run around the outside of the house and shake the sides of the house and door to the cellar. He used to laugh at things like that."

Before she had put on any weight, when Dianne was, she liked to say, a "bag of bones," her dad would never hit her. But soon after she began to gain weight, "I guess my father," she added, "felt he could finally start hitting me and not worry about breaking my bones."

It was right around this same time that her dad broke out the cat-o'-nine-tails, a long leather whip consisting of nine knotted fingers generally used by slave masters centuries ago to flog slaves as they worked. When he began to use it on her, she was about eleven or twelve years old, she recalled.

"I remember my mother was giving a party for somebody. There were balloons in the house."

Dianne claimed she climbed up onto her father's bed to reach for the balloons, which were rubbing up on top of the ceiling. Like any child might, she wanted one—and she didn't want to wait until someone told her it was okay.

The impatience of a child. It's part of their purity, part of their penchant for wanting to, quite fearlessly, take in everything life and their environment offers.

As she was jumping up on the bed, trying to reach the tails of the balloons, her dad walked in.

"What the *hell* do you think you're doing?" he shouted.

Dianne turned around quickly.

Just then, John Molina reached into the closet and pulled out his cat-o'-nine-tails and began whipping her back and legs.

When he finished, he said, "If I *ever* catch you doing anything like that again, I'll hit you *again* . . . and this time it'll be harder!"

Looking at her legs, Dianne wondered how much worse it could get.

"I had welts about six inches long. . . . Lucky for me,

I had a shirt on, which kind of stopped the welts from being too bad on my back."

The memory of that day was so deeply etched in Dianne's mind years later, she recalled in vivid detail how her legs looked after the beating. It was summertime, so she'd had shorts on. "My legs looked like an old barber's pole." There were red welts from the fingers of the cat-o'-nine-tails in circles—elongated like a candy cane—surrounding her legs.

Later, many would question whether Dianne was telling the truth. Was that beating and all the others, including a knife-wielding brother with a stocking over his head, mere figments of an active, clouded imagination? Were these events the product of hindsight?

Some would say yes. The real Dianne Molina was manipulative, callous, cruel, and selfish. According to others, above all else, a pathological liar who made up stories to support her own agenda.

3

Unraveling the third white bag, Thomas Bright took one look inside and knew exactly what it was that had caused such a foul odor.

"There was a third bag in thar," Bright recalled, "and I opened it up and I could see the side of a skull . . . a little *baby* skull."

When he saw the skull, Bright said, he knew what it was.

Oh Christ, he thought.

The skull was in bad shape. It looked like an artifact that an a archaeologist conducting a dig somewhere in the Middle East might uncover.

After Bright pulled the bag open a bit more, he confirmed his worst fear: staring back at him were tiny eye sockets and the deteriorated nose of what he believed was a baby. Yet, for a brief instant, it was a surreal moment, so far removed from Bright's perception of reality he thought he might be looking at a child's toy, an old doll or something.

"Hey," he yelled into the room where his grandson was, "call the sheriff's department. Tell 'em to send a deputy out."

4

"When he was drunk," Dianne later said of her father's rage, "it was a thousand times worse."

Oddly enough, John Molina never hit his wife, though.

"Something occurred at some point during their relationship that, I think, led my father to believe that if he hit my mother, she would probably kill him."

In February 1969, five months before Americans would sit glued in front of their television sets and watch the landing of *Apollo 11* on the moon, Dianne Molina, at fifteen, had thought she'd seen it all in her Jamaica, Queens, home. But the horrors she said she had endured up until that point were merely stepping-stones.

One day, "My brother came to the house to see my father, who was already partially drunk," Dianne recalled, "and sitting at the dining-room table."

From there, she said, Jim walked in and asked her father how he was doing. Jim and John Molina had been at odds for years. From what, exactly, Dianne couldn't remember.

"You can forget about the fucking car," John told his son, "you're not getting the fucking car!"

For no reason, John then picked up a drinking glass and cracked it over Jim's head, shattering the glass and breaking Jim's glasses. Jim ended up with a gash on his forehead and nose and started bleeding profusely from the top of his head down.

Dianne, standing in the room speechless, didn't know what to do.

Mabel jumped up from the chair she was sitting in and "threw my father off the chair he was sitting in," and then rushed to Jim's aid.

"Get the fuck out of my house!" John Molina screamed.

"Come on," Jim said, "let's go!"

Jim, Mabel, and Dianne piled into Jim's car and left the house.

Pulling out of the driveway, Dianne said she had a moment of contentment. She thought it was going to be the last time she ever saw her father again.

5

After calling the Graham County Sheriff's Office (GCSO), Thomas Bright's grandson walked over to where Bright was standing near the box.

"Did you really find a baby?"

"Take a look for yourself," Bright said, pointing to the bag.

Staring down into the bag, which was now ripped open even wider, Bright's grandson responded, "Yup, that's a baby all right. Jesus."

In the meantime, a call went out to all the available sheriff's deputies in the area. The first deputy to respond, Abner Upshaw, showed up at 4:30 P.M. Minutes later, Mark Smith, a second deputy, arrived.

Upshaw approached Bright immediately. "'Sometimes,'" Bright recalled Upshaw saying, "'people report things they *think* they see.'"

It was a sober calculation by an experienced cop. Upshaw undoubtedly had been called out numerous times for all sorts of crimes that had never materialized. What Bright and his grandson saw as a baby could—in reality—turn out to be nothing more than a dead animal or some sort of old, weathered doll, as Bright had thought.

Bright shrugged after Upshaw explained the situation. Then, "Go ahead . . . see for yourself then."

Back a few moments later, after looking inside the bag, Upshaw looked at Bright and said, "Yup, that looks like a baby all right."

Confident it was a baby, Upshaw put in a call to have a detective and the county coroner come out.

While they waited, Bright told Upshaw what had happened the past few days: the auction, the boxes, the baby.

At about 4:35 P.M., Bright handed Upshaw a large brown envelope that contained several documents. "I found this in another box."

There was a name on the envelope: Dianne Odell, a forty-nine-year-old female from Pima, Arizona. The document was dated 2002. Bright's earlier estimation that the unit hadn't been accessed in eight years had been wrong. Someone had apparently been inside the unit within the past year.

"This is helpful," Upshaw said. "Thanks."

As Bright, his grandson, and the two deputies stood in the mobile home staring at all the boxes, waiting for the coroner and a detective to arrive and begin an investigation, they had no idea that the one baby Bright had found was only the beginning. By the end of the evening, there would be more.

6

Dianne Molina was almost sixteen years old when she and her mother left their home in February 1969 after a bloody fight between her half brother and father. For Dianne, it felt as if the gods had answered her prayers: no more abuse from dad, no more drunkenness, no more living under the reign of a dictator.

Nothing in Dianne's early life, however, had been that cut-and-dry. There was always a price to pay. And, according to her later on, moving out of her childhood home would turn out to be no different.

"We went straight to my [half] brother's house in . . . Ozone Park," Dianne said. Ozone Park was only a few miles from Jamaica. "We stayed there for three days," she added. "My brother's wife was not happy with the fact that we were there and wanted us to leave."

When Mabel didn't respond to her daughter-in-law's request to leave, Dianne said her sister-in-law "concocted a story where she went to the landlord and he claimed we couldn't stay there."

If there was one positive aspect regarding Mabel Molina's character, it was the self-reliance she sometimes harbored. No one was going to carry her; no one was going tell her what to do or when to do it. As soon as Mabel got word that she wasn't wanted in her son's home, Dianne said, "she picked herself up and left."

Outside the home, bags in hand, Dianne was excited. She was going to live on her own with her mom. Just the two of them. No brothers. No dad.

"Here's some money for a cab," Mabel said to Dianne, handing her some spare change, "you're going back to your father's house."

Dianne was horrified.

"From that point on," she said later, "I was in prison."

Not only was she confined, but Dianne had no idea where her mother, at the time her only source of strength, had moved. Because for the next week, while living at her dad's, she never heard from her.

"It wasn't until about a week later that she showed up at my school and told me she had found us a place." Still, that "place" didn't yet include Dianne.

"I am going to find out if you can come stay with me," Mabel told Dianne.

Dianne started crying. "I can't stay there," she said, meaning her father's house. "I am scared to death."

"Don't you worry about it. Your father's not going to let anything happen to you," Mabel said.

"You *know* that's a lie!"

Mabel ignored Dianne's apparent worry.

"I'll keep looking for a place for the two of us. You go to school and make sure everything is nice and normal, and everything will be fine."

Because John Molina didn't want his only daughter to be out of his sight, Dianne claimed, he made Dianne's half brothers escort her to and from school. When Dianne returned from school for the day, she said, "that's as far as I went. I was put in my room, period."

For the next few months, Dianne lived under a strict routine of going to school in the morning, arriving home in the afternoon, and, like the prisoner she later saw herself as, was sent to her room for the remainder of the day and night.

One day, Dianne was in her room staring outside across the street at a neighbor's house. Sitting on her bed, crying, she watched her mother, she said, walk into the neighbor's house. With that, she ran down the stairs, where John was waiting for her.

"Can I go see Mom? She's across the street."

"No!" And that was all John Molina had to say. Dianne knew not to press him. It would do no good.

Broken, Dianne headed back upstairs. She felt her mother wanted to tell her something important.

"I knew that if I had tried to sneak across the street," Dianne said later in a tearful recollection, "when I got back, I would be picking my teeth up off the floor."

Dianne needed desperately to get away from her father's grasp. Furthermore, the reasons, she later claimed, were dark secrets between her and her father that Mabel knew about, yet did nothing to prevent.

"My dad," Dianne said, "was raping me. . . . It had started when I was fourteen."

CHAPTER 3

1

TO FORTY-SEVEN-YEAR-OLD GRAHAM County Sheriff's Office sergeant detective Dolores Diane Thomas, a mother of two, grandmother of seven, the thought of a dead baby left in a box to rot made her sick to her stomach.

"It was a human baby," Thomas said later, "I wondered what had happened to it."

Thomas had been employed by the GCSO for the past thirteen years, the past six working in the investigation division of the department, three of those as a sergeant. Primarily, Thomas's job consisted of "any type of follow-up on any case that the patrol deputy first on scene would determine required follow-up."

The GCSO employed some twenty-five sworn personnel and approximately fifty-five civilian officers. Thomas had fallen into the position of working for the investigation arm of the GCSO. Born and raised in Safford, she said later, she's "one hundred [percent] Hispanic . . . and probably related to half the valley." Her law enforcement career began in the Department of Corrections. She had worked for ten years as a records clerk, was promoted, and became the administrative secretary to the deputy warden, spending the better part of eight years on the job.

"When I turned thirty," Thomas recalled, "I thought, 'What the hell am I doing here? I don't want to do this all my life.'"

Thomas originally thought being a prison guard might help curb an urge she had for change, but realized quickly after taking the job that she "definitely didn't want to do that."

There had been an opening at the GCSO for a dispatcher in February 1990, so Thomas applied and, subsequently, got the job. Working dispatch offered Thomas a taste of life as a cop. She was the first one to take calls, listen in on what was transpiring out in the field, and would go on rides from time to time with cops to further her skills as a dispatcher. Knowing the layout of the towns helped her dispatch with "hands-on" experience, but that approach only lit the fire. Soon after, she developed a calling for law enforcement work that could only be satisfied one way.

Happily married for a second time—"[My second husband is] the most wonderful man to myself and my children any woman could ask for"—Thomas saw an opportunity when a job was posted for a sheriff. With no formal law enforcement experience, she assumed she'd fill out the application and never hear about it.

Nevertheless, after applying on a Monday and taking the written test on Tuesday, only a year or so into her career as a dispatcher, Thomas got the call later that afternoon. If she wanted the sheriff's job, she'd have to report to the academy the following Monday to live and train for thirteen weeks.

"I had four or five days to get everything I needed together . . . then I spent the next thirteen weeks getting screamed and yelled at and running my little tail off."

Among the many mental and physical challenges that

potential cops had to face at the academy, Thomas learned criminal and traffic law. Thirteen weeks later, though, she was let loose as a deputy sheriff—ready to take on any type of situation filling up a cop's day: from the clichéd cat-in-a-tree to a sniper picking off innocent people from atop a building, to investigating reports of sexual abuse against children, and everything in between. The outstanding criminal profile of Safford then (and even today) consisted of methamphetamine labs and sex crimes. Thomas viewed the job as a springboard to helping make the community a stronger, safer place. Safford was Thomas's home. She wanted to do her part to make it the best it could be.

Not two months into her new job, she got a taste of what the reality of police work was going to be like. She had been on her own one afternoon. The sheriff was out of town and her supervisor was patrolling Graham Mountain, a four-hour swing of time from start to finish.

While patrolling the city, Thomas received a rather odd call from dispatch. The mail lady had opened a mailbox and found a handwritten letter: "*Call the sheriff's office, I have just killed myself.*"

"As I'm driving out there to get the letter," Thomas recalled, "I was thinking about what I had been taught at the academy. They told us to think about what you're going to do when you arrive at a crime scene."

She was worried the guy might be holed up inside his home with a weapon, threatening to do himself in, and if anyone tried to stop him, he might use the weapon to hurt somebody.

When she pulled up, the place appeared quiet, uninhabited.

"I had my weapon drawn when I got out and began approaching the house," Thomas continued. "I got to the back of the home and . . . peeking around the corner, saw this gentleman laying on the front steps of a travel trailer he was using as his home while the main house was being built."

Pointing her weapon at the guy, Thomas called out.

No answer.

She could see a shotgun near his leg.

Again, "You okay, sir? Can you hear me?"

Silence.

"Slowly, as I made my way up to him, I could see he was deceased," Thomas said. There was blood everywhere. He had, in whatever turmoil he faced in life, chosen to end it, like thousands of others, with one blast to the head.

As Thomas stood and stared at the guy, she wondered, *Was this actually a suicide?* She had been taught to think that any scene could be a potential crime scene. Thus far, all indications pointed to suicide, but there was no guarantee. Was there someone else inside the home waiting to ambush her? Was there a spouse or someone else in need of medical assistance?

"What do I do?" Thomas questioned later. "This is my first call by myself. So, after checking his pulse to make sure he was dead, I backed away and made the appropriate calls to get everyone to the scene."

Detectives eventually found out the guy had been in a terrible financial jam and had, indeed, taken his own life. But the day—six or seven hours of which Thomas spent at the crime scene drawing maps, taking notes, going through the man's house, interviewing people—taught her several important lessons she would carry with her.

"I learned that you have to be so detailed," regardless of the situation.

It didn't matter that the guy had committed suicide; what mattered was that she shouldn't assume anything. Dig for facts and truths until all questions were answered. That one death, so seemingly inconsequential years later as Thomas was chosen to work in the investigation arm of the GCSO, told her that the truth was in the details and specifics, not in what a cop might "think" happened.

In 1995, Thomas began working in the children's sexual-crimes division of the GCSO. She was perfect for the job. Female, a mother and grandmother, she could talk to kids and get them to reveal secrets, a vital part of investigating crimes against children.

All of the skills she had learned throughout the years, Thomas found out as she began looking through Thomas Bright's trailer on May 12, 2003, were about to be put to the test.

2

Kew Gardens, New York, in Queens County, a tiny neighborhood a few miles from Jamaica, is known by some as the "Urban Village in the Big City." Today, the main thoroughfare running through downtown is called Metropolitan Avenue. It is a busy street, in a bustling section of town. In the early 1900s, that same busy street, however, then known as Williamsburg and Jamaica Turnpike, was but a dirt road dotted with massive colonials and large weeping willows. If one were to walk in the shoes of his forefathers during that era, Metropolitan Avenue would have looked like a backwoods street somewhere in South Carolina, with steep driveways and fenced-in yards. Rustic, seeping with nostalgia.

The apartment complex on Metropolitan Avenue that Dianne Molina moved into with her mother was typical for the region. It wasn't the Trump Tower, yet it wasn't skid row, either. Located above a retail carpet store, a second-story unit with access from the street, the apartment had a dining room, two bedrooms, kitchen, and pantry.

The infrastructure of the region enjoyed a building boom during the late '60s: multistory tenement buildings and large office complexes went up, while vendors of all kinds dotted the streets. For Dianne, as the world around her changed, it felt like she had been submerged in water while living with her dad and had now been allowed to breathe. Dad was a few miles away. But to Dianne, beginning a new life with Mom, free from the chains of Dad's abuse, Kew Gardens might as well have been on the other side of the world.

While children around her lived normal lives— going out on dates, having slumber parties, and just girls being girls—Dianne worked day and night to survive, she later said. She hadn't been with a boy yet, she said, only because it would have never been allowed, by her mom or dad.

"I couldn't even be involved in life," Dianne recalled, "better yet, *boys*."

What shocked Dianne most, she said, was that the world she believed she was heading into—a somewhat "normal" life with her mom—suddenly turned into something she never thought possible. For the past two years she had been sexually abused by her father, she claimed, anytime he felt like it. Mabel knew about the abuse, but did nothing to stop it, or even discourage it. Moving out with her mom, Dianne had every reason to believe the abuse was over. Yet, even after she moved away, her dad was allowed to come over and visit, where he would, she added, continue the abuse.

If the sexual abuse wasn't bad enough, what Mabel was about to make Dianne participate in within the next few months would prove to Dianne she was, indeed, invisible, as she had always believed—that her life, in the eyes of those who were supposed to care for and protect her, meant nothing.

3

One of the first things Detective Thomas did after walking into the trailer where Thomas Bright had found
the white bag containing the dead baby was have a photographer take several photographs of it. Everything
had to be documented: police reports, photographs,
interviews. It would be a long night for Thomas and
other members of the GCSO. As far as they could
tell, there was a baby killer on the loose. Whatever
needed to be done would get done.

To everyone on scene, after carefully studying the
skull of the baby, it appeared to have a hole in the top
of its skull, which could mean many things, one of
which included homicide, murder. Perhaps someone had shot the child and stuffed it into the bag to
cover up the murder?

By 6:31 P.M., Thomas had taken the baby out of the
bag and placed it into a "new, clear" plastic evidence
bag. After that, she started to remove the rest of the
contents of the box, laying them carefully out on the
floor next to her. Blankets. A sheet. Some personal
papers. Nothing really.

But then . . . a second plastic garbage bag.

On top of the box, Thomas noticed, someone had
written "Mommy's stuff" with a red marker. Then, as
she continued digging farther into the box, she came
upon a green-and-orange blanket. The outside of the
blanket appeared to be stained with a substance that
looked like old maroon-colored paint, brittle and flaky.

Looking at it closer, however, Thomas realized it was
old blood.

One little baby bled this much?

Removing the orange-and-green blanket, which
was rolled up like a sleeping bag, it occurred to
Thomas it was a bit heavier than it perhaps should be.

So she unraveled it to see if there was something inside.

Packed in the blanket was a second baby. In far better shape than the first baby, it had either not been in the box as long as the first baby, or had weathered the elements better for some reason no one could immediately explain.

Next, Thomas took the baby out of the blanket and placed it on the floor next to her so the deputy could photograph it. Then she placed it in an evidence bag and continued looking through the boxes.

Could there be another dead child somewhere?

4

August 7, 1969, should have been a night Dianne Molina remembered with happiness for the rest of her life. It appeared as though life was beginning to calm down and take shape. She had lived under oppression for her entire childhood. But this night—her "sweet sixteen" birthday—was a night no one could take away from her and ruin.

For Dianne, however, there would be no candles, no balloons, no birthday cakes, to celebrate what should have been a turning point in her life. There would be no surprise gifts or choruses of "Happy Birthday." Instead, her mother had a bizarre request.

Holding a piece of paper in her hand, Mabel looked at Dianne and said, "You have to go there and do what that man says."

Dianne was confused at first. She took the piece of paper and stared at it. There in front of her was the name of a man she had never seen before or recognized, and an address, just a few miles away, she had never been to.

"What . . . what is this?" Dianne asked. "I had a

funny feeling in my stomach," she recalled later. "Something was wrong."

"You will go and you will do what he says to do," Mabel stated firmly.

"I don't want to go. Please don't make me go."

"Well," Mabel said, turning, walking away casually, "if you don't go . . . I will send you back to your father's!"

"You know I can't go back there."

"Well, then, you'll do what I say."

Scared to death, Dianne left the house and walked to the address.

"What else could I do?" she said later, tearfully recalling that first night her mother "sold [her] into prostitution." She added, "I am thinking, 'How can I find a way to live with what is going to happen to me?' I am trying to figure out a way for me to get away from the both of them."

Dianne soon found out the man she went to service wasn't some drug pusher Mabel was paying off, as she might have assumed; he was a wealthy businessman "and old. . . . He wasn't young."

This one night turned into, according to Dianne, two to three times per week. She would sneak around at all hours of the night, going to strangers' houses and starring in whatever sick and twisted sexual fantasies the men had dreamed up. Soon she became numb to it all, she said, and after a while, it wasn't the abuse that bothered her most. It was the fear of being discovered by classmates.

"I was hiding . . . underneath jackets, wearing hats, sunglasses. . . . I'm doing everything I can do to hide. I began wearing outlandish makeup . . . just outlandish."

Over the course of the next few months, Dianne tried to stay in school, but her grades, as one might suspect, began to descend rapidly. She went from a B+ student to an F student, struggling to juggle schoolwork with the horror of being her mother's whore.

5

Finding a second baby led Detective Thomas and other investigators working the case to believe that, perhaps, there were more. Thus, a massive search got under way inside the trailer to see if Thomas's instincts were correct.

Within twenty minutes, the medical examiner, who was looking through some items in a box inside the kitchen area, yelled for Thomas.

"Another one?"

"Yes," the doctor said. There, before both of them, was a third baby, neatly wrapped and packaged in a garbage bag inside another box.

After photographs were taken of the baby, the doctor made an early determination that all three babies were, possibly, newborns. It was the way they had been wrapped. The babies, he believed, if they had been born alive, hadn't lived long.

Standing, staring at the three dead babies, Thomas could only come to one conclusion: how many more?

CHAPTER 4

1

ONE OF THE questions Dianne Molina asked herself, as she became entrenched in a world of prostitution that her mother facilitated, was why? What was it that drove Mabel to sell her only daughter's soul? If what Dianne later said was true, it was an act of evil no child could be expected to endure, a dark and sinister world of not knowing what was going to happen on any given night. Crime statistics have proven that men who sexually violate children are capable of just about any animalistic act imaginable. Dianne would leave her apartment, and wonder if she would ever return.

As the weeks and months wore on, and Dianne found herself sleeping with men of all types, a phone call she received one day began to explain things.

"I was the only one in the house," Dianne recalled. "The gentleman on the phone requested my mother."

"She's not home from work yet," Dianne told the man.

"Well, you tell your mother that if she doesn't pay me my money, I'm going to take care of her."

"All right."

Dianne said she immediately called Mabel at work, who had recently been hired as a housekeeper at a nearby hospital, working days.

"Don't worry about it," Mabel said. "It's nothing."

Dianne let it go. What else could she do? If Mabel told her to forget about something, she had better listen.

Two weeks went by. Dianne got out of school one afternoon and went straight home, as she normally did. On an average day, she would get home an hour or so before Mabel. It was, she recalled, the only time of the day or night when she could sit and be a kid.

No worries.

No wondering.

Just peaceful silence.

Minutes after she walked up the long stairwell into her apartment and put her books on the dining-room table, she heard the doorbell. "When I opened the door, there was a big man there. I mean, this guy was huge. . . ."

"Where is your mother?" the man asked.

"She's not here. Can I take a message?"

"Yes," the man said. Then, without another word, he "proceeded to put his large hands around my neck," Dianne recalled, "pushing me up against the wall."

"You tell your mother she has two weeks to come up with the money," he said, "or I am going to come back to take care of everybody."

One would have to speculate that Mabel was involved in either drugs or gambling. The woman worked a full-time job, yet was borrowing money from a shylock? Dianne said she worked for her mother two to three times per week, and although she never knew what her mother charged for her services, she had to believe it wasn't free. So, where was all the money going?

"For six weeks," Dianne said, "after that incident

occurred, everywhere I went I was looking over my shoulder."

As Dianne later thought about the phone call and episode with the large man, she realized what had perhaps "spurred my mother to put me to work. When she first put me to work, I thought it was just going to be long enough to pay off this debt to this person who had showed up at our door. I figured a month or so, maybe a little more."

But it continued. As the spring of 1970 came and went, Dianne was still being sent out to perform all sorts of sexual acts for money.

"Something had gone terribly wrong in what [my mother] was doing," Dianne recalled, "and there came a point in time when she called on my brother because, she told him, we had no food."

The call didn't make sense, however, to Dianne. Because although her mother had abused her emotionally and made her turn tricks, she never starved her.

One thing she noticed during the early part of 1970 was that her mom had begun to carry around a white envelope containing all of her money. Generally, Dianne said, there was always $400 or $500 inside it.

"Rather than give her money—none of my family members would ever give her money. But rather than give her money, when she asked my brother for food that day, my brother's wife went out and bought groceries for us."

Mabel was in her fifties when she left Dianne's father, rented her own apartment, and put Dianne to work. As soon as they moved out, Dianne claimed, Mabel had gotten herself mixed up in all sorts of things no one knew about.

"She would bring drugs home from the hospital and I don't know what she did with them."

As secretive a life as she led, Mabel was now begging one of her sons for food because she claimed she had no money. That envelope, Dianne remembered, with $400 or more in it, was full one day and empty the next.

After Dianne's brother brought the groceries over and left, Dianne went to Mabel and asked her why she lied. "You have money. I saw it in the envelope."

Without a word, Mabel pulled her hand back and slapped Dianne across the face. "What I do," she said through clenched teeth, "is *none* of your business! You do what you're told and take care of *your* end of things. You got that?"

Dianne shook her head in agreement. But she couldn't let it go.

"If you've paid this man off and you have extra money," she said as Mabel started walking away, "why did you lie and say you had no money for food, when I know you had four hundred dollars? I watched you count it. I don't know what you're charging for my services, but you're making money. Plus, you have your paycheck."

Dianne was tired of being a whipping post. She wanted answers.

"Well, I have to . . . I have to . . . do something."

"That was as far as I would ever get with her," Dianne recalled. "She always had *something* on her mind, *something* that she wanted to do, or she was thinking about *something*. It was always 'something, something, something' with her. She never would clarify what 'something' meant."

As Dianne stood in front of her mother that day questioning her about how much money they were making and where it was all going, Mabel, perhaps sick and tired of having to answer to a child, laid out her plans for the next few months.

"Well," she said, "you're going to have to continue to work because I'm broke now."

"Please don't make me do this anymore," Dianne said, crying, begging. "Please, Mother. Please . . ."

2

By the time the GCSO finished searching all of the boxes Thomas Bright had purchased, they had uncovered three dead babies, their remains carefully packaged and stored in bags and boxes for what appeared to be years, maybe even decades. During her investigation, Thomas had found out, from just looking at some of the paperwork inside the boxes, that a woman by the name of Dianne Odell was connected to the babies. The boxes were Odell's. There was no doubt about it. Odell's various addresses and phone numbers and Social Security number and other personal information were scattered all over paperwork found inside some of the boxes.

For the purpose of the investigation, Thomas gave the babies names: Baby Number One, Baby Number Two, Baby Number Three. It was, in the end, the only way to keep track of each one and begin trying to figure out what had happened and who they were.

From inside the trailer, the babies were repackaged in evidence bags and driven to the Pima County Medical Examiner's Office in Tucson, where they would undergo a meticulous forensic examination. It was late in the evening on May 12. Although anxious, Thomas would have to wait until at least the following afternoon—maybe even longer—before she could retrieve any type of information from the medical examiner regarding how the babies had died.

The following day, May 13, while Thomas waited for forensic results, she began to track down Dianne Odell so she could maybe get some answers as to what had happened. From the looks of things, there could be no sane explanation why someone would wrap three babies in garbage bags, wrap those bags in blankets, stuff them into several different boxes, and store them away like old family heirlooms. For Thomas, there had to be some sort of sinister, criminal act that had taken place. Even if the babies were stillborn, why would they be discarded so secretly and hidden?

Thomas got word early that afternoon from the medical examiner's office that the babies had been, in the medical examiner's early opinion, born full-term. This was significant. A back-alley abortion could be ruled out. If the babies had been born full-term, there was a good chance they were born alive, which meant they had somehow died *after* birth. The cause of death wouldn't be determined, Thomas was told, for another day or so.

Thomas was assigned as case agent. Graham County had developed a task force made up of several different officers from different agencies whose main focus was breaking cases. It would not be such a stretch to think this case in particular had hit every officer hard. Many, of course, had kids of their own. To think that a mother—or father—could discard babies like garbage fed an already burning desire among the cops to find out exactly what had happened.

As case agent, Thomas coordinated officers and handed out assignments in hope of locating Dianne Odell, who, as far as anyone could tell, was the one person who could provide the most answers at this point.

The first item of business was to conduct a computer search for Odell and find out her last place of residence. With just a few keystrokes, an officer came back to Thomas and reported Odell's last-known address as Rome, Pennsylvania.

Address in hand, Thomas contacted the Pennsylvania State Police (PSP) and had a trooper from the Towanda barracks, near Rome, conduct a more thorough search for a recent residence.

"From there," Thomas said later, "it was determined

another officer and myself would travel to Pennsylvania to try and find Miss Odell and interview her."

After speaking to the owner of the self-storage unit where the boxes had been purchased, Thomas determined that Odell had rented the units in question back in 1991, but throughout the years, she must have had some trouble keeping up with payments. In fact, she hadn't paid her bill since June 1994, nearly ten years ago, and hadn't been inside the unit since.

During a meeting of investigators and detectives, Bruce Weddle, a seasoned detective with the Arizona Department of Public Safety, was chosen to fly to Pennsylvania with Thomas to interview Odell. At six feet two inches, 175 pounds, the red-haired Weddle had been an Arizona state trooper, working the interstate, for eighteen years. For the past ten, he had been a detective, working mostly narcotics, where much of his time had been spent busting up large methamphetamine labs.

Weddle, who had just turned fifty, grew up in southeastern Arizona and had lived in the region all his life. From an early age, he said, the idea of becoming a cop interested him.

"My dad was in law enforcement, and from that I guess I got bit by the bug early on and realized that's what I wanted to do."

Leaving college, Weddle worked construction for a time and then went to work for a Pepsi-Cola bottling plant in the area. After a time with Pepsi, it only seemed natural for Weddle to then apply to the Arizona Department of Public Safety Police Academy, where he was quickly accepted.

For a number of reasons, Weddle and Thomas decided to take the earliest flight out of Arizona. Number one, Thomas recalled, "was to avoid the media."

Every major television station in Arizona wanted an interview with Thomas and other members of the GCSO. Reporters were calling the GCSO from all over the country. Thomas had fed them as little information as she could. CNN called. The Associated Press had run a story, as had many local newspapers. Everyone involved agreed the story was going to find legs. The quicker Thomas and Weddle got out of town and began uncovering facts, the better off everyone would be. There even had been a memorial set up at the self-storage unit. In the same fashion teenagers might leave flowers and candles and stuffed animals near a telephone pole after a peer had been killed in an automobile accident, people were leaving all sorts of mementos in front of the doors of unit number six. With that kind of emotion floating around, the GCSO knew the local media could really push the story into national status.

On Friday, May 16, 2003, Thomas found out she and Weddle could book a flight that night. All they had to do was steer clear of the media until then.

By Saturday morning, May 17, after an all-night flight, Weddle and Thomas touched down safely in Waverly, New York, and immediately drove to Towanda, Pennsylvania, where Trooper Robert McKee, a ten-year veteran of the force, was waiting to greet them.

As one might suspect, Thomas and Weddle were exhausted from their red-eye flight out of Arizona. Neither had slept much on the plane. Before they could focus on how to approach Dianne Odell, they needed rest.

Hours later, after a brief respite at the hotel, they met with McKee for lunch. McKee informed them how he had found out that Odell had been working at a local Rite Aid near Rome, but he couldn't confirm exactly which store. He did find out that Odell had been living with her paramour, Robert Sauerstein, for many years, a name also found on several pieces of documentation in storage unit number six.

Further, McKee explained, Odell was the mother of eight children. If those babies in the boxes were hers, that would make her the mother of eleven. She was nearly fifty years old, her youngest child just four. The woman had been pregnant just about every other year for the past twenty years. Some of her children had children, which made her a grandmother. Was it possible, Thomas and Weddle wondered as they listened to McKee, that the babies were born to one of her daughters?

After lunch, as Thomas, Weddle, and McKee worked their way toward the Towanda barracks to set up some type of mini task force, they passed a local pharmacy.

"Let's check it out," Thomas suggested. "Maybe we'll get lucky."

After a quick look inside and a brief talk with the manager, Thomas found out Odell had never worked there. Thomas was using a photograph of Odell that she had taken from one of the photo albums in the boxes.

Minutes later, they came up on a Rite Aid.

"Stop there," Thomas said. "Let's try it again."

"When we first walked in," Thomas recalled, "Miss Odell happened to be the first person I saw behind the cash register, and I recognized her from the photograph."

Thomas approached Odell. "Can we talk to the manager?"

"Sure," Odell said, then picked up the phone and dialed the back room.

Taking the manager aside moments later, Thomas asked if she employed a person by the name of Dianne Odell.

"Yes, we do."

"Can we have permission to speak with her?"

"Sure."

Thomas, Weddle, and McKee then walked back toward Odell, and after identifying themselves, they asked her if she would answer a few questions.

"Okay," she said. "Sure."

Later, Odell said she knew from the moment they entered the building who they were and why they were there. "As soon as I saw them," Odell recalled, "I knew they were from Arizona and when they came up to me and introduced themselves as detectives, I knew immediately what it was for."

Odell had gained a considerable amount of weight throughout the years. She was heavier now than she had been in quite some time. At about five feet six inches, 160 pounds, she had charcoal black hair with prominent streaks of gray and white running through in dramatic, checkerboardlike contrast. A mother of a four-year-old, with four teenagers at home, it was clear sleep wasn't something Odell had been getting a lot of: the pronounced bags under her eyes, the sagging, yellowed skin on her face, along with her tired walk, spoke of an exhausted woman, working hard in a dead-end job to support what was a rather large family.

"Is it possible," Thomas asked the manager as Odell began walking out from behind the counter, "for Miss Odell to leave for a time?"

"Can I get my purse and coat?" Odell asked.

"Yes, of course. Go ahead. Do you have a vehicle here, a car of your own?" Thomas wanted to know.

"Yes," Odell said minutes later, slipping on her coat.

"Do you want to drive your own vehicle, you know, follow us? Or ride with us to the barracks?"

"I'll drive with you," Odell said, staring at Thomas.

Odell, Thomas was quick to point out later, wasn't "under arrest for anything." They just wanted to speak to her and, hopefully, get some answers. Odell was extremely cooperative and willing to help in any way she could.

The Towanda barracks was a ten-minute ride from Rite Aid. Odell didn't say much. But she was certainly thinking about what was going to happen once she got inside the barracks and began talking. She would have some explaining to do, to say the least, regarding three dead babies found inside a self-storage unit she had rented.

"We did have some small talk during the ride to Towanda," Thomas remembered later. "'How long have you been working there? How long have you been here?' Nothing about the case was discussed. In fact, Miss Odell never once asked what we needed to talk to her about—which seemed odd to me."

Odell later said she asked Thomas and Weddle several times what they wanted to talk to her about, but they kept saying, "Let's wait until we get to the barracks."

Thomas, Weddle, and Trooper McKee denied Odell ever asked any questions about the case.

3

Concentrating on schoolwork became almost impossible for Dianne as the 1970 school year drew to a close. Likewise, homework and studying became a nuisance. Dianne said she couldn't focus on any of it when she spent much of her time wondering how to get out from underneath the grasp of her madam mother— especially now, since loan sharks and their goons were stopping by the apartment making threats. Life was a matter of survival, waiting and wondering what would happen next.

"For the most part, I left school because I was embarrassed to go. That was okay with Mom because she was home [most of] the day. So, she could keep me pretty much under her thumb and make sure I didn't do or say anything I wasn't supposed to."

Dianne said her father generally stayed away after they moved to Kew Gardens, but would visit occasionally. One of the times he did show up, she said, she happened to be home alone.

"He wasn't drunk, so he didn't bother to do anything to me. But he was really quite nasty to me about why my mother wasn't there. So I said to him, 'I don't know where she went. . . .' I then asked him if he wanted coffee. He said no and left."

As the chilly air rolled into New York during the fall of 1970, Mabel made a decision to move after being mugged in front of the apartment. It was the latest in a string of robberies she had endured since moving to Kew Gardens. The final incident happened at a bus stop up the street from the apartment. Mabel had gotten out of work at 4:00, which would generally put her in the apartment by about 5:00 A.M. On this morning, someone who had been apparently waiting for her at the bus stop sneaked up from behind as she walked home and pistol-whipped her in the back of the head. With blood running down her forehead, she had to go back and get stitches at the same hospital she had just come from. When she finally made it home later that morning, she told Dianne they were moving.

"My life," Mabel said, "is worth more than a lousy paycheck."

And my life is worth more than turning tricks for you! Dianne thought, but she didn't say anything.

With no way physically to move—neither Mabel nor Dianne had a driver's license or car—Mabel said she'd pay for Dianne to get a driver's license and ask her father to buy her a car, an El Camino, so they could pack up everything when they were ready and go.

"But don't you tell him we're moving," Mabel warned.

Mabel had a location picked out upstate. It was on a lake in the Catskill Mountains. Comfortable. Relaxing. No big-city problems. No pollution. No muggings. Just fresh air and the pungent smell of pine needles, dry leaves, and fresh water.

John Molina agreed to buy the car, but once word got back to him they were going to use it to move, he laughed and told them to forget it.

"He ended up showing up on our doorstep one day," Dianne recalled, "and he was almost three sheets to the wind at the time. Right about then, I went into my own protective mode. My mother was there and they started getting into it."

As they argued, Dianne stepped away, trying to remain, she said, "invisible." But her father, at one point during the argument, said, "Dianne, I want you to come down to the house with me."

Dianne knew what that meant.

"Whenever he was angry, he would never take his anger out on the person he was angry with. It was always me."

"No, no, no," Dianne said. "I have to do something else. I can't go."

I can't go. . . . I can't go. . . . I can't go. This was what Dianne thought as she stared at her father. *I know you're going to rape me again.*

Mabel stepped up and said, "No! She's got something to do for *me.* She has to go somewhere for me." While talking, Mabel took out her address book and pointed to an address. "You have to go here, Dianne," she said.

John looked at the both of them—*What the hell is going on?*—and asked, "Where is she going? What's this about, Mabel?" He seemed confused.

"She has to go to Flushing and take care of an errand for me."

With that, John left.

"You get your ass upstairs," Mabel told Dianne after John left, "get dressed in those clothes I bought you and go now."

Since Dianne had started turning tricks, Mabel had purchased her an entire new wardrobe of provocative clothing, which went along with the job. But Dianne had a hard time wearing any of it.

"Let's put it this way," she said later, "even if I had Marilyn Monroe's body, I would not have been caught dead in those clothes!"

The obvious questions one might ask looking back on all this would be: Why didn't Dianne go to her father—or anyone else, for that matter—and explain what was happening? Why keep it all secret? Why not tell her brother? The police? Anyone who could possibly put an end to it.

"I tried always to be invisible . . . ," Dianne said. "You have to look at it from my point of view: there were other situations that occurred in the house . . . my father would not have believed me if I told him what my mother was doing."

Experts claim this type of severe emotional and sexual abuse would have prevented most people in Dianne's situation from believing she could report the abuse without suffering repercussions. Psychologists claim some of the main reasons why kids don't report such savage sexual abuse are that they "may have been threatened by the offender regarding telling," or "may not know it is wrong." Some may even "assume responsibility."

In Dianne's case, she later said, she felt a bit of each. She felt, for example, if she ever went to someone and explained what was happening, she wouldn't be believed.

One story Dianne later told that led her to believe her father, especially, would have written off her allegations against her mom as preposterous involved her dog. When she lived in Jamaica, her father used to make Dianne keep the hallway area of the house free from any dog hair. Dianne would sweep it often, but the dog would shed throughout the day. By the time her dad got home, the hallway was generally full of hair. If he found as much as one hair in the hallway, she claimed, he would beat her, accusing her of not having swept the hallway at all. How, she asked, could she have gone to that same man and reported what her mother was making her do? On top of that, she said her father was raping her. Would he want to get the authorities involved at the expense of perhaps exposing his own behavior?

"He used to bash my head up against the wall whenever he saw hair in that hallway. He'd grab me by the back of my hair—which was down to my knees then—and bash me against the wall, calling me all kinds of names: 'slut, whore, bitch.' I wasn't going to talk to him about *anything*, even if I was dying."

If all of what Dianne said was true, it was a situation where there was no end and no beginning for her. She was caught in the middle, just trying to survive as best she could. The move upstate, at least at first, seemed like a new beginning. Dianne was getting older. In a year or two, she could think about leaving home. The move up north would be the start of something different. Maybe things *would* change. Dianne didn't see Mabel sending her 100 miles south to turn tricks with johns in the city. At the least, the prostitution would end.

Mabel had a friend, Marie Hess, a woman who had lived near them in Jamaica, but she had moved up north many years ago. When Mabel found herself without a vehicle and no one to help her move, she called Hess and asked for help.

"Mrs. Hess," Dianne recalled later, "sent her husband down to Kew Gardens in his truck to help us."

The move didn't happen as quickly as Dianne might have hoped. In fact, it would be a few years before Dianne and Mabel relocated. Dianne was almost eighteen years old, she said, when they finally moved.

It was the summer of 1972. Tucked deep in the heart of the Catskill Mountains, Kauneonga Lake, Sullivan County, New York, seemed like a tranquil, quiet place for Dianne and Mabel to begin a new chapter. Arriving there, it was everything Dianne had pictured it would be: peaceful, serene, colorful, secluded. Dad couldn't just pop over anymore and give her any problems; he would have to drive for hours. Mom couldn't pull an address out of her smock and say, "Go here, Dianne, and do what he says." In a way, her life of emotional imprisonment with her mom would continue, but it might be tolerable now that they had moved. Yet, inside the first few months of living next to Mrs. Hess on Kauneonga Lake, Dianne made an announcement that ultimately changed the entire dynamic of her and her mom's relationship—and sparked a debate between them that would soon turn deadly.

4

When Odell, Thomas, Weddle, and McKee arrived at the Towanda state police barracks, Odell began thinking about how she was going to explain to her children and common-law husband, Robert Sauerstein, what she had left behind in Safford.

"What was going through my mind," Odell recalled, "was I now have to brace my family for what is to come. I need to get back to my family, sit down, talk to my husband, and tell my children what occurred. I was going to tell them what had actually happened."

Odell had never, in the nearly two decades she had been with Sauerstein, told him about the babies. "I wasn't going to say anything to anybody until I had a chance to inform my family."

The last thing Odell wanted to do was to sucker punch everyone. They were all at home, going about their day—school, work, television, bedtime—and now this ugly secret from decades ago was going to unearth itself. What if they turned on the nightly news and there was Odell being branded a baby killer?

"I wasn't trying to protect my family," Odell later insisted. "I was trying to *prepare* them. I knew what was going to come about—but I also knew the truth at that time of what had taken place. And I figured, as long as I tell the truth in this, I am going to be okay."

Regardless of how Odell felt, Thomas and Weddle wanted answers. They had three dead babies found in boxes, wrapped in plastic garbage bags, and, obviously, packaged in a way that led them to believe that the person(s) who had stored them away didn't want them to be found. They needed to know what happened. Their job, in effect, was to find that truth Odell was referring to—whatever it was. No one in law enforcement was pointing a finger at Odell; at this point, she was merely the likely person to begin questioning.

Thus far, Odell hadn't been read her Miranda rights. There was no mention of the babies, or why, in fact, Thomas and Weddle wanted to talk to her. As far as Odell could determine, she was there to talk about "seized items discovered in a storage shed in Arizona."

Weddle looked on as Thomas took out an audiotape recorder and set it in front of Odell on the table. Trooper McKee was there to observe.

It was around 3:00 P.M. when Thomas turned on the audio recorder and stated her name, credentials, and the person she and Weddle were preparing to interview.

After Odell recited her vitals—birthday, address, Social Security number—Thomas made something clear: "You are not under arrest. What we are doing here from Arizona is we are investigating a situation that has been discovered in the last week . . . and what's happened is your name has come up as a possible lead in the case that we are working. Do you recall when and if you've ever lived in Arizona?"

"Yes . . ."

"Could you tell us about that?"

Odell said she had lived in Pima back in 1993 in a house with seven of her eight children: four daughters and three sons, ranging in age from four to twenty-three years old.

For the most part, Odell was "unemotional," Thomas recalled. "In total denial of having any knowledge or involvement. . . . She appeared very calm and confident."

"Was there a father or husband involved?" Thomas asked.

"Yes," Odell said, "the father of my children, Robert Sauerstein." Sauerstein had fathered five of Odell's eight living children.

"The two of you are not married?"

"No."

"Okay, are you still with Sauerstein?"

"Yes."

"And may I ask how many children you still have at home?"

This was, of course, vitally important to Thomas and Weddle. Their entire investigation focused on children. There was a chance the mother of the three dead babies was somehow responsible for their demise.

Odell named her children, but she also mentioned a grandson who had been staying at the house.

Detective Weddle piped in, asking, "Who does that grandson belong to . . . ?"

Odell said the child was her daughter's.

"Does she live there also?" Thomas asked.

"No."

"So, you just have custody of your grandson?"

"No," Odell answered, "I don't have custody. She just walked away from him. She left him with neighbors and they called me and asked me if they could bring him to me."

The statement didn't prove anything, but it did tell Weddle and Thomas there was some sort of friction in the home where the children and Odell were concerned. Even more important, the child had been with Odell for five years, not one or two weeks.

"She never came back for him?" Thomas asked, puzzled and, perhaps, a bit shocked. *How in the hell does a mother abandon her child?*

"No." Then Odell talked about the contact she'd had with her other daughters throughout the years. Beyond the one daughter whose child Odell was looking after, and her oldest daughter, it was clear, at least from her point of view, she hadn't any real problems with her older children.

"My grandson and my youngest son," Odell recalled later, "are almost inseparable; they're like brothers. I had my grandson since he was eight months old. I'm the only mother he's ever known. Although I've shown him pictures of his mother, he'd shake his head and say, 'No, you're my mommy.'"

Later in the interview, Thomas sat back and said, "Okay," taking a deep breath, trying to digest what amounted to a large family tree involving many different children and grandchildren, "when you lived in Pima, were there any other children involved in the home, or that you gave birth to, or anything like that?"

It was the first time Thomas or Weddle had broached—even remotely—the subject of babies and what might have happened to the three dead children. After all, this was the main purpose of the interview: to find out what happened to the babies who hadn't lived—as far as anyone could tell thus far—for more than a few hours. The medical examiner was still trying to figure out how the children had died, but it was clear from early tests the babies were newborns.

"No," Odell said stoically.

Thomas didn't pressure Odell immediately. Instead, she did what any experienced investigator might have done: she began to float the opportunity for Odell to come up with an explanation. It was clear from the energy in the room—the aura of the conversation and the demeanor between the detectives and Odell—that there was an awfully large white elephant hanging around, and sooner or later, it was going to have to be talked about. For Thomas and Weddle, however, they had traveled nearly twenty-five hundred miles. They had all day and night to talk to Odell. There was no need to push the subject now. Once Odell invoked her right to remain silent and asked for a lawyer, the conversation was over. Up to now, though, according to Thomas, Weddle, and Trooper McKee, she was calm and, as far as they could tell, somewhat cooperative, and at no point mentioned that she wanted a lawyer.

"When you moved to Arizona," Thomas asked, "where did you come from?"

"Pennsylvania," Odell shot back, adding, "No, excuse me, Utah."

"How long did you live in Utah?"

"About a year."

"Where have you lived most of your life?"

"New York."

For the next few moments, Thomas and Odell traded dialogue about Odell's children and where they were born. Most of her children were born in New York—all in hospitals. Odell said Sauerstein had fathered the youngest of the children, and James Odell, a man she had been married to at one time, fathered her three oldest daughters: twenty-two, twenty-three, and twenty-four years old.

"When you moved to Arizona, did you bring a lot of property with you for your home?" Thomas asked.

"I had a truckful."

"Did it all go into your home?"

Weddle, sitting patiently, studying Odell's body language, knew where Thomas was heading.

"No, no," Odell said.

"Do you recall what you did with that property?"

"Had to put some of it into storage."

Okay, now we're getting somewhere, Weddle told himself.

"Where at?"

"I don't remember his name," Odell said, sipping from a cup of water. "He was the mayor of the town where we lived."

"So, there was a storage shed there in Pima?"

"No, I think it was in Safford," Odell said.

Indeed.

Thomas and Weddle did everything they could not to look at each other at that moment. All of their previous questions seemingly didn't matter when compared to what was transpiring now. Getting Odell to admit she had rented a storage shed in Safford was important. She was offering significant, relevant information pertaining to the dead children.

"When was the last time you've been to the storage shed?" Thomas asked.

"Maybe . . . I think it was April '93."

"And you only took some of the things out?"

"Yeah."

"Do you know what happened to the rest of your things?"

"No."

Thomas then changed the subject and asked if Odell was still legally married to James Odell. Odell said she hadn't been married to James for over twenty years. She met Sauerstein in 1985 in New York and had been with him ever since.

"And since you've been with Mr. Sauerstein, you've had several children?"

"Yes."

"Okay . . . no other children?"

"No."

"Did you ever have any miscarriages or abortions?"

Odell thought about it for a minute. "I had miscarriages in New York."

"Do you recall, one, two . . . ?"

"I think it was three."

Weddle and Thomas looked at each other. *How convenient: three dead babies, three miscarriages.*

CHAPTER 5

1

DIANNE AND MABEL adjusted comfortably to their new surroundings. Their apartment was on the second floor of Mrs. Hess's main house. Scattered around the grounds, along the banks of the lake, were several bungalows Mrs. Hess rented, generally to summer vacationers or folks just passing through town. During colder months, the Hesses closed the nonwinterized bungalows for the season.

Mabel hadn't worked since the pistol-whipping incident back in Kew Gardens. As she and Dianne got settled into their new digs at Kauneonga Lake, Dianne began wondering what they were going to do for money. Here they were starting a new life and neither one of them had an income. Had Mabel saved any money from Dianne's days as a prostitute? Was the mattress stuffed with hundreds and fifties?

According to Dianne, when she asked Mabel how they were going to live, Mabel looked at her and, as serious as she had ever been, said, "Now it's *your* turn to take care of *me*!"

Dianne said she felt as if she owed her mother for

raising her, like there was some sort of debt to be paid for her upbringing. Taking on a job at this point, however, wasn't something Dianne could physically do, even if she wanted. It wasn't that she was lazy, or didn't want to work. No, Dianne had a secret. There was a baby on the way, which she later said she was happy about when she found out. What ate at her—more than Mabel demanding she go to work and take care of them—as she tried to figure out how to tell her mom she was pregnant, was who the father of the child was.

2

The startling fact that Odell—sitting, sipping water, openly giving Thomas and Weddle information about her life so they could try to wrap up the case of the three dead babies found in boxes—would admit to having three miscarriages was a significant break-through during the interview. By this point, neither Thomas nor Weddle had mentioned they were inves-tigating the deaths of three babies, or that the re-mains of three babies had been found. Yet here was Odell admitting to renting a self-storage unit in Saf-ford and having three miscarriages.

Two plus two equals four.

Thomas asked Odell, after she admitted to the three miscarriages, to explain the circumstances.

"I started hemorrhaging," Odell offered. Again, unemotional. All business.

"Do you know what caused that? Did *they*—your doctors—know?"

"No," Odell said. "I was bouncing and I felt like a tear . . . like a pull, and I just started bleeding." She paused for a moment. Looked down at the table. Took a deep breath. "I mean *uncontrollable* bleeding."

"Now, was that three times in a row, or was that in between your other children that it happened?"

"For a long period there after my son was born, I had miscarriages. One was in Arizona after [my son in 1991] was born and I went to the emergency room there and they did an emergency [procedure] on me, and there were two in New York when we came back here."

None of it added up to what Thomas and Weddle knew by that point. It was clear the babies in the boxes were much older. Odell was talking about 1991 and beyond.

"Do you know . . . how far along you were in your pregnancy when this happened?"

"I would say not even two months."

It didn't make sense with the approximate ages of the babies in the boxes. The thought was, someone had delivered the children at home and, perhaps embarrassed or scared, discarded the babies without alerting anyone.

Weddle and Thomas wanted to pinpoint dates and perhaps tie the dates of Odell's miscarriages to her having rented the self-storage unit. Maybe the children hadn't met with ill harm, after all? Perhaps Odell, if she was indeed responsible for leaving the children in the boxes, had delivered and wanted to hide the births for some reason? Maybe she had misjudged how long she was pregnant?

"And you said," Thomas asked, "the last time you were in your storage shed in Safford would be approximately April of '93? Do you know what happened with the rest of the property there?"

"No, I don't have a clue."

"Well, let me tell you what we found—"

Before Thomas could finish, Odell said, "Okay," and looked at Thomas and Weddle with a confused, serious stare, as if to say, "What is going on here?"

Thomas explained how the contents of Odell's storage unit had been auctioned off about a week ago. "What was found," she added, "is why we are here."

Odell sat up in her chair.

"Do you have any idea what would be in that storage shed that would cause law enforcement to be involved?" Thomas paused for a moment. Then, "Any idea whatsoever, ma'am?"

"None."

"Has anyone else ever had access to that storage shed?" Thomas still hadn't come out with it. She was still giving Odell the benefit of the doubt to come up with some sort of explanation.

"There was," Odell started to say, then stumbled a bit with her words, "there was . . . another key, yeah."

"And who had that key?"

"It wasn't my neighbor across the street . . . I'm trying to think of her name."

"Do you recall what type of things you might have left behind?"

"Mostly bed frames, fishing poles, crib stuff . . . I don't think so."

Detective Weddle leaned toward Odell: "What's your mother's name?"

"Good cop, bad cop," Odell said later. Thomas acted sympathetic while Weddle presented himself as passive, but then changed his tone, projecting a more abrasive approach.

"Mabel," Odell said.

"Do you remember having boxes," Weddle asked, "I mean, boxes of photographs that were left in there?"

"Some of them were left there, yeah."

"We found that strange," Weddle said. "You know, Miss Odell, that somebody would go off and leave photographs, family photographs that had been collected for years, and especially photographs of your mother. Is your mother still alive?"

"No," Odell said, "she's not. . . ."

Weddle, a large man in stature, Western all the way around the edges (cowboy boots, plaid shirt, big belt buckle), hardened by what he'd seen as a cop throughout the years, got up from his seat and walked around the room for a moment. After running his hand across his chin, sighing a bit, he looked at Odell. "I got another question for ya," he said, raising his finger in the air as if he were thinking. "You said that you removed stuff one other time." He paused. Turned around. "Was that *after* you had moved that you came back and removed some of the items, the last time you moved the items out of there? Had you moved at that point and came back and removed items?"

By itself, the question alone seemed confusing. A mixed bag of winding words.

"No, no," Odell said immediately. She was getting a bit panicked now, as if she were being accused of something.

"Or was that *before* you moved?"

"That was before I had moved, yeah."

"So after you moved, you *never* returned and removed anything out of that storage shed?"

"No, no. I had lost [*sic*] the key . . . umm . . . umm . . . with one of my daughters' friends, just in case I had lost the keys when I came back I could get in and get stuff, you know if I had decided."

Thomas had been studying Odell as Weddle took control of the questioning, watching her mannerisms and movements. Although Odell was shifting a bit in her seat and answering questions with more enthusiasm, she still seemed confident. It was clear in the way she thought about her answers. Thomas and Weddle knew that a suspect who thought about what she said was a suspect hiding something. Nerves fray. Lies build on top of lies and become hard to keep track of. Thus, the suspect had to think about what she had said previously so she could mold responses to those particular questions and answers.

Odell was definitely hiding something. Weddle and Thomas were sure of it.

3

Dianne was in a remarkable predicament during the first few weeks of her pregnancy in early 1972: what was she going to do about the baby she was carrying as she and her mother settled into their new home? She had broken down and told Mabel about the baby, whereby Mabel acted as if she had known all along. That wasn't the problem. Instead, according to Dianne, it was who the father of the child was: John Molina, who, Dianne claimed later, had allegedly fathered the child while raping her one last time before she moved north.

As would be the case with many of the stories Dianne later told, there was no way to prove John had fathered the 1972 child. Nevertheless, Dianne insisted her father was responsible for both the life *and* death of the child she would later call Matthew.

"When we moved up to the lake," Dianne said later, "I was already pregnant with Matthew. . . . [My mother] didn't want me to have the child. We kept arguing about what I wanted and what she wanted."

During a brief argument one day, Mabel ended up "slapping" Dianne around.

"That was when I said I'd had enough."

She couldn't recall how, but after Mabel hit her, Dianne "managed to get down to [her] father's house" in Jamaica, Queens. When she arrived, she asked him, "Can I stay long enough to have the child?"

John looked at her for a moment. He was amazed, shocked by the mere sight of her. While he stood there contemplating what to do, Dianne said, she "thought he would say no."

So, what do I do then? she asked herself while standing in the archway, waiting for a response.

"My mother's words kept echoing in my head." Mabel had laughed when Dianne told her where she was going, telling Dianne her father would never let her stay. "He doesn't want you there," Mabel said as Dianne left. "You're a constant reminder."

After John thought things through for a moment, he told Dianne to "go into the other room," where, she remembered, the television was on. John headed for the kitchen, his favorite area of the house. Apparently, he was going to sit and contemplate the situation and then let Dianne know. Until then, he expected her to sit, watch television, and be quiet.

Whenever John had to make any major decision, he began drinking, according to Dianne, to help him through it. There he sat, "for hours," she said, sitting at the kitchen table, drinking and thinking.

At some point, he finally spoke. "Come in here, Dianne!"

"I heard the anger and slur in his voice. I was scared."

Dianne sat at the table across from him and they just stared at each other for a brief period.

"How could you do this?" she said John asked at one point. "Why did you bring this to *my* door? People will see you." He paused, and as he began to say, "You should be ashamed of yourself for coming back and asking for my help," he raised his hand.

"With all of his might," Dianne recalled, "he came up and punched me in the head."

With the force of the blow, Dianne fell off the chair.

As she lay on the floor, John grabbed his cat-o'-nine-tails and, like an Egyptian guard whipping a slave, began mauling her "across" her "back, legs, and head."

As he did that, Dianne said, she "curled into a ball" on the floor.

Then he starting "kicking" her violently.

"I felt like I was being hit everywhere, all at once."

When her father ran out of energy and stopped, Dianne said, she crawled on all fours into the living room to "try to recoup some energy."

With his whip, her dad had spoken; he obviously didn't want Dianne around. So, after "resting until early morning," she said, she went back up to the lake.

The subject of who the father of the 1972 child was would come under considerable scrutiny later. Dianne changed her story several times throughout the years. In April 1989, for example, she was interviewed by the New York State Police (NYSP), where she signed a two-page statement in which she had given the police a detailed description of those months she spent at the lake with Mabel while carrying that first child.

". . . [In] the early part of 1972 I became pregnant by a person in New York City," Dianne told police when they asked her who the father of the child was.

Now, if she would have left her statement at that, there would have been no controversy later on. A "person in New York City" could have certainly meant her dad.

But she didn't stop there.

"I only had met this person," she continued, "once, and don't remember his name."

This second part of the statement lent itself more to the obvious conclusion—that she became pregnant by one of the johns her mother had set her up with, or some random sexual encounter.

In 1972, Dianne weighed approximately two hundred pounds. Later, however, she described herself during that same period as "skinny" and "average." Was Dianne manipulating the police in 1989? Was she trying to save herself? What was her motive? John Molina was dead at that point. There was no reason for her to lie if, in fact, her dad had fathered the child. Furthermore, she had every opportunity to tell the truth. There was no reason to hide anything by then.

Her motive would become clear much later when authorities found out what happened to Matthew, as she called the child, and what she had done with it—a fourth dead child, incidentally, who was not among the three dead babies found in Arizona.

4

Odell traded jabs with Thomas and Weddle regarding who else could have had a key to her self-storage unit. For about five minutes, they went back and forth: Odell swore it was a friend of her daughter's, but wasn't sure; while Thomas and Weddle tried to allow her to come up with another explanation, which she couldn't.

Finally Weddle asked Odell if she ever went back to the storage unit after abandoning it. Odell said she and her "common-law husband," Sauerstein, had moved to Texas with the kids at one point, and "on my way back [to Safford], the car I was driving died. So I pretty much had to stay there and try to work to get another car and to put the kids in school. . . ."

"Was Mr. Sauerstein with you at that point?" Weddle asked.

"Yeah."

"So when you left Pima, Arizona, that's when you moved to Texas?"

"Yes."

Odell was in an emotional jam back then, she explained later. She had never told Sauerstein, or anyone else, about her secret children, so getting back to Safford to clean out the storage unit was extremely important to her—but for reasons unknown to anyone else.

After a few more questions, Thomas, a mother herself, wanted to know why Odell and Sauerstein had moved around so much, especially with "all these kids." Thomas had worked child abuse cases for years. She knew the signs: a family that was always on the move was, generally speaking, a family running from something—usually child abuse charges.

"I guess we were looking for that perfect place, you know. Like they say: The grass is always greener on the other side. But when you get there, it's not so green."

For the record, Thomas had Odell then recite the names of her children and their ages. It was simple questioning; a prelude, perhaps, for what was coming.

"Have you ever had a child anyplace other than a hospital? Like natural childbirth? Like in the home? Anything like that?"

"No," Odell said.

It was a lie.

"Have you ever been a midwife? Have you ever delivered children for anyone else?" Thomas was being thorough, giving Odell a chance to explain herself.

"No."

"So you've had how many children?"

"Eight."

"Eight?"

"Not counting the miscarriages."

Thomas and Odell had another brief exchange regarding Odell's youngest children. Then Thomas looked at Weddle. "You have any questions?"

"No," Weddle said. "I'd go right ahead with it."

"Okay . . . ," Thomas said while looking down at her notes. She paused a moment, then looked directly at Odell: "When we . . . When the individual purchased your storage shed, the contents of your storage shed, he took everything out and took them home. Going through the boxes, what he found, and what we continued to find after we were called, were three dead babies. What do you know about that?"

"Nothing. Three dead babies?" Odell seemed appalled, shocked, even confused.

"Wrapped up in sheets," Weddle added.

"Blankets," Thomas corrected. "They were in blankets." And now she looked at Odell. "They were in boxes that contained all your property, all your clothing that was marked, your photo albums in there, letters, the kids' immunization records; these boxes had all your other identifiable property in there, along with these three dead babies."

The facts of the case spoke for themselves. One box, in particular, had "Mommy's stuff" written in red marker on top of it. The box had been sealed. The handwriting, at least from an early comparison to Odell's, was unmistakably a match. It didn't necessarily mean Odell had placed those babies in the boxes, but there was a good chance—by the sheer coincidence of all the evidence—that if she didn't, she knew who did.

5

When Dianne arrived back at the lake after suffering what she claimed was a brutal beating by her father, Mabel took one look at her and said, "I told you he wouldn't want the 'little bitch' you are when you're around."

"I need to go to the hospital, Mother," Dianne said. *Contractions?*

"Lay down. You'll feel better," Mabel said.

Dianne didn't realize it, but she was in labor. "I didn't know . . . but I laid down until I felt like I had to go to the bathroom really, really bad. I felt a lot of pressure."

"I think I'm in labor, Mother."

"Lay down on the floor and push," Dianne recalled Mabel telling her at that point.

So she did.

As Dianne pushed, she felt the baby coming. She then asked Mabel to call an ambulance, but, she said, "my mother convinced me it was a bad idea."

"It will destroy the family," Mabel said. "Do you want everyone to find out that your father is having sex with you? You won't have anyone left after that."

"I gave in," Dianne said later, "because I knew I would never survive if everyone knew that."

"Matthew was born," Dianne recalled, "and *never* moved."

After Dianne felt better, Mabel told her to "get rid of Matthew . . . bury him in the yard." So she put the baby in a blue suitcase, she said, because if she had "buried him" in the yard, she "would never be able to find him. He would be gone forever."

From there, she put the blue suitcase in the closet and went on with her life.

CHAPTER 6

1

A FEW YEARS before Dianne and Mabel moved to Kauneonga Lake, not a mile away from where they would ultimately live in one of Marie Hess's bungalows, the largest gathering of musicians and music fans of its day took place just up the road. The Woodstock Music and Arts Festival drew in the neighborhood of a five hundred thousand people—a weekend of love, sex, booze, drugs, and, of course, music. Some of the biggest names in the business hit the stage: Jimi Hendrix, the Jefferson Airplane, Santana, Crosby, Stills, Nash and Young, along with many more. Because of the festival, Bethel, New York, had become famous. People have been known to flock to the region to visit Max Yasgur's dairy farm and experience, if only in memory, the place where it all happened, as if the region held some sort of sacred aura.

For Dianne and Mabel, small-town life and the historic relevance of the town where they now lived mattered little. To them, Kauneonga Lake was simply a new place to live. Getting out of the city and moving to the country, as they settled into the ebb and flow of what was a somewhat normal way of life, seemed to fit them well. The dead baby in the blue suitcase was a memory now. With the pace of life slower up north, it seemed easier for Dianne to forget about what had happened in her life and move on.

According to Dianne, she started dating when she hit her late teens, early twenties. As a woman, she felt she had a lot to offer. She said she still saw herself as a virgin, even though she had bedded down with more men than she could count and had given birth to her father's child. The sexual acts she had been *forced* into weren't about love, commitment, or sex; they were about power and money.

At twenty, Dianne wasn't looking for a man, she insisted, but wasn't about to shy away from love if it happened. Life had become a routine of work and home as the years progressed after the baby she called Matthew had died. Soon she found a job as a clerk in Monticello, a nearby town, at a retail-clothing outlet. It wasn't what she wanted to do, she said, but it passed the time, kept her away from her mom, and, simultaneously, earned her a little cash.

Jonathan Schwartz, a broad-shouldered man with a square jawline and Cary Grant–type allure, had caught Dianne's eye from the moment she saw him at work. Jonathan spent his days in the warehouse. He and Dianne would run into each other every so often. Throughout 1973 and partly into 1974, they developed a close friendship that grew, she said, into love.

The relationship, however, was flawed from the get-go. Jonathan grew up in a Jewish family and had never dated a Gentile. Dianne was Latino and white. She looked more white than Latino, and race or religion meant little to her. She liked Jonathan and they got along well. He treated her with respect and turned out to be the first male figure in her life to show her any type of admiration and respect, which she believed she deserved.

"I really, really did love him," Dianne recalled.

On January 8, 1974, Dianne and Jonathan, in what was a small ceremony, got married. After a brief honeymoon, they moved into an apartment near the lake, just below where Dianne had been living with Mabel for the past few years. Inside the first year of their marriage, though, things didn't go as Dianne or Jonathan might have planned. In great physical shape most of his life, Jonathan developed severe health problems not long after he and Dianne married.

"He got very, very sick and ended up having complete renal shutdown," Dianne said, "and had to go on dialysis."

What made it hard for Dianne to care for Jonathan, she said, was Mabel, who was stuck on the notion of Dianne marrying into wealth and insisted she do whatever Jonathan wanted. Despite Mabel's hatred for Jews, she would tell Dianne, "You take care of him, Dianne, and do what he says." Mabel believed Jonathan had money, and if Dianne catered to his every need, some of it would trickle down into Mabel's hands.

Jonathan was soon placed on a list. As soon as a replacement kidney was available, he would get it. Until then, Dianne believed it was her job as his wife to care for him.

2

Thomas and Weddle had always viewed the babies in boxes as a homicide case. Homicide and murder cases are entirely different from both a legal and investigative perspective. By definition, murder is not an act of contrition; it is an act of "willful killing." One person sets out to kill another and completes the act, generally, in a violent manner. Most of the time, there is premeditation involved and the person committing the crime is considered to be of sane mind. Homicide, on the other hand, is the killing of one person by another in "which intention is not considered." A drunk driver doesn't necessarily set out to kill another human being when he gets into a vehicle drunk and begins driving down a crowded street.

"Officially, homicide—under New York state penal law—includes murder, manslaughter, criminal negligent homicide, and abortion (illegal)," a former New York state cop with over twenty-five years of law enforcement experience explained. "Murder first and second are actual charges, whereas homicide is not. When you investigate a 'homicide,' it's not necessarily a murder. But when you investigate a murder, it's *always* a homicide."

At first, Thomas and Weddle believed that whoever was responsible for wrapping up those babies and hiding their bodies had not, perhaps, intended to kill them, but rather had been there when something terrible happened and decided to cover it up. They weren't so sure it was Odell, yet they had good reason to consider she either knew who had done it, or had participated in it with that person.

After Weddle explained to Odell how they had found photographs of family members among her items, Odell admitted she had left the photographs behind. It was, essentially, the first time she had admitted to anything.

"I didn't take anything," she said, "that wasn't absolutely necessary, like the kids' clothing, my clothing, clothing that they needed, you know, that we needed to change into."

Thomas and Weddle wondered why a mother—obviously a poor mother, struggling to make ends meet, someone who couldn't even afford to pay for the storage unit—wouldn't take her children's clothing. The only conclusion that made any sense was that Odell and her family were running when they left Arizona. Otherwise, why would they just up and leave without taking all of their personal possessions?

Thomas, sitting, listening, decided to take the questioning down a different path. It was time to stop dodging the issue, put the facts on the table, and see how Odell reacted.

"Do you have any idea," Thomas asked, "why the bodies of three babies would be in these boxes inside the boxes that were taped shut and marked with your identification, such as 'Mom's, *Doris's, Alice's*, all your court papers, anything like that?"

Whoever had packed those babies had packed them in such a way that he or she didn't want them to be found. It was clear from the way they were packaged so carefully.

Odell shot back immediately, "No, no idea. Holy cow. I would have no idea. I'm sorry. I wish I did."

"We would, too," Weddle said. He was understandably frustrated. He could sense Odell knew more than she was willing to concede.

"This is . . . all new to me," Odell said.

"Is there any way any of these babies could have come from any of your kids without your knowledge? Did anything like that ever happen in your home, or did your daughters ever say anything to you about being pregnant? Anything like that?"

"Not that I'm aware of. No."

"These aren't miscarried fetuses," Weddle added, letting Odell know they knew more than they had been giving away, "just a few weeks old. These are full-term babies."

Neither Thomas nor Weddle had heard from forensics by this point, but every doctor involved had given an early opinion that the babies were born full-term, which meant the babies could have been delivered alive and killed afterward, or had died during delivery. It wasn't a long shot to think someone Odell knew had hidden pregnancies, decided to deliver by herself, and discarded the children. It happened. Today, perhaps, more than any other time, teens were having children. Every year, there were stories of girls showing up at their high-school proms, giving birth in the bathroom, and trying to flush the babies down the toilet. Babies were found in Dumpsters, on the side of the road, in back alleys. It wasn't such a stretch, Thomas and Weddle assumed, to believe one of Odell's children had delivered the children and discarded them.

"Now, these babies," Thomas said, "are currently being processed for DNA. Would you be willing to give us your DNA so we can compare it to these babies?"

"Sure," Odell said.

Over the course of the next fifteen minutes, Thomas questioned Odell about Sauerstein, asking if he had any knowledge of the babies. Odell said he didn't. After that, they talked about Odell and Sauerstein's move from Utah to Arizona, and if she had remembered ever moving boxes that were never opened. Finally Weddle asked why Odell had left so many personal items behind, adding, "That was hard for us to understand. Why a family that has so many children, why they would leave behind that many things."

Odell had no answer. She just shook her head, shrugged her shoulders.

Next they talked about the storage unit and asked if Odell had ever been contacted about not paying her bill. It seemed entirely unbelievable that if Odell had indeed left the babies behind, she would have stopped paying the bill. Why would someone do that, knowing what the eventual outcome would be?

Odell said she was never contacted. She had even called the owner of the storage facility at one point, she added, but never followed up or received word back.

"Do you have any ideas where those babies would have come from?" Thomas asked.

"No, I don't. . . ."

Weddle asked Odell if she watched television— especially the news.

Odell said no. With kids at home, where would she find the time?

"This is national news," Weddle insisted, "'cause it's been on the news the last three or four days."

Odell became scared at that point, as if she could feel the spotlight on her now. *What's waiting at home? Are they waiting in my driveway?* she contemplated while picturing satellite trucks parked around the block where she lived. Reporters waiting at her doorstep. Headlines: BABY KILLER . . . MOTHER KILLS KIDS . . . MONSTER MOTHER.

As Odell sat in deep thought, Weddle continued, "It's just a matter of time, probably today, that [the media] are going to find out who the locker was rented to (which is you) and that's more likely going to come out in the news. So be prepared for it."

Thomas said she and Weddle were likely going to be speaking with Sauerstein, and they wondered if Odell thought he'd have a problem with talking to them.

"I don't think so."

Weddle mentioned the DNA sample again. "We don't know what happened out there, ma'am. We're not trying to point the blame at you, but obviously—"

Odell interrupted. "Well, it sure sounds like it's coming down my way!" She was irritated. The tone of the questioning had gone from casual to accusatory. She felt pressured.

"Well, this has to start somewhere," Weddle said after Odell became visibly upset. "Where else would our investigators look?"

"I . . . I understand what you're saying, but, you know, I'm also getting innuendos from just the inflections in your voices, and it's just not him, it's you, too," Odell said, looking now at Thomas.

One might question Odell's tactics here. As she sat and talked, she knew what had happened to the children. If she chose, she didn't have to go through the rigorous questioning she was now undergoing. She could have left the barracks at any time, or demanded a lawyer, which would have suspended the interview.

But she didn't.

The media kept coming up in conversation. Thomas, Weddle, and now Trooper McKee, who had been there the entire time, kept telling Odell to prepare herself. This was going to be a huge story. A mom who possibly could have killed her babies meant ratings—and the media wouldn't stop until it tracked down the current owner of the storage shed. From there, Thomas Bright would be found. There was a good chance Odell was going to be "breaking news" in the hours and days to come. Trooper McKee, like Weddle and Thomas, had made it clear to Odell that her life was going to change, whether she had done anything or not.

"We're not pointing a finger at anybody," McKee said, standing up, walking toward Odell, "until we do an investigation. And that's what we're doing here now. You know, put yourself in our shoes. Who would *you* first start with?"

This seemed to calm Odell down some. "I understand completely," she said, "but, you know, I'm just saying this is how, this is what is coming across to me, judging by the expressions."

In truth, they had found three—not one or two, but *three*—dead babies in boxes marked with Odell's name. Was it such a stretch to think Odell had had something to do with the deaths of the babies, or that she knew what happened? Cops followed evidence. Thus far, there was no reason for them to believe Odell hadn't been involved.

3

As Jonathan Schwartz maintained what had become a life of waiting in bed for a kidney, Dianne worked hard to support the family. She was twenty-one years old now, and had left behind a life of horror: beatings, sexual abuse, emotional abuse. Still, she hadn't graduated high school and was stuck, one could say, in small-town America working in retail, making minimum wage, now taking care of an ill husband and a mother, who had made it clear she was responsible for providing a life of leisure she thought she deserved.

By early 1975, Jonathan received a kidney, and almost immediately after the transplant, he began to get his strength back. He was his own man again, entirely self-sufficient.

"When he got better," Dianne recalled, "he realized he didn't want to be married any longer."

So they split up and eventually divorced.

With Jonathan gone and Dianne once again single, she moved back upstairs with Mabel and started living in the same tangle of dysfunction she had grown up in. Mom, Dianne insisted, began to work on her the moment she moved back in. "Find a new job! Make more money! You need to take care of me." Mabel would say that Dianne had made a promise when she was nine years old to care for her mom—and promises were made to keep.

Around the end of the year 1975, a "fine-looking man" Dianne would come to know as *Hubert* Odell, and his brother, James, rented the apartment below Mabel and Dianne. James, with a smile that caught

Dianne's eye immediately, seemed like the perfect gentleman. As he and Hubert moved in and began hanging around, she worked her way slowly into getting to know them.

Dianne had changed jobs. She had found an opening at a local ice-cream plant and started working full-time.

At first, she said, she and James were just "good friends."

"He was a backwoods, country-type guy. . . . I kind of accepted him the way he was. I looked at him as a friend."

While Dianne continued a friendship with James well into 1976, her relationship with her mom became fragile. Dianne would push certain issues and her mom would back off—one in particular was Baby Matthew. There was a dead child in a suitcase in the closet. Sooner or later, something would have to be done about it.

"I would broach the subject a couple of times with what had happened to Matthew and she would give me a stone-cold look," Dianne recalled. "She would say things like, 'If you open your mouth to me about [Matthew], I'm going to kill you. I don't want to talk about it.' My mother had a way of looking at you that would drop you in your tracks."

Furthermore, Dianne said she was terrified of what Mabel would do to her if the subject of Matthew was brought to light. She believed her mom would kill her if she went to the police, or mentioned Matthew to anyone.

"When she said, 'I will kill you,' it was something I took seriously."

James Odell and Dianne spent the next year or so just kicking back, playing cards, and talking about life. James, Dianne said, was a homebody. He liked to stay in the house. Whereas Hubert, James's brother, was what Dianne described as someone who was out and about much of the time "with the ladies."

By August 1977, Dianne and James found their relationship had turned from friendship to love, and on August 22, they decided to get married. James had recently joined the navy. There was a good chance, Dianne knew, he was going to be shipped out soon after the wedding. But she still wanted to be his wife, she said, and support whatever he wanted to do.

Indeed, no sooner did they get married than James got the call for boot camp.

James wrote Dianne while he was away. In one letter, she learned about a lawsuit he had been involved in. It was going to be settled within the next six months to a year, he said.

This was good news, Dianne thought. They could use the money. Why?

She was pregnant.

After finding and reading the letter, Mabel was under the impression the lawsuit would bring a large amount of money into Dianne's hands. This, Dianne later claimed, was something Mabel viewed as the possible windfall of cash she had been looking for all her life. All of a sudden, James was this great person. While Mabel could barely dredge up a good word about him before, now she was praising him any chance she got.

One afternoon, Mabel approached Dianne. "You have to go down to the dock when James gets back and meet him."

"No, I don't think I want to make that trip," Dianne said. "I don't even know where he's coming in."

"No! I think you should *really* try."

"I'm not going, Mother. Anyway, James's mother doesn't want me to go."

Mabel kept pushing Dianne to "kiss James's ass" whenever she could, all the while seeing that pot of gold when

James returned. She wanted James to feel comfortable, so he would have no ill feelings over sharing the lawsuit money.

"She wanted me to do a lot more than make him feel comfortable. The difference between my mother and I, you see, is that my mother had this god-awful love of money. And I never did. As long as I had enough to survive and make sure my kids had food and shoes, I was fine. I would go out and work hard, even if I had to clean someone's toilets. My mother was never like that."

In a way, Mabel thought the world owed her a good life.

Shortly after James returned, Mrs. Hess, who owned the lake house Mabel, Dianne, and James were renting, announced she was selling the house. They would all have to leave.

Dianne and James found an apartment on Lake Road, right down the street. It was a quaint little place above the town's post office. The missing shingles and weather-beaten paint on the home mattered little to Dianne. It was a place to live. Pregnant, she and James were starting a family.

The only problem with the new living conditions became what to do with Mabel: Where would she live? She didn't work. She had no money. Who would take care of her?

"At that time," Dianne said, "James treated me beyond belief. My relationship with him was phenomenal."

Still, Dianne hadn't told Mabel she was pregnant. James accepted it, she claimed, and remained "ecstatic," but she was scared what her mom would say.

Mabel ended up moving in with James and Dianne. There was, Dianne said, nowhere else for her to go. It was clear, from what Dianne later said, that Mabel became a nuisance more than anything else. She was always there in Dianne's face, and Dianne had a hard time letting her go.

Regarding James and Mabel's relationship while they set up a family in the new apartment, Dianne said, "[They] were getting along fabulously then. She was big-time kissing his ass. And he thinks she's the greatest thing since sliced white bread. She went out of her way to cook everything he wanted, make him every kind of pie imaginable, did everything he wanted. . . . As a matter of fact, in the house we were living, he told me that the kitchen was my mother's, not mine."

As the winter of 1978 fell on the Catskills, packing a wallop of snow and subzero temperatures, the apartment Dianne, James, and Mabel were renting turned into an icebox. After the first few nights of below-freezing temperatures, Dianne and James realized quickly that it wasn't the best place to raise an infant.

Alice Odell had been born on June 16, 1978. When Alice was about five months old, Dianne worried the apartment was much too cold for her. In what would become an important point to law enforcement some twenty-five years later, Alice was born at Community General Hospital in Harris, New York—without any complications. Dianne had delivered Alice in the setting of a maternity ward, like thousands of other mothers who passed through the doors of the hospital. The baby Dianne called Matthew, whose resting place amounted to a suitcase in a closet, had *not* been born at a hospital, but rather inside the apartment Mabel and Dianne shared. What would become an even bigger issue was that there was no male figure around the house when Matthew was born; yet, when beautiful Alice came into the world, James was part of Dianne's life.

With the cold air bleeding through the slats of the apartment on Lake Road, a constant reminder that it was just too cold for Alice, Dianne spoke to James about moving. James agreed. It was time, he and

Dianne decided, to look for a home of their own. James had money. Why not?

The house they found was not too far away. James didn't purchase the home outright, but instead he paid the owner a year's rent. After the year was up, they would see how things had gone and decide what to do. Anyway, moving anytime soon wouldn't be a good idea. Dianne had another announcement to make.

She was pregnant again.

CHAPTER 7

1

THERE ARE, FOR many cops, defining moments in their careers that they remember for a lifetime. For Detective Bruce Weddle—a happily married man of a few decades, with children and grandchildren of his own—the babies-in-boxes homicide case was beginning to weigh on him emotionally as bits and pieces of the story started coming together. It wasn't a case of a common drug pusher who had robbed a fellow druggie and ended up with a bullet behind his ear; these were children, infants, three babies who hadn't a chance at life. Another case, Weddle recalled, that bothered him nearly as much happened in the late '70s.

There was a strike at one of Arizona's largest copper mines and union workers had been picketing for a few days out in front of the mines.

"During the strike," Weddle recalled, "we were put in a position where we were working against the strikers."

Over a period of a few days, thousands of townspeople had converged and sided with the union. The scene grew intense, building in size and energy as time went on.

"We were on the strike line trying to keep the road open. It put me in an awkward position, because several of the people who were on strike were people I had known very well and grew up with."

Neighbor against neighbor. Brother against brother.

"It became a very volatile situation, where, at one point, we had somewhere between four hundred and five hundred police officers working the scene."

It was a moment in Weddle's career when he found himself conflicted. But what could he do? It was his job. He had to leave friendship and family out of it.

Here now, a proud grandfather and father, Weddle saw three babies wrapped up and placed in boxes as if they didn't deserve life. This, Weddle said, was something he *could* control. He could find out what happened to the children and allow justice its due course.

But the interview on May 17, 2003, that Thomas and Weddle had conducted with Odell ended up yielding more questions than answers. For one, it was clear Odell was either hiding the truth for some reason, perhaps protecting someone, or she was responsible. Second, neither Thomas nor Weddle had a clear understanding of what had happened to the three dead babies. There was no doubt the children had died shortly after birth. Still, for a murder to have occurred, the children would have to have been born alive. Thus far, there was no proof supporting that theory.

As Odell collected her belongings and prepared to leave the Towanda barracks, Thomas offered her a ride back to Rite Aid, where her car was parked. Odell said sure. But before Thomas had a trooper bring Odell back to Rite Aid, Odell asked Thomas and Weddle for a favor.

"Please don't mention anything to Robert [Sauerstein] about what we talked about here."

Odell said she wanted time to talk to Sauerstein. According to Odell, he had no idea the babies even existed. As one might guess, he would be surprised by the news. Sauerstein had been with Odell for eighteen years. Here was this deep, dark secret between them that was now going to be exposed.

No sooner did Odell leave the Towanda barracks did Thomas, Weddle, and McKee drive to Odell and Sauerstein's home in Rome, Pennsylvania, hoping to speak with Sauerstein before Odell had a chance to talk to him.

"One of the girls at the store (Rite Aid) called me, got me all kind of nervous," Sauerstein said after Weddle and Thomas knocked on the door and introduced themselves. "I've been expecting you."

"Okay," Weddle said casually, "what the deal is, we got involved in an investigation"—he looked at Thomas, looked back at Sauerstein—"and your—you and your wife's name came up as the—as the lead in the investigation back when you lived in Arizona."

Weddle wasn't so good at getting his words to flow clearly, but what he said surely piqued Sauerstein's interest.

"I thought you were here for me," Sauerstein said, as though a weight had been lifted. Thomas recalled later that Sauerstein, when they first approached him, assumed they were serving an outstanding warrant for previous allegations of child abuse in Arizona.

At first blush, Weddle saw a guy who, he recalled, "grew up in the country. He wasn't a city-type fella, or anything like that." The community of Rome, where Odell and Sauerstein had been living, was very rural: one church, town green, general store, local sheriff. "Sauerstein was a little bit on the offensive when we first got there," Weddle continued. "You see, when he left Arizona, he had a situation there that was possibly pending. He thought it was going to warrant and he thought he was going to be arrested, a child abuse case he was involved in."

Sauerstein presented himself as a bit standoffish and defensive, but Thomas reassured him that they were there for another reason entirely. It had nothing to do with an outstanding warrant. "No, no," she said, "we have other things to talk about."

Sauerstein just stood at the doorway as they continued asking questions. In six months, he would turn fifty-three years old. A small man, compared to his husky common-law wife, Odell, who was five feet six inches, approximately 155 pounds, Sauerstein had needle-straight brown hair tinged with streaks of gray and black. He wore a multicolored shirt—blue, maroon, white—with the logo "Pony" tattooed on the left breast. His pencil-thin beardline merged into a point with his salt-and-pepper goatee. His blue eyes looked tired, worn. He had a pair of reading glasses hanging from his shirt collar.

"Huh!" Sauerstein said when he realized why they were there. He was relieved, but at the same time curious about what was going on.

"You remember," Weddle asked, "the . . . You remember, when you lived there [in Arizona]?"

"Yeah."

Weddle and Thomas stepped back onto the porch, passing an old oven on the front steps; 217 was written in Magic Marker on a wooden pole next to it. The house was small, a bit run-down. For the next few moments, Weddle questioned Sauerstein regarding the time frame he and Odell had lived in Safford.

Then, "What was the purpose of leaving?"

Sauerstein paused and looked down at the wooden slats making up the porch floor. "Well," he said, "Dianne's . . . one of Dianne's daughters accused me of hitting her, which I didn't do. And I just, I got scared . . . I took off."

Weddle asked if there was an outstanding warrant.

"I hope to God not, 'cause everything is going pretty good for us, I mean, swell."

"I better tell you that's not the reason we're here."

This seemed to relax Sauerstein, who, according to Odell later, had a "mean streak to him" at times. There was an indication he had run into some trouble in Arizona with law enforcement regarding one of Odell's daughters, and he had taken off to Texas to avoid possible charges. Investigators and the prosecutor who would go after Odell later said they believed Sauerstein had "abused" some of the children, but he was never prosecuted or convicted.

Thomas and Weddle knew little about Sauerstein. It was a developing case. They were still gathering evidence—information about everyone involved, including Sauerstein, who had to believe that if Thomas and Weddle had traveled all the way from Arizona to ask him questions, it wasn't for an outstanding warrant.

As the conversation continued, Weddle thought it odd that Sauerstein would allow his children, who were in the house and wandering around the porch area, to listen to what was being said.

"We wanted to get to the point about the babies, and his oldest daughter worked in a small store that was adjacent to the house, almost on the same property," Weddle recalled. "We suggested to him several times that he might want to ask his children to go inside the house so they couldn't hear the whole conversation."

But Sauerstein didn't. Instead, Weddle said, Sauerstein allowed the children to hover around him and soak up what was being said.

"Sounds like you're doing a pretty good job," Weddle said after some small talk, reassuring Sauerstein again that they weren't there to serve a warrant, "from what I've seen so far."

"Well . . ."

While Weddle and Sauerstein talked, Thomas sat and listened, being sure not to disturb the flow of the conversation.

Sauerstein started talking about the self-storage unit Odell had rented. Obviously, he didn't know much about it. He explained how, when he took off to Texas, he didn't take anything from the unit. Why? Because there was a get-the-hell-out-of-Dodge element to his leaving. Why chance it?

"Do you remember ever making any, ah, rental payments for the storage locker?"

"I don't handle them," Sauerstein said, laughing. "I'm bad with money."

Thomas and Weddle cracked smiles.

"I'm going to tell you why we're here," Weddle said.

"Yeah?" Sauerstein said, looking at the two of them.

"Just this week," Weddle said more seriously, "it's a week ago today, they had an auction in Safford. What they did and particular storage lockers that y'all rented, to this date nothing's been done with them."

"You got to be kidding me?"

Sauerstein had figured—perhaps like Odell—that the items in the storage units had been sold years ago.

"Nope, no, I'm not kidding you."

"All that stuff been sitting there all this time?"

Weddle explained how the contents had been sold at auction and how Sauerstein and Odell's names both came up on several of the items inside the boxes. If Sauerstein knew what was inside the boxes, he was doing a fairly decent job of hiding it. It was obvious he had no idea where Weddle was heading with his questioning. As the conversation continued, Sauerstein seemed more interested in where his artwork was than anything else.

"Yeah," Weddle said, "a couple of pieces of paperwork that might have had your name on it."

"Some pictures maybe?"

"Pictures, yeah. . . ."

"Art pictures! There was a couple, right? We took the two good ones," Sauerstein said.

"This would be the tools, clothing, ah, some boxes with some bedding stuff in it."

"Okay . . ."

"And inside the boxes with bedding and stuff, in it there was three *dead* babies."

"What?" Sauerstein said, looking surprised. "You got to be kidding?"

"No, I'm not kidding at all," Weddle said, and then, with perhaps not the best choice of words, added, "I'm dead serious. . . . That's why we're here."

Sauerstein hung his head in his hands.

Jesus Christ. Three dead babies?

2

Sixty-six-year-old George Hess and his wife, Marie, had lived in Sullivan County, New York, for forty years. In 1973, George and Marie purchased the Rest Bungalows on Kauneonga Lake. They lived in the main house, on the bottom floor, and rented additional rooms and bungalows on the same property.

George later backed up Odell's story of her and Mabel moving to Kauneonga Lake when Odell was nearly eighteen years old, and, in fact, said he had driven down to Jamaica to pick Odell and Mabel up and move them up to Kauneonga Lake.

"She [was not married]," George recalled later. "My wife and I have known the Molinas for many years. They [lived] in our upstairs apartment." George knew Dianne was pregnant when she first moved in, he recalled, but "I never knew if [she] had her baby, nor did I ask."

The Hesses were people, one could speculate, who

minded their own business. *Pay the rent on time and we'll leave you alone.* Marie had been friends with Mabel since they met in Jamaica during the '30s, and they had written to each other periodically throughout the years after Marie and George moved up north. Some of the letters depicted a mother-daughter type of relationship. It was clear Mabel and Marie were fond of each other.

During the spring of 1979, George and Marie decided to sell the bungalows, and Odell, Mabel, and James moved. Running a hotel, if you will, was too much work for an aging couple. Retirement meant leisure and relaxation. Keeping up a place like the Rest Bungalows took time, hard work, a youthful spirit, and passion for the work that neither of the Hesses had anymore.

"As we were getting ready to move," George recalled, "I wanted to clean out the attic."

So George got himself a fold-up ladder and went up into the attic with a flashlight to see how dirty it was. As he began looking around, the first thing he noticed was an old suitcase: " . . . solid in color with two latches."

Curious, George decided to open it and look inside. *Maybe someone had left a bundle of money?*

As George opened it, a foul odor consumed him. Then he looked down and saw what he thought to be a rubber doll.

"I toyed with the idea of throwing it at my wife," George recalled jokingly. Marie was standing at the bottom of the stairs waiting for him.

But as quick as George thought about scaring his wife, he said, the smell inside the suitcase overtook him.

Oh, my God Almighty, George remembered thinking, standing on the ladder, staring at the doll-like figure, taking in the awful odor.

Then he pulled the suitcase closer and took a more

concerted look inside. As he did that, he realized it was "the body of a small baby. . . ."

George yelled down, "Marie, you're not going to believe this."

With Marie helping him, George lifted the suitcase down the stairs and placed it out by the rear door of the bungalow. After that, he called Mabel.

"I found this suitcase in the attic that is not mine," he said, "and if it's yours, well, you had better come and get it."

"Okay," Mabel said, and hung up.

Ten, then fifteen minutes went by, George recalled. Mabel lived, at the time, two minutes away. So George called again.

"If you don't come over and get this suitcase, I am going to call the state police!"

"Okay. . . ."

A minute later, Mabel was standing at the door. "Where is it?"

George handed her the suitcase, and "that was the last time I saw her."

Not long after Odell, Mabel, and James got comfortable in the house James rented, James came home one night, Odell recalled, with what would turn out to be bad news.

"While James was overseas and before he left to go overseas," Odell said later, "we were getting along famously. But I didn't know at that point in time, when he came home permanently, that it was going to be the downfall."

Was it a matter of perhaps not knowing each other well enough before jumping into marriage? Odell said no. "I knew him. It was James who changed."

Around this same time, Odell said, Mabel began to "meddle" even more in her and James's life, causing problems and coming in between them. It wasn't anything specific. Mabel was just always there, always in their face, always saying something to make them feel uncomfortable. Whereas James liked Mabel when he didn't have to see her all that much, being home all the time began to wear on him.

"It was at that time that he decided he didn't like being around the house, so he started hanging out with his brother, Hubert. Drinking [and doing other things], shall we say, fool around."

With an eggshell-type atmosphere inside her home, Odell decided it was not time to announce she was pregnant again. It was the summer of 1979. They had not been in the house quite a year and yet everything seemed to be falling apart. But after several attempts to try to get along better, Odell and James agreed to split.

"He went his way and I went mine."

With nowhere left to go, Odell moved back up to the lake, a small bungalow on Horseshoe Lake Road. Kauneonga Lake had become a sort of safe haven for her by this point—somewhere to return to always. She had spent many years living at (or near) the lake. She was twenty-five years old, had one young child, another on the way, and had given birth to a child out of wedlock (Matthew), who was dead and locked inside a suitcase.

Now she was on her own again.

The bungalow was part of a larger house. With Odell pregnant, living with a child in a one-room apartment, Mabel decided to move in.

Then, on November 12, 1979, after being in the new home just a few months, *Maryann Odell* was born at Community General Hospital in Harris, New York, the same facility where Odell's now one-year-old daughter, Alice, had been born the previous year.

As Dianne once again began what was a new life,

James started stopping by the bungalow to see how she was doing. They had been married for a little over two years. They had two children. Life was about second chances. It was worth giving it a shot.

"I'd like to try and keep our marriage together," Odell remembered James asking her one day.

She believed in love. Better yet, she believed the children deserved to have a father. "Okay," she said.

James had one stipulation, however, regarding the reinvention of their marriage. "I want us to get out of here—and away from your mother!"

"Where do you want to go?"

"Florida. My sister will put us up until we find a place."

It was February 1980, and deathly cold in upstate New York. Florida not only offered Odell a break from her mom, but the climate would certainly be a welcome change. James had gone down in December to look for a place. He promised he'd be back in February to get her.

Little did Odell know as she, James, and their two daughters made the twenty-four-hour trip down to New Smyrna Beach, Florida, to move in with James's sister, that she wouldn't be there long. Nor did she foresee that the problems they were essentially running from in New York would only get worse as, she claimed, she got to know the "real" James Odell while in Florida.

3

The main purpose of talking to Robert Sauerstein before Odell got a chance to speak with him was, for Weddle and Thomas, to get a reading on his initial reaction to the situation. The first few days of any investigation were crucial. Cops will tell you: homicide investigation is a "specialized undertaking," a craft that takes an experienced investigator not afraid to learn new techniques as he or she goes along. Practical thinking—that's what many cops claim is one of their biggest assets going into a homicide investigation. With three dead babies, whose parched, leathery remains had been mummified and decomposed to the point of fossils, and no forensics or eyewitness testimony to deconstruct, it was a case of narrowing down the most likely scenario and following it. For Weddle and Thomas, their investigation consisted of going from person to person, collecting stories, and then sitting down and putting the information together. As a cop, when you have several different people who could potentially be involved, you have to get to them as soon as you can so their memories don't get clouded with pressure from outside sources—and, most important, they don't have a chance to get together and collaborate on stories. From everything Weddle and Thomas could discern thus far, Odell hadn't spoken to Sauerstein.

Still, Weddle later said, it might have been a mistake to interview Odell when they did.

"On that particular day, it may have been a mistake on our part . . . but the media was going to find her before we did. And that was our main reason for leaving [so quickly]. But on the day [May 17] we first interviewed her, I had been up all the previous day; then we flew that night, and drove right to our hotel and found Odell. We were both exhausted. We look back on it now and think, 'If we would have been fresh, we would have waited until the following day, we would have probably ended the whole deal with one interview.'"

Instead, Weddle and Thomas now found themselves at Odell's house, interviewing a man they knew little about, and not having much information from Odell to draw on.

After mentioning the fact that three dead babies had been found in the self-storage unit Odell had rented, Weddle and Thomas were confident that Sauerstein hadn't a clue as to what was going on.

As the interview progressed, he spoke of the many children he'd had with Odell.

"All your kids are accounted for, as far as you know?" Weddle asked. It seemed like an odd question, but in the scheme of Weddle and Thomas's investigation, it was something they needed to know.

A cop never *assumed* anything.

"Yup," Sauerstein said. As he said it, one of the children walked onto the porch. "As a matter of fact, there's one of my little guys right now," Sauerstein, a proud father, said.

Weddle then asked Sauerstein if he was willing to give them a DNA sample.

"Yes, I would."

The interview then took on a rather chronological scope as Sauerstein and Weddle discussed the self-storage unit, who had visited it, how often, and when. Then Weddle got into Odell's children from her marriage to James Odell. He wanted to know if, perhaps, any of her older girls could have had a miscarriage.

"Oh, no, they were kids then," Sauerstein said.

"The one wasn't fourteen, fifteen years old, which is . . . ?" Weddle started to say.

"That was Alice," Sauerstein said, "she was a real troublemaker."

A rebellious teenager was one thing. It was in a teen's nature to be antieverything. What Weddle wanted to know, however, was "Did she have any miscarriages?"

"She had it against me. . . ."

Weddle and Thomas looked at each other. *What the hell is he talking about?* Maybe he didn't understand the question.

"Did she *have* any miscarriages, or anything of that nature, that you know of?"

"I know that she had, according to her, she was raped up in Oregon," Sauerstein said. "That was one of the main reasons we left. They were investigating, they were looking at his [*sic*] uncle, who supposedly was a child molester or whatever. And they knew we were leaving. But nothing ever panned out. I don't think she was ever pregnant. . . ."

Standing quietly throughout most of the interview, Thomas spoke up again. She could feel Weddle getting somewhere. Sauerstein, if he didn't know what had happened to the babies, certainly could be helpful in a number of ways. It was more than likely he knew things about the case without even realizing it.

"You don't have any idea where these babies came from?" Thomas asked.

Turning quickly, perhaps surprised by the tone Thomas used, Sauerstein said, "Hell no." He was a bit incensed, and began pacing back and forth on the porch. "We were there [in Utah] maybe three or four months. Can't have three babies in three or four months—not unless you're a cat!"

"These babies," Thomas continued, "were wrapped inside and packaged up in boxes that had all your other stuff in them. It could have been moved from—"

"All right, all right," Sauerstein said, throwing up his hands.

"It doesn't mean she"—Thomas stopped herself from pointing a finger at Odell—"I mean, anybody had them there in Arizona. They could have been moved from somewhere else. We just don't know. So—"

"We don't know how long they've been there," Weddle added. "That's what we're saying."

"What are your thoughts on that?" Thomas asked.

"You got to be a sick son of a bitch to be traveling around with three dead babies," Sauerstein said.

"A person might have a rational reason," Weddle added, "why they ought to do it. I don't know, but I can't think of one offhand, but—"

Sauerstein interrupted. He wanted his point to be understood clearly. "No! Hell no! I don't think anybody would do that kind of thing that was rational. . . . Ah . . . you said something and I lost my train of thought."

There was a quick exchange regarding whether Sauerstein had been back to Arizona since he and Odell left.

He said no.

Then, "Let me ask you this," Weddle posed, "we've requested that your wife submit to a polygraph test tomorrow. She said she would. Are you going to have a problem with that?"

"Me doing it?" Sauerstein pointed to himself.

"No, for *her* doing it."

"No, no, I mean, Dianne's the type of person where you go into the supermarket and you hand the woman twenty dollars, right, and the woman gives you back twenty dollars . . . and me, I'm like shut up." He laughed at the situation. There was no way, he said, he would give the money back in the same position. But Odell, he insisted, was such an honest person that she would speak up.

"That's a good person," Weddle said.

"You know, I mean, she does good with the kids."

"How 'bout you," Thomas asked, "would you take a polygraph?"

"Yeah," Sauerstein said, "but I don't think it would work on me."

"Why's that?"

"I have a nervous condition."

"Would you be willing to try, see how?"

"All right."

* * *

After getting dropped off by Gerald Williams, a PSP trooper, Odell left Rite Aid and drove straight home. She was flustered, worried about what she was going to do next. What would she tell everyone? How does one explain three dead babies left in boxes? How does one tell family members about a secret she's been harboring for decades? The following days were going to be filled with explanations, interviews, polygraph tests, fingerprints, and DNA results, Odell knew as she made her way down the interstate. The media was going to be calling, knocking on the front door, hovering around the neighborhood, asking questions of neighbors and coworkers. How would she explain it all? What options did she have, really, when it came down to it? Her only course of emotional stability at this point was the comfort in knowing she would be able to tell Sauerstein and her children before Weddle and Thomas (or the media) got a crack at them.

After all, in Odell's mind, Thomas had promised her that she and Weddle wouldn't speak to Sauerstein before she had a chance to.

She was nervous as she drove. When she arrived home, as soon as she walked in, Sauerstein said, "They've already been here!"

Odell dropped her head. "Robert was already frothing at the mouth. He was pissed," she recalled later. All she wanted to do was cook dinner, calm Sauerstein down, and figure out a way to break the news to everyone. She wanted to talk to Sauerstein "rationally," she said. "Because . . . I knew if I tried to sit down and explain it to him right away, we were going to get into a major fight."

"I'll cook dinner," she told Sauerstein, "and we'll talk later."

That comment seemed to appease Sauerstein for the moment. However, as Odell began taking out pots and pans, getting dinner started, he wouldn't let it go.

"He never gave me the opportunity to sit down and really talk to him. . . ."

Odell kept thinking, *How am I going to deal with all of this?* Her main objective was to keep the cops off her back while she explained the situation to her family. She wanted to tell them everything: about her mom, her dad, the rapes, and the babies. Everything that had brought her to this point in her life. She believed they would understand why she had packaged and toted the babies around. After that, she planned on talking to a lawyer—she claimed later—and then going back in to talk to Weddle and Thomas. Once everyone had a clear understanding of the circumstances, she was convinced the matter would resolve itself without any major legal problems.

On that night, Odell said she couldn't bring herself to sit down and eat while everything was going on. *My God,* she kept telling herself, *the media, the kids. This is going to hit the news. My kids still have to go to school, still have to take the bus, still have to come home and live in this neighborhood.*

In retrospect, the situation, as Odell later explained it, was quite remarkable: here was a woman whose main objective, she insisted later, was to protect her children. Noted essayist and author Steven Pinker, the Johnstone Family Professor in the Department of Psychology at Harvard University, has dedicated his life to researching language and cognition. Among his many books, including *The Language Instinct, Words and Rules,* and *The Blank Slate,* Pinker is probably best-known for his book *How the Mind Works.* In 1997, Pinker wrote an essay for the *New York Times* titled "Why They Kill Their Newborns," a probative analysis of mothers who kill their children.

"For a woman to destroy the fruit of her womb,"

Pinker wrote, "would seem like an ultimate violation of the natural order. . . . Most [of these deaths] remain undiscovered, but every once in a while a janitor follows a trail of blood to a tiny body in a trash bin, or a woman faints and doctors find the remains of a placenta inside her."

Quite surprising to some, Pinker suggested in the piece that this type of murder "has been practiced and accepted in most cultures throughout history." Furthermore, other psychologists "found that [while] mothers who kill their older children are frequently psychotic, depressed or suicidal . . . mothers who kill their newborns are usually not."

This bizarre dynamic, Pinker explained, led Phillip Resnick, a psychiatrist who published a rather now-famous study of child killing in 1970, to split "the category of infanticide"—by definition, infanticide is "the act of killing an infant; the practice of killing newborn infants"—"into neonaticide, the killing of a baby on the day of its birth; and filicide, the killing of a child older than one day."

Killing any human being, most would agree, is, as Pinker proposed, an "immoral act, and [most] often expresses our outrage at the immoral. . . .

"If a newborn is sickly," Pinker continued, "or if its survival is not promising, they [those mothers who kill] may cut their losses and favor the healthiest in the litter, or try again later on."

Although Diane Thomas and Bruce Weddle had no idea as of yet, Odell had a fourth dead child, whom she was would later call Matthew. Truth be told, she would give birth several times throughout her life and deliver healthy children without complication. Yet in between those healthy, living children, after Matthew died, there were three dead babies, and then still, several more healthy births in hospitals after the births and deaths of the three dead babies. Could Dianne

Odell fit into the category Dr. Phillip Resnick described as neonaticide? Had Odell been discarding
those children she viewed as sickly or unwanted? Was
this her motive?

After Sauerstein agreed to take a polygraph, *Clarissa*,
Odell and Sauerstein's seventeen-year-old daughter,
who had been working at the store adjacent to the
house, wandered over to the porch. As she approached
Weddle, Thomas, and Sauerstein, wondering what
was going on, Sauerstein looked at her and said, "Well,
all that stuff [in the self-storage unit in Safford] been
there all this time."

"Oh?" Clarissa said.

"Except for some personal items, I don't know."

"So they want to give us our stuff back, or what?"
Clarissa asked, obviously confused. Why would the
storage company send someone all the way across the
country for that purpose?

"No," Sauerstein said, "in one of the boxes they
opened, there was three babies wrapped . . ."

Sauerstein, apparently, was having trouble finding
the right words. So Thomas stepped in and said,
"There was three dead babies we found in the box."

There was no other way to put it.

"Huh?" Clarissa said. She had a stoic, almost impen-
etrable look about her. "I'll phone Gram and I'll be
back."

Sauerstein stumbled to say, "That ought to : . . will
light up . . ."

"And that's probably good to tell her," Thomas said,
"'cause like we were telling Dianne, the media . . ."

"It's all over the news already," Weddle added.

"The media's already had it for days."

"Up there?" Sauerstein queried, meaning Arizona.

"Nationwide!" Thomas said.

Weddle, Thomas, and Sauerstein then discussed how the media would find out where they now lived, but Thomas reassured him they wouldn't give out any information that breached their privacy.

As Thomas spoke, Sauerstein began smiling.

"I know I'm laughing about this, but, you know, I'm kinda nervous and tryin' . . ."

"Well, you know," Weddle said.

"Somebody out there is a real freak," Sauerstein added.

Thomas explained that Odell had agreed to meet at the Towanda barracks at ten o'clock in the morning on the following day. They expected her to keep the appointment.

For some reason, they then began talking about Odell's oldest daughter, Alice, and the trouble Sauerstein had admitted to having with her years ago.

"I was the stepfather. I came into the house and I took control. . . . We didn't find out until later on when the sisters started talking to me, [but Alice] used to plan this and plan that, say Dad did this and Dad did that."

Pressed further by Thomas, Sauerstein said that Alice had come running at him one day—"I'll never forget the day"—from inside the kitchen and there was a step down—"and she had socks, and she came, I seen her comin' and I put my hands up . . . and she just slid, and the next thing you know . . ."—according to Sauerstein—"Alice said, 'He hit me. He hit me.'" After that, Sauerstein said, "Oh, shit, ha, because I had!"

"The cops were called?" Thomas wanted to know.

"I did get into trouble," Sauerstein said. He was talking about another one of Odell's children that happened to be there the same day. *Doris Odell,* after hearing her sister scream, ran into the kitchen to protect her sister and began yelling in Sauerstein's face. "So I picked her up." The cop who answered the call,

Sauerstein added, saw it as physical abuse. The judge, however, felt different. The judge "just took me out of the jail and said, 'If everybody that spanked their kids went to jail, everybody would be in jail.' Ha, ha, ha! I said I didn't even spank her. I just picked her up and said shut up. She was screaming."

It was certainly clear to Thomas and Weddle that there was negative energy in the house between Sauerstein and Odell's kids. But for now, Thomas didn't want to hear about it. She wanted a DNA swab from Sauerstein's cheek and a photograph.

After taking a scrape of DNA from Sauerstein's cheek and a photogrpah, Thomas and Weddle began preparing to leave.

But Sauerstein had a question. "How old were the babies?"

"They were estimated at forty-weeks gestation," Thomas said.

Sauerstein seemed shocked by the answer.

After pausing for a moment, Thomas added, "They were newborns, Mr. Sauerstein. Newborn *babies*."

CHAPTER 8

1

A DESTINATION THAT usually beckoned a call later in life, Florida offered sunshine, beach sand as soft and white as Styrofoam, warm days, cool nights, and a life of serenity and leisure. Dianne Odell, in early 1980, didn't quite see her move down south in that same manner, but she certainly saw it as an opportunity to mend a relationship with her husband that had been severed. They could start fresh somewhere new.

When James left for Florida in late 1979, Odell and Mabel, stuck with no place to live, moved back to John Molina's house, where it all began, in Jamaica, Queens.

The obvious question one might ask: Why would a mother with two young daughters go live with a man who had beaten and raped her, she claimed, for a better part of her childhood? Why would she put her children in a position where that cycle of abuse could continue?

"It was okay," Odell said later, "because he, my father, had a boarder living in the house with us." In Mabel and Odell's ten-year absence, John had been renting out rooms. "I felt fairly protected." The boarder, she continued, was home all the time. With someone else living in the house—an outsider, no less—she didn't think her dad would go back to his abusive ways. On top of that, she wasn't a petrified fifteen-year-old living in a world of fear. She was a woman now: older, bigger, stronger.

"I figured he wasn't going to pull any stunts on me."

But what about the children?

"The woman (the renter) was retired. She never went anywhere or did anything. But as protected as I felt being back there with the boarder in the house, I still felt uncomfortable." And for that reason, she said, she started calling James in Florida routinely, begging him to come and get her.

Are my kids safe here? Odell said she frequently asked herself.

"I never left my kids alone with him."

Additionally, she never went anywhere without her children—even Matthew, who was in that same blue suitcase, only now in one of her dad's closets.

Right before James drove up from Florida to get Dianne, Mabel and John got into a "huge fight. And [my mom] moved back to Kauneonga Lake and got a job taking care of an elderly woman."

Two weeks later, James finally showed up to get Dianne and thus she found herself living in Florida.

But things took a turn for the worse, according to Dianne Odell, almost immediately. Once James picked up alcohol, she said, "he ran with it, hell yes."

As time went on, the situation only worsened. On certain nights, James would leave and not come home, generally staying out with his brother until the following morning. There was one time, Dianne claimed, when "two young girls, crying and hysterical, and a young man in the same car" pulled up in the front of the house while Dianne was outside with the kids and, after trying to "take my daughter," accused James of doing horrible things to them.

This scared the hell out of her, she said. She began crying. Things were too chaotic, dysfunctional. Nothing had changed—the only difference now was that she had two children: Alice, just over a year old, and Maryann, just under a year.

Complicating things even further, however, Odell realized around this same time she was once again pregnant.

2

Pennsylvania is considered one of America's more historic states, Philadelphia often given the brand "the cradle of the American Nation" because it was in the city of "Brotherly Love" that the Declaration of Independence and the Constitution were written by America's Founding Fathers. Deeper into the state's mostly mountainous terrain, with some flatland scattered conservatively about, the "Pennsylvania Dutch" region in the south-central portion of the state is what many who visit the state come to see. The Amish and the Mennonites have lived for many, many decades in the area around Lancaster, York, and Harrisburg, with smaller bands to the northeast into Allentown, Bethlehem, and Easton, as well as the picturesque Susquehanna River Valley, having manifested quiet, solemn lives among themselves, entirely immune to the luxuries most Americans are accustomed to.

The small town of Towanda, tucked up in the North Country, close to the border of New York, became the hub of the babies-in-boxes murder investigation for Dianne Thomas and Bruce Weddle. But they had been in town now for two days and hadn't really gotten any closer to finding out what had happened than they were before they left Arizona. The case was weighing on Thomas especially, who had hoped to have it wrapped up quickly so she could send the babies to their final resting place. In a sense, for over twenty years the babies had been in a state of purgatory, decomposing, mummifying, waiting for someone to come along and claim them. The flower and candle memorial at the self-storage unit in Safford had only grown in size. Thomas and Weddle wanted answers.

After leaving Sauerstein and Odell's home, Weddle and Thomas located Odell's daughter, Doris, who was twenty-two years old and living about an hour and a half away in New York.

After Thomas and Weddle explained why they were there, Doris was "shocked," Thomas recalled later, "at the news. . . ." As Thomas explained how the babies likely traveled with the family from state to state, Doris put her hands over her mouth. *Oh, my, God . . . I don't believe it.* She turned white, Thomas said, to a point where they thought she might faint.

"I had no idea about those babies or that they traveled with us," Doris said.

It was okay, Thomas said. She could rest easy. They weren't there to cause her any trouble. They just wanted to know a few things.

As Doris talked, Thomas and Weddle became concerned that perhaps they had missed something—because Doris talked about a *fourth* dead baby.

"My older sister, Alice, called me a few years ago and told me the New York authorities were looking for my mom. Alice told me they had found a baby in a suitcase . . . but I can't recall anything more than that."

Thomas and Weddle looked at each other. *A fourth dead baby?*

Then Thomas learned that Alice and Doris hadn't had any contact with their mother for the past five years.

"My mother took my first son," Doris said, "and would

not return him! I've been trying to find her for some time."

"The only help Doris ended up being," Weddle said later, "was that we could check her off the list of being the potential mother of the children." More than that, Weddle and Thomas had it under good information now that there was some conflict between Odell, Sauerstein, and Doris. "And we hoped that if she knew anything, she could fill in some of the blanks."

"I believe the interview with Doris was productive," Thomas recalled. "We at least eliminated her as the possible mother [of] the children. We were thinking that maybe Dianne's daughters were having babies and hiding the pregnancies and births. Doris was surprised to hear her mother lived so close to her."

As frustration built, even mildly, for Thomas and Weddle, patience would prove to be their biggest asset in the coming days. Because within the next twenty-four hours the case would unravel into an intricate myriad of odd circumstances that began to answer, at least, some of the questions everyone was asking.

For now, though, as Weddle and Thomas settled into their hotel suites and said good night to May 17, 2003, the focus was on the following morning, when Odell would hopefully be back at the Towanda barracks answering more questions.

3

By July 1980, stuck in Florida with a man Dianne Odell later described as an "alcoholic husband" who was staying out all night doing God-knows-what, it was time for her to make a decision. Before she did that, James suggested they get out of his sister's house and move into a place of their own. Soon to be a mother again, Dianne felt the change might do them both some good. Maybe she could still salvage the relationship.

"We moved into this trailer . . . and he's getting progressively worse. Umm, he's living on one end of the trailer and I'm living on the other."

Faced with the prospect of not wanting to wait around for James to change, Dianne convinced him to bring her back to upstate New York, a place she had called home for the past ten years.

When they arrived in New York, Dianne Odell said, "James went his way and I went mine."

But this time, it was for good.

Dianne Odell moved into what was called Hamilton House on White Lake, where Mabel had been living since she left Queens after the argument with John. White Lake was about a mile south of where Odell had lived on Kauneonga Lake. White Lake and Kauneonga Lake are, actually, one in the same. In the shape of an inkblot, White Lake and Kauneonga Lake, technically speaking, are the same body of water. The north side is called Kauneonga Lake and the south side, by Route 17B, White Lake. For ten years, Dianne had lived on the north side, Kauneonga Lake.

"James needed to be free—and I needed to be stress free."

With the split, Diane Odell said, she assumed James was going to still be a dad; he just wouldn't be living with the kids. She wondered how she was going to make it on her own with two kids and one on the way. She assumed James would help out financially.

"I figured he was going to put some money into their upbringing and want to see them. But he doesn't. He takes off, and that's the end of it."

Nine months pregnant, living again in Sullivan County, on February 19, 1981, Dianne Odell received news that her father, a man who had, she claimed, sexually and physically abused her for years, had died.

"I went down to the funeral," Odell said later, "pregnant. I wasn't going to go, but my mother had to have a way down there, and I had to drive her. So I loaded the kids in the car, and, if nothing else, I thought I might wait at the house while my mother went to the funeral."

She was furious at her father.

"I was happy he was gone, but angry I had never gotten an apology. I hated him. I was glad he died a slow and agonizing death."

At eighty years old, John had lost a battle with stomach cancer, Odell said. It had gradually eaten away at his body, putting him through a tremendous amount of pain and suffering at the end.

"He had never realized what he had done to me. And he never acknowledged it. When he looked at me, he looked right through me."

Three days after her father's funeral, on February 22, 1981, Odell found herself back at Community General Hospital, in Harris, New York, giving birth to her third daughter, Doris.

For the past few months, save for six weeks or so after Doris's birth, Odell had been working at a local newspaper in the proofing room. It was hard work, she said, but it helped pay the bills. As things seemed to be going as best they could, given the life she had built for herself, she ran into a snag near the end of 1981, beginning of 1982. The owner of Hamilton House, where she and Mabel were living in a three-room apartment, decided to raise the rent, which Odell and Mabel couldn't swing. While Odell worked, Mabel watched the children. But the hours she was working and the money coming in weren't enough to keep up with everything. Mabel had given up her job watching an elderly woman when Odell moved back to New York from Florida, and Odell, of course, didn't think Mabel was the best person to watch the children, but, she said, she had no other alternative.

4

Weddle and Thomas greeted Sunday morning, May 18, 2003, with the understanding that Odell was going to meet them at the Towanda barracks and submit to a polygraph test. With any luck, they'd get a chance to interview her afterward. They were feeling much more composed after finally getting a good night's sleep. Still, now wasn't any time to hold back on their investigation. They had some hardball questions for Odell, which might clear things up, but she was going to have to agree to be questioned. A polygraph, although not admissible in a court of law, would give them a good understanding of how much she knew about the life (and, possibly, the death) of the children. But it was only the beginning.

Surprising to both detectives, Sauerstein showed up at Towanda in Odell's place. "We need to talk," Sauerstein said upon greeting Thomas.

"What's the problem?"

Weddle shook his head. *What's going on? Shoot, she's lawyered up.*

"Dianne's had a change of heart," Sauerstein said.

"Oh?" Thomas replied.

Hearing that, Thomas decided to call Odell at home. After four rings, she got the answering machine. "This is Detective Thomas at the Towanda barracks. Could you please call me when you get a chance."

A few minutes later, as if Odell was at home screening her calls, she called back. "What do *you* want?" Odell asked bitterly.

"We thought you were coming in this morning to, you know, give us those fingerprints so we can—"

Odell interrupted. "No! I'm mad at you."

"Why's that, Miss Odell?" Thomas wondered.

"I didn't want you to speak to Robert before I did. I thought I made that clear."

Thomas played dumb. "I wasn't aware of that, Miss Odell. I have a job to do, anyway. That's our investigative procedure."

"Well, I . . . I wanted to tell them."

"Sorry, Miss Odell. Where are we today?"

"I need to speak to an attorney first, before I come in. I want to get my house in order before I talk to you again."

"And then what?"

"I'll come in and tell you *everything.*"

Odell was apparently calling the shots now, letting Thomas know that she had broken an agreement between them and, because of that, she and Weddle would have to pay a price.

Thomas explained to Weddle that Odell wasn't coming in—at least not right away. Weddle, disappointed, suggested they ask Sauerstein, who had himself agreed to take a polygraph test and was finishing it up in another room, to phone her. Maybe he could talk her into coming in?

"We need her fingerprints before we leave for Arizona," Weddle told Sauerstein. He said they were scheduled for a flight the following day and "really needed Dianne's fingerprints" to be on that plane with them. The truth was, Weddle and Thomas could stay as long as they needed. It was an intense moment, really, in the investigation. A turning point. But intensity bred commitment. Weddle and Thomas knew that. As cops, they fed off it. They were sticking with their case, no matter where it led or how much opposition they faced.

Sauerstein agreed to call Odell, but said he couldn't make any promises.

"I told them," Sauerstein said later, "that Dianne wanted to talk to a lawyer first, which I agreed with."

After a few brief moments on the phone with Odell, Sauerstein indicated she was willing to come in and talk, providing she had a ride.

"Great," Thomas said, "we can wrap this thing up and get back home."

Weddle took off to Rome with a PSP trooper while Thomas stayed behind with Sauerstein. Round-trip, it would take about thirty minutes to return with Odell.

When Odell arrived, the first thing she did was walk off with PSP trooper Gerald Williams into the fingerprinting area of the barracks and "voluntarily," Williams said later in his report, submit to fingerprinting. Williams had been a member of the PSP for twelve years, the last seven as a criminal investigator. He worked out of the Wyoming, Pennsylvania, barracks, which covered Luzerne County, or the northeastern section of the state. As a criminal investigator, he was part of a task force responsible for four different counties: Luzerne, Wyoming, Sullivan, Branford. Part of his job was to assist in all counties. Having heard that investigators from Arizona were working on a case in Rome, Williams was brought in to help out where he could.

It was 3:30 P.M. when Williams fingerprinted Odell. The day was getting long for everyone. Odell looked tired and worn down, most likely from a night without much sleep. Her hair was uncombed, hugging her shoulders. She wore little makeup, had dark yellow-and-black—bruiselike—bags under her brown eyes. As she sat on a bench in front of a white-brick wall and Williams photographed her, she frowned and looked away. In another photograph, she stared blankly into the camera, her face bearing an expression of guilt: *Let's get this over with.*

After Williams finished fingerprinting her, Odell wiped the ink off her hands. Williams asked her if she was willing to speak to Thomas, Weddle, and himself about the three dead babies.

"You're not under arrest," Williams added, "and you can decline to speak to us. You're free, in fact, to leave if you want, anytime you wish."

Williams later said Odell thought about it for a moment and said, "Okay. Let's talk."

Odell remembered this same scenario a bit differently. She insisted that Williams told her she "couldn't have a lawyer."

Odell recalled, "There was about fifteen minutes of conversation that day that wasn't recorded. I never decided anything. I went in to give them my fingerprints and they moved me into a conference room and that's when . . . Williams said, 'This isn't going to go away; you're going to have to talk to us.' My reply to him was 'I want to talk to a lawyer.'"

At that point, she claimed, Williams folded his hands over his chest and said, "No, you don't need a lawyer. What would you need a lawyer for? The only thing a lawyer is going to do is tell you to keep your mouth shut."

"Those were his words to me," she added. "And my husband was there to hear it."

Sauerstein claimed Odell asked for an attorney "several times," but she was denied each request.

Trooper Williams later testified under oath that everything he, Thomas, and Weddle did that day was done with Odell's consent. After all, Odell could have left the barracks anytime she wanted. She was never under arrest. On top of that, she had expressed to Thomas over the phone before returning to the barracks that she wanted to converse with an attorney, yet she didn't bring one with her when she voluntarily returned to Towanda.

As Odell talked to Williams in one room, Weddle and Thomas, in another room, discussed how they were going to go about questioning her, banking on the notion she would agree to be questioned. It couldn't be a touch-and-go–type interview; they had been down that road once already and Odell seemed to be, they now believed, evasive, hiding things.

"I have an idea," Weddle suggested to Thomas. "Let's lay out the photos of the babies as we found them in the boxes and bags."

"Good, Bruce," Thomas said. "Let's give it a shot."

A time usually came in any investigation when a suspect needed to be nudged. Generally speaking, a photo, or piece of evidence, might push a suspect over the edge and take them back to the time of the crime, stirring their memory a bit. Not that Odell had killed the babies, but maybe she knew what had happened. Seeing the horrific photographs, their tiny mummified and decomposed bodies wrapped in plastic, might break her.

Weddle took out a half-dozen photographs and scattered them on the table in the interview room, which was directly down the hallway and around the corner from where Odell had been fingerprinted. Then he placed white pieces of paper over each photograph. When the time came, he would ask Odell to look down, then remove the paper and expose the photographs. It was a hit-or-miss opportunity. She would either open up or leave.

"We were hoping it might shock her," Weddle said, "to the point that she's going to know that we know about the babies and the jig is up and it's time to get down to business."

As Odell and Williams walked out of the finger-print area toward the interview room, Odell told him she "wanted to get her house in order" before she spoke to anyone else.

"It's my younger son," she said. "I'll come back to the station tomorrow. I need to make sure *Brendon* is going to be okay."

"Let me ask you something," Williams said, walking with Odell, "why would you have to 'get your house in order' and provide for Brendon?"

Odell bowed her head, spoke in a low voice, almost a whisper. "I want to speak to an attorney for civil purposes; mainly, to arrange living arrangements for Brendon because . . . Robert, my husband, doesn't treat Brendon very well."

In retrospect, it was an odd statement—as if Odell knew she was going to be detained by Weddle and Thomas. No one had mentioned the idea of her being arrested. She hadn't been read her Miranda rights, but she took it upon herself to insinuate that whatever she was going to be talking about would somehow keep her at the barracks.

"They don't get along so well," Odell continued, meaning Brendon and Sauerstein. "I fear for his safety. Their relationship is like water and rock. They don't mix well together."

Once again, Odell later explained this same conversation with Williams—as she would with many of the conversations she had with law enforcement during that same period—differently.

"It wasn't even Brendon," she claimed, "that I wanted taken care of. They don't even have the facts correct! That's what I'm saying. . . ." Brendon was 14 at the time. "It was *Adam*" who was fifteen and ". . . had reached that age of rebellion. I wanted to make sure he was taken care of. And without me there . . . who knows?" Odell wanted Adam to go down to Florida to live with one of his sisters, she said, where "he could have a fairly normal life. [His sister] would make sure he toed the mark. But more important, I wouldn't have to worry about him and his father getting into it. There was a clash of personalities from the beginning. I didn't want my son to feel the weight of what was about to happen because he had always been extremely close to me."

"Is that the only reason why you would want to speak to an attorney?" Williams later said he asked Odell as they continued walking toward the room where Weddle and Thomas were waiting.

"Yes."

"Listen, I want to be clear on this: you are not under arrest, you can leave here at any time. No matter what you have to say to us, you are going home tonight. Do you understand that?"

Odell started crying. "Okay, I am willing to speak with you. . . ."

Just then, Williams and Odell reached the room. Weddle and Thomas were outside the room, buzzing around, waiting for them.

Then, as Odell and Williams made their way down the hallway, with Thomas standing by the doorway of the interview room, Weddle said, "Dianne, do you think we could talk to you for a minute?"

"Sure," she said, heading into the room; Thomas, Sauerstein, Williams, and Weddle were behind her.

When they got into the room, Sauerstein said, Odell sat in between Williams and Thomas.

"They were kind of [nice to her]," Sauerstein remembered. "There was no bad cop/good cop. Now it's nice cop/nice cop."

"I want to talk to a lawyer," Sauerstein remembered Odell saying again as she sat there.

At that point, Sauerstein said, Trooper Williams blurted out: "Why would you want to talk to a lawyer? A lawyer will just tell you not to say anything!"

Within a few minutes, Weddle walked over to the table where the photographs were covered with white paper and exposed a photograph showing one of the boxes the babies had been found in. The garbage bag the baby had been wrapped with was open, revealing the decomposing corpse. Thomas and Weddle were a bit flustered, only because they weren't set up for a formal interview, meaning they didn't have their tape recorder running. If Odell was ready to confess to a crime, having a confession on tape would be essential to the case later on.

"Do you know what those are?" Weddle asked, looking at Odell, pointing to the photographs.

Odell shook her head. "They look like bags of garbage," Weddle recalled Odell saying at that point.

"Well, Miss Odell, that's what they've been treated like—garbage."

Thomas and Williams looked at each other.

This is it. . . .

Weddle continued: "There's dead babies in those bags, and you're the one who knows what the situation was and why those babies were in those bags." Weddle, who spoke with a noticeable Western brogue, paused for a moment to allow Odell a chance to think about the images. Then, "We don't intend on leaving Pennsylvania, Miss Odell," he continued, "until we find out from you what happened."

Odell, looking at the photograph, then blurted out, "If that's what you need, okay, the babies are mine. I've withheld this information for years. . . ."

Weddle, Thomas, and Williams later corroborated the statement.

"It seemed to me," Williams recalled, "as if it was like a big burden would be relieved off of her shoulders. That's how it appeared to me."

With that information now exposed, Thomas immediately went for her tape recorder and explained to Odell how they needed to get her statement, and whatever else she wanted to say, on tape.

Sauerstein, who had been in the room, was asked to leave and stand on the opposite side of a two-way mirror, in another room, where he could watch and listen.

By 4:00 P.M., Thomas had her tape recorder on the table in front of Odell, the wheels of the cassette tape squeaking and turning.

"You have already indicated a few things to us," Thomas said into the microphone, "that we would like to have you go through again so that we have it on the tape recording. You agreed to speak to us?"

"I already agreed to that," Odell said, crying.

"Okay, go ahead if you would, please, the first thing that we were talking about is the babies that we in Arizona had found that were in the storage unit. Okay, go ahead."

Odell took a deep breath. *It'll be okay. Just tell the truth. Get it over with.* She kept repeating this to herself as she tried to figure out what to say first.

CHAPTER 9

1

"THERE WAS A gentleman," Odell recalled, "between James and his brother, I dated."

It was 1981, she explained. *Mark Ingalls* was a good-looking man in his late thirties who had worked around the apartment as a handyman. Odell said she noticed him, of course, because he was always around, but he meant little to her. Just another drifter who had showed up one day and wound up sticking around after finding work.

It was Mabel, Odell claimed, who pursued Mark, professing to be acting on her behalf. Mabel had heard that Mark, a Vietnam veteran, had filed a "large class-action lawsuit against the government over an Agent Orange" issue. Mabel saw a huge payoff coming his way. So she pressured Odell into dating him in order to get her hands on what was a potential windfall of cash.

"He was nice enough," Odell recalled, "but he was *not* what I was looking for. I did not want this relationship. I wanted to be left alone. . . . I had had enough of men being in my life. I was angry at any man who would ask me to do anything. Because all of my life, all of the men in my life, in my family, all the way up to my husband, always telling me what I could do and when I could do it, what I should be saying."

It was because of this controlling atmosphere, coupled with the fact that she had lived under the power of her mother's hand for so long, that drove Odell to push men away entirely. Still, to appease Mabel, she began dating Mark—and, within a few months, guess what?

She was pregnant. But Mark never knew, she claimed.

"It [the relationship] was long gone and finished" by the time she found out she was pregnant. But there she was, once again pregnant and husbandless, wondering what she was going to do. She'd had three (living) children already, no child support coming in, and was working a dead-end job just to survive.

One of the first things Odell said she did was go to her mother with the news: "I'm pregnant, Mom."

Mabel just stared at her. Then, "I can help. One phone call and everything can be taken care of."

"I don't think so, *Mother.* I don't want *that* kind of help."

Mabel was talking about an abortion, of course. She had mentioned it many times before, during Odell's previous pregnancies.

Unlike the preceding three living children Odell had given birth to, she claimed she didn't receive prenatal care for this child because she didn't want Mabel "squawking about money." Additionally, she said she was scared of leaving her living children alone with Mabel "any more than I absolutely had to."

Moreover, she said she learned a lesson during her three previous births: that the hospital would send her home if her contractions weren't close enough apart. Because of that, she claimed, she waited until "the pains were close enough not to send me back home." When the time came, she said, she gave her three girls—Alice, Maryann, and Doris—a bath and put them to bed. "Just like a normal night."

Earlier that same day, she'd warned Mabel she was in labor. "You'll probably have to watch the girls for a while. . . . I won't be able to get up and take care of them."

As the pains became unbearable later on, Mabel began soothing her. "Lay down for a while, take the stress off of your back," she said, rubbing Odell's shoulders, massaging her back.

Odell rested for a while, she remembered, and "when I stood up, my water broke."

"Call an ambulance, Mother," she said she "begged." Mabel was in another room. At that point, she knew she couldn't drive herself to the hospital, so she began pleading with Mabel for help—that is, help with finding a way to the hospital.

Sitting on the couch, waiting, wondering where the ambulance was, she believed Mabel had called 911. With the pain now so severe she could hardly move, everything became secondary to the fact that the baby was coming, regardless of whether there was an ambulance on the way.

Moments later, as the pain "became so bad" it felt as though the baby was "coming out," natural instinct took over as Odell said she began to push. As she did that, she started experiencing a "loud ringing or buzzing in [her] ears.

"I couldn't hear myself speaking anymore."

The next thing she remembered, when she recalled the episode later, was "my mother by my feet, bent down with her hands moving." She doesn't recall "hearing or seeing" the baby, contrary to what would become a major legal issue later on.

"I started to panic," she said, "and I tried to stand up."

That was when "my mother got up with the baby in her arms and walked away."

As Odell stood, she said, she "passed out."

"When I woke up, the baby was wrapped in a blanket lying next to me."

Mabel then walked into the room.

"What happened?" Odell asked, looking at her mother.

"It had breathing difficulties," Mabel said.

"We *have* to get an ambulance here right now!"

"Okay . . . but you know what they'll say: that it was done deliberately!"

"*What*, Mother, was done deliberately?"

"You know, Dianne, what was done."

Odell just looked at Mabel: *what are you talking about?*

"Come to think of it, you better go bury that thing and throw it out!" Odell recalled Mabel telling her at that point.

"When she said that to me, I felt like I was going to break into a million pieces."

"I'll get the girls, Dianne, and *you* won't be around anymore," Mabel continued, referring to how it would play out if the police were called in and eventually found out what happened.

"My mind felt like it was in a blender," Odell recalled, speaking of that day when she says her mother killed Baby Number One. "Knowing what she was capable of, I made the only choice I could make."

"I wasn't letting her take my girls."

2

So Thomas and Weddle were at the Towanda barracks on May 18, 2003, ready to hear from Odell what had happened to the three babies. Thomas had her tape recorder running and Odell, in tears, was finally going to give them an account of what would be the first of two different versions of what had happened.

Thomas stared at Odell while Weddle, waiting patiently, said, "Come on, Dianne, it's okay. Take your time."

"They're my children," Odell said. "The first one occurred as a—as a rape, umm. . . . I went the whole nine months, didn't see a doctor, didn't have any medical attention at all. The delivery came and I knew the baby was coming because I had already had [three other children] and I had tried to, I felt I could deliver this myself."

There was no mention of Mabel standing below her and then handing her a dead child after she had passed out and woken up.

Thomas and Weddle were well-trained investigators; they knew to allow Odell the space she needed to talk it through.

Don't cut in. Don't stop her. Let her go.

On the other hand, what Odell was now saying, in many ways, was a lot to swallow. According to Odell, she had given birth to three healthy children, all in hospitals without complication, but decided, for whatever the reason, to deliver a fourth baby by herself at home.

"Unfortunately, what had happened," Odell continued, "once the baby came out and I ended up passing out and I don't know for how long, but I don't know, umm . . . anything more than I pushed and went back, that was it."

She took a break for a moment and sipped from a glass of water in front of her. Then, "I don't know if the baby cried, I don't. I have no knowledge of that. When I woke, when I came to, I kind of leaned on my side and I felt like I was going to pass out again, and I leaned back, umm . . . kind of caught a deep breath and I remember taking, oh, whatever was underneath me, towels or whatever it was, and trying to prop my body half up so that I could try and sit up."

So far, she hadn't admitted to a crime. She was careful to say she hadn't heard the baby cry. Thus, if the baby hadn't been born alive, there's no way it could have been murdered. But interestingly enough—and, of course, Weddle and Thomas had no idea how large a role it would play later on—was that nowhere in Odell's statement was Mabel participating in the birth.

"I succeeded in doing that," Odell continued, referring to propping herself up, "but as I did, I must have started to bleed heavily again because I could feel that, not tunnel vision, it's kind of like a light-headedness and darkness comes over you and you're . . . and that's it, and that happened."

She was nervous. Shaking. Taking sips of water. Blowing her nose. Wiping away tears.

"And when I came to, I had tried to . . . umm . . . clean the baby's throat out and see if the baby would breathe on its own because I had no way of knowing how long I had been out and it didn't. . . . And then panic took over, panic and fear and confusion, and I don't know what all else. . . ."

"What year was that?" Weddle asked.

"Maybe 1982, 1983, or 1984."

"Was this your fourth child?"

"Yes."

"So you had three girls . . . and this would have been your fourth?"

The three girls Weddle was referring to had been fathered by James Odell.

"Right."

"Where did the birth occur?"

"In a place called Hamilton House in White Lake, New York."

After Weddle tried getting Odell to pin down an exact time of year, he asked her to continue.

"Well, I knew the baby was, umm . . . That it was at nighttime, but it was getting late in the morning and I knew my mother would be showing up . . . and umm . . . I took the baby and wrapped it up in what it was laying in. I think it was a towel, but I'm not even sure, and I put the baby in the closet. I had climbed into bed and I propped my bottom up so I would stop feeling that feeling of passing out. And I stayed in bed for three days until I had, I felt I had enough strength to get up, because between the time I got into bed and I felt well enough to get up. When I had to go to the bathroom, I used to crawl on my hands and knees to go to the bathroom."

So, Mabel hadn't even been there at the time of the birth.

Furthermore, as Thomas and Weddle listened, it occurred to them that the scenario Odell had just described could have happened once—but *three* times? Not a chance.

Weddle wanted to know how Odell provided care for her living children while she was laid up in bed for the three days.

Odell said the children "went into a different kind of mode, you know, like they were taking care of mom—"

Thomas cut in. "You said you put the baby in the closet because you knew your mother was coming over. Did she ever show up the next morning, or in the next few days?"

"Yes, she did. Yes." Odell looked down.

"Did she notice anything? Had you been able to clean up your bed area, or wherever you had the baby?"

"Everything was on those towels and the towels were folded up and around the baby and in the closet."

"Okay."

"There really wasn't too much to be cleaned up. I remember at one point or another, I had to, there was a spot on the rug or on the floor, I forget which it was, but there was a spot that I needed to clean up and I, umm, managed to get myself to the bathroom and get a washcloth and I just washed that up."

In the context of time, it appeared that Odell had an incredible memory. It had been at least twenty years since the incident. Yet, here she was recalling, in vivid detail, spots on the rug, towels, washcloths, as though it had taken place a week ago.

Odell then explained how she "healed up" without the help of a doctor.

"Do you know the name of the father of this child?" Weddle asked.

"No."

"It was just a rape incident, by an unknown assailant, an unknown person?"

Odell shook her head. "Uh-huh."

"So you were never able to obtain the name of that person, the father?"

"No."

"Were you even able to obtain or find out, did you know the sex of the baby?"

"I probably did, but I couldn't recall to you. I don't remember."

Remarkable. She could recall precise details about the birth and spots on the rug she had cleaned up, but not the sex of her child? It was as if the baby were an anomaly—some nuisance that had no name, no father, no gender, no life. Could a woman carry a baby for nine months, give birth to it, and *not* know the sex of that child?

As the interview progressed, Odell began to somewhat change her story. But what she was about to tell Weddle and Thomas, as Williams sat and listened, would turn an investigation of the life and death of three babies into three separate cases of murder.

3

Hubert Odell, James Odell's brother, showed up at the lake toward the end of 1982, not too long after Odell had given birth to Baby Number One.

"I don't know how true this is on his end," Odell

said, "but [Hubert] said he came up to the lake to visit his nieces. I never had a problem with any of James's brothers, so it was okay."

Odell never tried to get too involved in that end of the Odell family because "each member . . . had their own set of problems." Moreover, it was hard to be around an Odell because certain members of the family "reminded me of my father."

Regardless, she and Hubert struck up a friendship that turned into an intimate relationship, but again, only at the urging, she claimed, of Mabel.

"At that point in time, [Hubert] had the potential to make a tremendous amount of money . . . dollar signs in my mother's eyes. She believed if I was able to get close to him, she could manipulate some of that money out of him."

Again and again, Odell said, Mabel's quest for the cash-cow husband led her down a path of meeting men, sleeping with them, and becoming pregnant.

Hubert ended up getting into a bad car accident one day, which set him back. Then, Odell said, he borrowed some money from Mabel.

"He borrowed, I think it was, five hundred dollars. And the moment he borrowed that five hundred, that was it for him: he was screwed royally. You never borrowed money from my mother. You *gave* her money, but you *never* borrowed it."

Odell had simple goals in life at that point: work, home, and spending time with her children.

"I didn't want any man in my life. I didn't want to be bothered by anybody. I wanted to be left alone."

What she meant by "spend time with my children" was obviously all of them. Baby Matthew was in a suitcase in her closet and now she had Baby Number One in a box next to Matthew in that same closet. It was important for her to keep the babies in her closet in her room, she insisted, so they were within her grasp at all times.

"I am going to be totally blunt," she admitted, "I knew it was my secret. But I also knew at some point or another that it was also my weapon. My mother knew they [the babies] were there and I knew they were there and she was horrified I had not taken them and thrown them away—because that's what she had wanted done."

Odell insisted Mabel knew the babies in the closet were going to one day set Odell free.

"I would go to the police and I would explain everything. And the babies would be my proof. I never expected it to take on the connotation it took [later] on, where I would have to worry and think about my children going to school and the reaction of their peers . . . and the taunting my kids would take. . . . No one wanted to find out the truth, and that started with the police and went all the way down the line."

4

It was getting close to 5:30 p.m. on Sunday, May 18, as Odell sat with Weddle, Thomas, and Williams, trying to sort out what had happened to the babies. It was important for Thomas and Weddle to get Odell to lock down what she was saying. If she decided to change her story later, at least Weddle and Thomas would have something to work from.

"What eventually happened and what did you eventually do with the babies' remains while you were at [the lake]?" Weddle asked.

Odell said she put the baby in a closet.

It was hard to grasp. Right there, among the children's toys, winter jackets and hats and mittens, was this dead child, as if it, too, was some household item Mabel and Odell had no use for.

Thomas and Weddle then asked Odell to describe exactly where the baby was stored.

"A broken-down cabin," she said. "A cottage." It was in back of the main house where she had been living. Totally "[un]inhabitable by anyone. . . ." This important fact told Weddle and Thomas that, regardless how the baby died, Odell knew what she was doing and had purposely hid the body.

Then came the question everyone—the media, family, friends—would be asking in the coming days and months.

"It may be hard to describe or explain, but why, what was your thinking process as you were keeping this child rather than doing other things with it?" Meaning, going to the authorities and maybe explaining what had happened. Odell was a grown woman, almost thirty years old at the time. Why wasn't the child given a proper burial?

"Eventually doing exactly what I'm doing now and laying them to rest in a peaceful manner," Odell said, as if she had facilitated the events of the past week.

For a few moments, Thomas asked Odell about the color of the blankets she had used to wrap the babies in, but she couldn't remember.

"Okay, then you said the second baby you had, how long after the first baby, do you think you could have delivered the second baby?"

"It was no less than a year. It might have been a little longer, but I can't . . . give you the dates exactly, my memory is extremely fuzzy."

"And this second baby," Thomas asked, "you said it was from a boyfriend, a relationship with a man?"

"Right." Odell seemed more relaxed. Perhaps the relief of exposing such deep-seated secrets she had been carrying around with her for two decades had settled her.

"Do you recall who he was?"

"No, I don't."

"Can you tell us what happened with that infant?"

What was odd about how Odell reacted to the question was how she immediately began to talk about the relationship with the man, not what had happened to the child. Had the relationship with the man affected the future of the child? Is that what she was implying?

"That lasted approximately six weeks," she said. "It started out on a fairly even level, and about three weeks into the relationship, he started to get physical, a side of him I hadn't seen come out. He wasn't very nice to the girls and I decided it was time for him to go!"

As she continued to talk, she failed to mention the baby. Instead, she kept talking about how abusive the man had been and how abusive her former husband had been, along with the "toll" it had taken on her girls.

"Is that before you knew you were pregnant?"

"Yes."

"So, he never knew you were pregnant?"

"No."

The conversation then shifted to whether *anyone* knew she was pregnant: Her mom? The kids?

Over and over, Odell insisted no one—not even Mabel—knew.

"I could wear regular clothes. I was wearing regular jeans, regular shirts."

"Okay," Weddle said.

"I'm heavier now than I ever have been in my life."

Again, she said she never saw a doctor and never received prenatal care.

Mabel had moved in with her, she explained, at about the same time because the elderly woman she had been caring for had passed away.

"Okay, tell us about the birth of that baby."

As Odell explained it, she was on the couch in her living room. "I could feel contractions starting, and I didn't think anything of it because I thought I had some time, and I had put the girls to bed and, umm, right after they had gone to sleep, which I couldn't even tell you what time it was, but I know that it was dark."

From there, she claimed, she went into the bathroom—same as she had done the previous year—and as she was taking cloths and towels off the towel rack, her water broke. After that, she said, she sat down on the floor with all of the towels and cloths and "propped [them] underneath me because I could feel that pressure, that pressure coming, that need to push . . . and I did, and when I did, everything came out—*swoosh*—and then I went again."

Weddle and Thomas were confused: "*And then I went again?*"

"I'm sorry?" Weddle asked.

"Out I went again!" Odell said, snapping her fingers.

"Oh, shit, you passed out?"

"Yup!"

CHAPTER 10

1

BABY NUMBER TWO never had a chance at life, same as Baby Number One.

"The father would be," Odell said later, "my ex-brother-in-law."

Odell said she had sex with Hubert Odell, her husband James's brother, "maybe four times." During one of those intimate moments, she became pregnant. When she found out, Hubert was out of her life entirely. It was the middle of 1983. He had borrowed money from Mabel and taken off.

"I told my mother I was going to keep the baby," Odell said. Mabel compared the "situation" to Odell's "divorce from James: 'James didn't want to be responsible [for the children] and neither would anyone else.'"

When Odell went into labor, she said, she "did all the things" she "would normally do, except for working." Mabel knew she was in labor, even though Odell had never told her.

"After I put the girls to bed, I went to sit down for a moment."

Mabel then walked up to her and said, "How far apart are the pains?"

"Ten minutes."

"I was going to catch my breath," Odell recalled, "and then drive to the hospital while I still could."

She gave no reason for not doing the obvious: calling 911. If she couldn't drive herself to the hospital, she certainly could pick up a phone. Instead, she said, she got up to go to the bathroom, and "when I stood up, the pain was so bad it brought me to my knees. It felt like I had a basketball between my legs. I was afraid to move for fear of hurting both myself and the baby."

Odell screamed at that point, "Mother, please help me. . . . Call an ambulance."

Again Mabel walked into the room and bent down in front of her.

"The baby's right there. . . . There's no time."

"I won't do anything until you call!"

"The pain was so unbearable," Odell explained later, "she knew I wouldn't hold out long. . . That was when the ringing started along with something like tunnel vision. When the baby was born, I saw her holding the baby. . . . She turned to walk away and I tried to get up and run after her, but I blacked out. And when I woke up, the baby was already gone. Once again, she said to me, 'Go throw this thing out or bury it somewhere.'

"I was so upset. I felt so much anger . . . I knew if I said anything . . . she would have taken the girls. I wanted her to pay for what she had done. So I put [the babies] away to wait for the right moment."

2

If there ever was a "right moment," it was May 18, as Odell sat with Weddle and Thomas. Obviously, though, something about the moment wasn't working for Odell, because she explained how she had passed out again while giving birth in the bathroom, which was quite a different story from what she had said later.

This seemed odd to the detectives, for the simple reason of convenience, suffice it to say she was sitting inside a police station being questioned about the circumstances surrounding the deaths of three of her babies.

"What did you see when you awoke?" Weddle asked.

"Not much, because I had, umm, I had tried to sit up and I wasn't even thinking about it this time. But I tried to sit up because I wanted to see if I could just clean everything out and I remember I went like this"—she made a motion, reenacting how she had passed out—"and that's all I remember."

"You went back out again?"

"I must have."

"Like what, what did you do?"

"I went to reach, like this." She reached underneath her leg.

"To reach over, to get, to touch the baby?" Weddle wanted to know.

"Yeah. I . . . My feet were kind of like this, and I went like this, and everything like in here kind of like scrunched together."

"My feet like this and everything like in here. . . ." What did she mean? A jumble of words. It was as if she were making it up as she went along. Vague details offered Weddle and Thomas nothing. What had started out as a detailed account had turned suddenly—as they were getting down to the mechanics of what happened and how the babies actually died—into ambiguous descriptions and mimelike reenactments.

Odell then explained her "intention" was to grab the child and clean its mouth out so it could breathe.

Weddle wasn't buying it. He wanted to know if she

had tried to bring the baby up and onto her chest to prop it up so it could breathe easier.

"Yeah, and maybe try to pat out whatever was in there and clean it out, and, you know, just bring it air."

There wasn't much emotion now on Odell's face. She was calm, concentrating exclusively on telling her story.

"And I . . . don't have a clue as to what happened. But when I woke up, I must have hit my head on the tub or something, because I had a lump here." She pointed to the right side of her head, above her temple.

After they discussed where the bump was, Weddle brought up probably one of the most important aspects of the interview so far. "When did . . . you clean up everything? Did you cut the umbilical cords off?"

Surprisingly, Odell had no trouble recalling exactly where she had bumped her head, the exact location on her body, or even pointing to it, but she couldn't remember when and if she cut either of the babies' umbilical cords.

"You don't know? On either one?" Weddle asked.

"I don't think I did, but I'm not going to . . ."

"So, you're not sure, then?"

"I'm not sure. . . ."

For Weddle and Thomas, one of the most important facts that could perhaps come out of the interview was whether the babies had been born alive. This would have to come from Odell. No one else, as far as they could tell, had been with her.

"Okay," Weddle said, getting up from his chair, "did you ever hear either one of these babies cry?"

"No!" Odell said quickly, without thinking about it.

"You didn't hear when you awoke from being out?"

"No. The only thing I remember hearing was, umm, you know"—she stumbled a bit with her words and paused—"when people say your ears are ringing? That's what I remember hearing—that ringing in my ears."

"But you never heard either baby crying?"

Odell, a bit taken aback by the continued questioning, then said, "They might have. I'm not going to say that they didn't, but I didn't hear it."

Weddle wanted a firm answer. Yes or no?

"You didn't hear it?"

Before Odell could answer, Thomas piped in, "What happened next after you passed out again?"

It was getting late, she explained. She said she could see out the window that "daybreak" was coming. The sun, signifying another day of life, was just creeping up above the bathroom window. Then, "And this baby"—Baby Number Two—"was already gone," she said, "and I wrapped it up and put it"— she stumbled again, trying to hold back tears—"I put it in the closet." The closet was "adjacent to the bathroom."

Time and again, Odell recalled certain definitive details.

"I put the baby in the closet and I closed the door and I went to go back into the bathroom because I had . . . had blood all over my legs, and I went to just get water, and I had to go forward to get water, and as I did, I passed out again."

Then she crawled on her hands and knees to the couch in the living room and just lay there.

"I remember by the time I reached the couch, I could hear that ringing in my ears again and I was afraid I was going to pass out. It was one of those couches that opened into a bed. . . ."

Another piece of minutia.

Odell said she stayed on the couch for the next "three or four days."

"And the girls"—Odell's three daughters—"just kind of took care of themselves again?" Thomas asked. She was curious how the heck three girls —five, four, and three years old—could have fended for themselves.

"The girls kind of took care of *me*," Odell said.

Thomas and Weddle looked at each other. *What?*

Odell stuck to her story. She was saying that her three daughters, questionably old enough to go to the bathroom without the help of an adult, had taken care of her while she got her strength back.

Weddle and Odell then discussed how the babies were wrapped.

"There might have been a bedspread . . . I can't say for sure."

"So," Thomas asked, "how long do you think the baby was in the closet?"

"I know it was at least three days. . . ."

"After the three days, what did you do?"

"Umm . . . those—those three days, ah . . . I guess the stuff in the bottom of the closet was stuff that I decided I didn't—I didn't need to use every day, and I put it all in the box along with the baby."

"Do you remember at all . . . did your mother come over in those three days that you were in bed, with the second baby, I mean?"

"Yeah, yeah," Odell said excitedly, as if the mere mention of Mabel had sparked a memory.

"Did she notice anything? Ask anything?"

Odell said Mabel was upset because Odell hadn't kept a promise to bring her "someplace." Whether Mabel knew anything about the birth, she added, "I don't, I couldn't answer you, 'cause she had never said anything to me."

"She had never said anything to me."

"Did you ever tell her about this baby?" This would become one of the most crucial questions of the interview.

"I would rather cut off my arm than tell [my mother]," Odell said without hesitation.

3

Shortly after being impregnated in late 1984 by a man named David, who had moved into the house Odell and Mabel were living in, according to Odell later, he moved out in early 1985 and she never saw him again.

Alone in the house with Mabel, Odell went into labor one afternoon a few months later.

"I don't remember too much about this, because nothing is clear. . . . Everything is like one fluid movement.

"I had coffee with my mother—she fixed everything in the kitchen. When I got up, I lost my balance and I couldn't stand. She had said, 'This will help you.' When I woke up, I was on the floor . . . and my baby was next to me. It felt like I cried for days."

Beyond that, Odell couldn't recall much else about giving birth to the child and what happened to it afterward—only that her mother had killed it and she put it next to the others in a box.

By the middle of 1985, Odell had gotten a job at a local warehouse that imported lighting material from overseas to manufacture and sell in the United States. She had been through a plethora of men since divorcing James, one of whom was, in fact, James's brother. At thirty-two years old, she had given birth out of wedlock to three children between 1982 and 1985, to bring her child bearing total up to seven, four of whom were dead. The three children between 1982 and 1985 were killed by her mother, she claimed. She was hanging on to their corpses, which were inside her closet, carefully packaged in garbage bags, boxes, and a suitcase, because she wanted to give the children a proper burial someday, and, most important, she wanted to have proof of what Mabel had done to the kids when she went to authorities. Holding on to the bodies, she insisted, was going to later prove that Mabel had murdered them.

"Whenever I would broach the subject with Mom," Odell said, "she would give me one of those stares. . . . I kept the babies with me, in *my* room, I made sure she didn't have access to them, because I didn't want them disappearing. I wanted people to understand the things that were done to me. . . . I wanted to let them know my mother was as crazy as a bedbug, and they were my proof. And if I let them go and never saw them again, I would never get to lay them to rest properly. I would never have a grave site to go to. I knew what she had taken away from me. I didn't have the strength, tenacity, or the courage to break away from her. That's my ghost, my monster—that's the beast I deal with every day. My downfall. I could not, for the life of me, break away from her to do what I had to do."

Yet, that emotional bondage, Odell claimed, which had been with her for the better part of her thirty-two years, would begin to subside after she met the man who would later become her soul mate, confidant, and friend, Robert Sauerstein.

Late in 1985, after taking a few days off from work, Odell walked in one morning and saw Sauerstein. She walked past him the first time, she said, and didn't pay much attention. Soon, though, they were talking and, a while later, dating.

Obviously, from what Odell said later, any man she dated would have to pass Mabel's litmus test: Did he fit her qualifications for the ideal man? Or, rather, did he have the means to make money? Lots of money.

"She didn't like him," Odell said, "and I had asked her why, and she said, 'He has no potential.'"

"Well, he's a friend," Odell said, "and I like him.

"'You just make sure it doesn't become any more than that!'"

Odell and Sauerstein were still friends at that point.

Sauerstein had only been over to the lake house a few times for dinner.

"We laughed. We talked. We joked around. We did all those things."

Months later, as the friendship between Odell and Sauerstein turned into intimacy and romance, she and Mabel got into a financial jam. She couldn't recall the exact circumstances, but she remembered they needed extra money and Odell's checks from the factory weren't cutting it.

"That's when she came to me and asked me to ask Robert to move in with us, so he could help with the bills."

Following a pattern that seemed to dominate Odell's life as an adult, no sooner did Sauerstein move in during the fall of 1985, than Odell became pregnant for the eighth time.

4

Odell, sitting at attention, told Weddle and Thomas, near the end of that May 18 interview, that she would have rather lapped off her arm than tell Mabel she was pregnant. Still, Weddle and Thomas wanted to be certain they understood her correctly.

"So the answer is no?" Weddle asked. "You never told Mabel you were pregnant?"

"The answer is no!"

"She was just that type of person, huh?"

"Very stoic," Odell said.

"Is that . . . Was she a factor in . . . why you didn't take these babies to the hospital?"

"Oh, very much so."

"She was that much of an influence on you?"

"Oh yeah!"

"Is she living now?"

"No."

* * *

Mabel was diagnosed with congestive heart failure in 1993, generally a fatal disease of the heart. In 1995, she died. Was it a time of celebration for Odell, who had lived, she claimed, under Mabel's dysfunctional reign for the better part of forty years?

Odell said it wasn't. She felt a sense of relief, for obvious reasons, but it was no time to break out the champagne.

"My mother had used her disease as a crutch," she said, "to draw sympathy from me, guilt from me."

In many respects, one could say it worked, because it was Dianne Odell who had taken Mabel to the doctor's office whenever she needed to go.

"She wouldn't go by herself. She wouldn't take care of herself. . . . Even though I went out of my way to make sure she had her medications and shit, she wouldn't take them. At that point in time, I had drawn a line: I could lead a horse to water, but I couldn't force it to drink. I could get her pills, but I couldn't make her take them."

Near the end of her life, Mabel was having "ministrokes," Odell recalled. She started losing her ability to speak. Finally she died of an aneurism one afternoon.

"I felt unbelievable relief when she was finally gone. Unbelievable guilt. And then I spent two weeks waiting for her to come back and *get* me."

According to Odell, Mabel had said at various times that she was "*never* going to let [Odell] go." Even death, Mabel said, wouldn't stop her return from the grave to haunt her. Mabel had gotten into her head to a point, Odell claimed, where she believed she would *never* be rid of her.

"And she still tortures me to this day."

* * *

Questioned further about Mabel by Weddle, Odell said, "Her and my father were a good pair, they were."

"Meaning what?"

"Well, my father spent his life torturing me, and she—she spent her time trying to make me feel like it was okay."

"In what way do you mean 'torture'?"

"I used to get hit for nothing!"

"Physical, physically . . . ."

"Physical, yeah, something like that."

Odell then gave Weddle and Thomas an example, telling them a story about being hit in the face by her father's "closed fist" after being slashed with a belt.

"So very strong-personality-type parents?"

"Yeah."

For a few moments, Odell talked about her brothers, explaining how the abuse, as far as she could tell, was directed only at her. Afterward, she said she believed that if Mabel had never been in her life none of what was occurring at the moment—the babies in boxes, cops, the questioning—would have happened.

Weddle was curious, as was Thomas, why she thought her life would have turned out differently if Mabel hadn't been part of it.

"I would have . . . I would have done what any normal person does."

"Was there a question because you were an unwed mother?"

"Oh yes."

"That there would have been problems between you and your mother?"

"Yes."

"What would she have done?" Thomas asked. "You had the baby, the baby was deceased. What do you *think* she would have done if you were to have told her. . . . What would have happened?"

"She probably would have hit me. She didn't hit me very often, but when she did, she *did.*"

Weddle seemed interested in Odell's answer. Was Mabel one of the "underlying reasons" why her life had turned into such a mess?

"Yes."

"I mean why . . . why this happened? Why the three babies were found deceased and not buried?"

"A *very* big factor," Odell said. "I'm not blaming . . . I'm not blaming this on her—"

"No, I understand that," Weddle said.

"This is me, okay."

This statement by Odell fell more in line with a statement she had given to police back in 1989, when she was questioned about the death of Baby Matthew.

"For the length of my pregnancy," Odell said in 1989, "I did not receive any medical assistance, nor did I tell my mother I was pregnant."

Weddle and Thomas had found out only recently about Baby Matthew.

"One of the Towanda district attorneys, Stephen Downs," Thomas recalled later, "was also there [that second day we interviewed Odell], and he remembered something about that first baby. He made some phone calls and found a report dated 1989."

So Thomas and Weddle now had a clear picture of what had happened to Odell's first child. According to the report, Odell said "somewhere around" September or October 1989, "I went to Jamaica, New York, to see my father, John Molina. I did not get along well with my father." Odell was thirty-five years old at the time of the interview. "We sat at the kitchen table and I told my father I was pregnant and my mother did not have much money, and would he help me? He was disgusted with me. He told me to go into the TV room while he thought about whether I could stay there or not."

For several reasons, Weddle and Thomas viewed Odell's previous statement as contradictory. One, Odell would later claim her father had fathered the child during a rape. Two, she said she feared her father—that he was the last person in the world she would have ever turned to for help.

Although they now knew about Baby Matthew, Weddle and Thomas wanted to keep the focus on what had happened to the three babies found in Safford a little over a week ago. Odell had explained how Baby Number One and Baby Number Two could have died. But what about Baby Number Three? What were the circumstances surrounding the third baby's death?

"To be really honest with you," Odell said when Thomas asked about the third baby, "I can't recall much about [it] at all."

Thomas pushed her. "Do you know . . . How did you get pregnant? Did you have another relationship?"

"Yes."

Then the interview centered on Odell meeting Robert Sauerstein and the reasons why they moved from state to state: New York to Pennsylvania, Utah to Arizona, Texas to Pennsylvania. Throughout the interview, Odell was asked several times if she wanted something to eat, if she wanted to take a break, or if she needed to use the rest room. Essentially, she was being questioned under her own free will. She could leave at any time.

Interestingly enough, at one point, Thomas asked, "And you never told your mother [about the dead babies in boxes], even before she passed away?"

"No! Like I said, I would rather have had my arm cut off and be beaten to death before [I would do] that!"

Soon after the interview concluded, Odell collected her things and prepared to leave. Before she stepped out the door, Thomas walked over to her and told her there was a possibility the case would be handed over to New York authorities and they would be getting in touch with her soon.

Odell was tired and beaten down by the emotional toll the interview had taken on her. In a sense, she had dredged up feelings and thoughts she had perhaps long ago parted with. "Okay," she said to Thomas.

Just then, as she was walking toward the door with Sauerstein, Trooper Williams approached her. "Take care of yourself. Thanks for coming in and speaking with us. We appreciate it."

"Thank *you*, Trooper Williams," Odell said, "and thank Diane Thomas and Bruce Weddle, all of you, for . . . for treating me with respect and dignity."

"Okay," Williams said as Odell walked over to him and, he said later, hugged him, said good-bye, and walked out the door.

CHAPTER 11

1

ON AUGUST 18, 1986, with Mabel and Robert Sauerstein by her side, Dianne Odell went into labor. By the end of the day, she would give birth to Clarissa, her eighth child, her fourth living child. With Sauerstein now part of the family, living in the house, the father of the child, Odell was brought to Community General Hospital once again while Mabel stayed at home. This would become an important issue later—because whenever Odell had a man in her life who knew she was pregnant and she went into labor, she ended up having the child at a hospital.

Was it a coincidence?

Odell later said she "never" told Mabel she was pregnant with Clarissa. She was afraid, she claimed, "that if Robert left," she would be alone and pregnant with only Mabel to look after her.

"What I did was, I told her on the way out the door that I was on my way to the hospital."

Odell had been pregnant seven times previously, had four of those children in the house, Mabel by her side, so she claimed. But this one, the eighth child,

Mabel didn't know about? Authorities would find this hard to believe—the fact that Mabel, whom Odell had described as someone who was constantly in her face and trying to control her, wouldn't have known she was pregnant. It was a near impossibility.

2

At the conclusion of the May 18 interview, Odell, who hadn't really admitted to much of anything substantial, was free to go. She was not under arrest, nor was she in custody. Thomas, however, warned Odell that New York authorities would be contacting her about the case. As of now, though, she was a free woman.

None of what had taken place had comforted Odell. In a way, her past was beginning to catch up with her. Soon, she knew, everything was going to have to come out. There was still that shadowing aura of the media hovering around, trying to sniff out a story, and Odell was fully prepared for it, though she had no idea, really, just how big a story it was going to be within the next twenty-four hours.

What was important to Weddle and Thomas, as they sat back and talked about the interview after Odell left, was where the babies had been born— that much Odell had admitted: Kauneonga Lake, New York.

"In law enforcement," Thomas said, "that meant that the jurisdiction of this case was no longer in Arizona. It now belonged to New York."

Weddle and Thomas knew their work was finished once they heard the babies were born in New York. They would have to stick around and debrief New York authorities on what they had uncovered, but the case would fall on the shoulders of the NYSP—if, in fact, they felt they had enough evidence to pursue it. There were all sorts of questions lingering regarding statue of limitations, manslaughter, first- and second-degree murder. But the main question, the one piece of information no one seemed to know: had the children been born alive?

As of yet, there was no proof they had been. Odell was sure of her story and had, if nothing else, thought it out thoroughly. When Weddle had asked her if she recalled one of the babies crying, she said she couldn't remember. Thus, if the babies were stillborn, there was no case, and the only person who could vouch for the childrens' well-being was the same person who had said she couldn't remember. Essentially, the entire case fell on Dianne Odell and what she would do next.

3

As Mabel, Odell, Sauerstein, and Odell's four living children—one of whom had been fathered by Sauerstein—began a new stage of their lives at the lake, things seemed to be going rather well as the new year, 1987, approached. For Odell, it was about stability. She had a man in her life who loved her, which was all she had ever wanted. But Mabel wasn't going anywhere. She became, at this point, a nuisance for Odell, a ball and chain that would seemingly never detach itself. Wherever Odell and her family went, Mabel was there tagging along.

"We're not living high on the hog at this point," Odell remembered, "but I'm happy. I'm coming out of the darkness and into the light."

Indeed, since 1972 she had given birth to eight children—four of whom were dead. Just having Clarissa and keeping her alive, one could speculate, was a step in the right direction.

By this time, Baby Matthew, still locked inside the

blue suitcase, decomposing, had been moved from attics to closets to toolsheds. Along with Matthew, though, there were three more dead children in boxes, wrapped in plastic bags and blankets, also being moved from place to place. When Odell, Sauerstein, Mabel, and the living children moved again during the summer of 1987, they abandoned an old Volkswagen, which hadn't run in years. Either mistakenly or on purpose—the truth would never be known—the blue suitcase containing Matthew's remains was left inside the trunk of the car.

"When we got evicted from that brown-and-white house," Odell said, "we only had three days to get out."

Apparently, within the struggle to gather her personal items, Odell must have failed to realize the suitcase was inside the trunk of the car, where Mabel had put it after getting that call from George Hess, who had found the baby in an attic he had cleaned out one day.

Sauerstein, who had recently gotten laid off, had been offered a job in Hawley, Pennsylvania, a small town outside of Scranton, on the northern tip of Lake Wallenpaupack.

Because Sauerstein had to find a home big enough for Odell, the kids, and, of course, Mabel, he went ahead to Hawley while Odell, the kids, and Mabel moved into a motel in Cochecton, New York, just outside of Monticello.

By the time Sauerstein got settled in his new construction job, it was January 1988. By then, he had found an apartment on Main Street in Hawley. Four months later, however, after the place didn't work out, they moved to Paupack Street, not too far away, near downtown Hawley.

As they settled into their new home, Sauerstein worked hard to support all of them. Yet, as they were still just getting by, Odell had *another* announcement to make.

"I'm pregnant."

Her ninth pregnancy. But still, the reality of Odell being pregnant again wouldn't center on whether she would have the child; it came down to whether the child would live—and that, of course, as history had proven, depended on how Odell's relationship with Sauerstein went.

4

At six o'clock on Sunday night, May 18, 2003, Sullivan County, New York, district attorney Steve Lungen received a call that introduced him to the Safford, Arizona, case of the three dead babies found in boxes. Lungen had just gotten home from a day of riding his Harley-Davidson, a bike he had purchased in 2001 as, he said jokingly, "part of a midlife crisis." Before buying the bike, Lungen had never driven a motorcycle. Yet, he fell in love immediately with the wind on his face and the meditative sound of the tar humming underneath his feet.

"When I bought the Harley," Lungen recounted, "I thought my wife was going to divorce me . . . but now she gets mad at me if I don't take her when I go out for a ride. I love it. It's the only thing that really relaxes me."

The spring air was mild in the Northeast in May 2003. Summer was in the air. One of the ways Lungen was able to get away from the daily grind of prosecuting murderers and rapists, thieves and child molesters, was to hop on his bike with his wife, hit the road, and forget about the madness that infused his daily life as one of Sullivan County's most dedicated and esteemed prosecutors.

As Lungen rolled his bike into his garage, his cell phone rang. It was Rick Sauer, a NYSP investigator.

"I just got off the phone with the Pennsylvania State

Police," Sauer said. "They are investigating a case involving a woman with babies. There's a claim that maybe she had another baby we found back in the 1980s."

Lungen sat down on a crate in his garage and caught his breath. He hadn't been home five minutes. It was a Sunday. Dead babies? A mother? *Can I ever catch a break from this?*

"Do you remember the case at all, Steve?" Sauer asked.

Lungen shot back a few questions, more specific in nature, and then a bell went off. "Yes!" he told Sauer. "There was a fetus found in the trunk of a car out by Kauneonga Lake."

As Sauer began to say something, Lungen thought: *The fetus had been found in the trunk of a Volkswagen back in the late '80s and I had considered prosecuting the case. I tracked down the woman who had abandoned the newborn inside the suitcase, but . . .* Then, "I don't recall her name, Rick. But I remember we found the woman and determined we couldn't proceed with a criminal case because of her position that she claimed the baby was stillborn." Lungen paused and took a sip from a bottle of water he generally always kept by his side. "Why, what's going on?"

"Okay, let me get back to you," Sauer said. "You're going to get a call from the DA in Pennsylvania. They're investigating this case in Arizona where they think this mother killed three of her babies. And we think that maybe this baby in the 1980s might be related. But let me call you back."

"Right. Okay."

Lungen put his bike away and didn't think too much about the call. It had been a long day of riding and forgetting about work. The last thing he expected on a Sunday night was getting mixed up with three dead babies and a case he had tried to prosecute nearly twenty years ago.

For any district attorney who had harbored truth and justice as a sixth sense, however, work *was* life, life *was* work. It was a twenty-four-hour, seven-day-a-week job. There were no breaks.

Fifteen minutes later, while Lungen was sitting in his kitchen preparing to eat dinner with his wife, the phone rang again.

"Listen, Steve," Sauer said, "we've been questioning this woman, Dianne Odell, in Pennsylvania. Based on our conversations with her, three babies that were found in a storage shed in Safford, Arizona, were traced back to Pennsylvania and eventually back to New York—which is *your* jurisdiction."

Lungen stared at the kitchen table, ran his hand across his forehead. "What has she said?"

"Well, she said the babies were born in Sullivan County, which makes it *your* case."

"Okay," Lungen said, "let me think about this."

"We're not arresting her. I want to make that clear," Sauer added. They weren't even sure, Sauer continued, that they had a case. He was calling to inform Lungen what was going on. In fact, after interviewing Odell that afternoon, the PSP had allowed her to go home, Sauer explained.

"We weren't exactly sure what it was she had said to the Pennsylvania State Police during what had turned out to be four hours of taped interviews," Lungen recalled. "Had we known at the time, it may have changed our position."

After he and his wife ate dinner, Lungen put in a call to one of his investigators and had him set up a meeting with the Pennsylvania authorities—a sort of get-acquainted-with-the-case gathering. He told him to schedule the meeting for the first thing Monday morning. Lungen and his two investigators, along with an investigator from the NYSP, would drive down to Wilkes-Barre, Pennsylvania, and sort out what was going on. If Odell was admitting to murdering the babies in Sullivan County, then it was indeed Lungen's case. But who knew at this point? Odell, Lungen soon learned, hadn't really admitted to much of anything just yet.

Immediately Lungen began to worry about the media. He was told the story was about to blow up, which would generally hamper an investigation and make cops and attorneys conduct business differently. But the media in this case, Lungen recalled, would ultimately be an asset. The pressure the media was about to put on Odell as she left the interview with Thomas and Weddle would, in effect, break the case open.

5

On July 10, 1988, Adam Sauerstein was born to Odell and Robert Sauerstein. A healthy baby, Adam was given life by the wonderful doctors and nurses at Wayne Memorial Hospital in Honesdale, Pennsylvania. Odell, now almost thirty-five years old, had five small children at home and four dead children still waiting for, in her words, a proper burial.

For the next eight months, Odell lived a life she later described once again as "a constant state of fear." She began to suspect Mabel might do something to her living children. Yet, at the same time, she claimed, she was happier than she had ever been. Sauerstein, for the most part, treated her well, and because he was around, Mabel's abusive behavior had been kept to a minimum. Still, there was always, she said, that lingering notion that Mabel would hurt the children if she decided to either tell Sauerstein about the dead children or run to the police and explain how Mabel had murdered them.

The life Odell was managing—a life that included stowing away four dead babies as if they were hand-me-down clothes—was all about to change, however.

Near the beginning of 1989, Max Shapiro, a forty-eight-year-old junk dealer who owned and operated a small junkyard behind his home in Bethel, not too far from where Odell and Mabel had spent much of the past fifteen years living on Kauneonga Lake, received a call from a woman who lived on the lake. The woman asked Max to come to the lake and tow an "abandoned vehicle" off her property. A family who had recently moved out of the area, she explained, had left the car behind.

Always looking for quality used auto parts, Max drove up to the lake a day or so later and towed the Volkswagen away.

For months, the vehicle sat in Max's junkyard collecting more rust than it already had. Then, on March 14, after it had been stripped of all of its valuable parts, Max decided to ready it for the press so he could sell it for scrap metal.

With most vehicles, Max liked to go through them one last time before he fed them into the press. With the trunk of a Volkswagen in the front of the vehicle, Max took out a crowbar and *snapped* the lip open to see if someone may have left anything of value behind.

"Inside was a gray plastic garbage bag," Max later told police, "containing a blue suitcase, a blanket, and a fancy picture with different-colored glass."

Max took the items out, put them off to the side, and continued salvaging the vehicle.

After he finished pressing the Volkswagen, he took the items from the trunk inside his house. Then, with his wife nearby, Max took the same crowbar and opened the suitcase. Immediately Max and his wife,

Elita, a registered nurse, discovered what they believed to be a fetus.

Without touching anything, Max phoned the NYSP. "I think I've found what appears to be a decomposed infant body."

Trooper James Schultz took the call. After a few detailed questions, he said, "Thanks. We'll send somebody right out."

The first trooper to arrive on scene was Michael Hunter, who interviewed Max and his wife. After realizing how accurate they were in their description of the baby, Hunter then contacted the Bureau of Criminal Investigation (BCI) in Ferndale.

While Hunter waited for BCI to show up, he secured the scene.

It didn't take long. A few hours after Max Shapiro's call, a swarm of cops were scouring the junkyard as if they were looking for a bomb. What was interesting about the case from the get-go for cops was the fact that the woman who had discarded the Volkswagen hadn't done anything to conceal her identity. In fact, the picture frame found next to the suitcase had the name Dianne Gail [Ingalls] printed on the front of the frame, Ingalls being Odell's first married name. Furthermore, a quick check of the license plate Max had lifted from the car before pulverizing it proved that the last-known owner of the vehicle was a local woman named Dianne Odell.

Elita Shapiro, Max's wife, indicated to one of the officers that she had known Odell at one time. "She once lived in Kauneonga Lake across the street from the telephone building," Elita said, "but has since moved, I think, to Pennsylvania. I believe she has three girls."

A day or so later, two investigators tracked down James Odell's brother and sister. They said they hadn't seen her for about eight years.

The one BCI investigator who seemed to take control of the investigation from the beginning was Roy Streever, a tall, good-looking cop who had a reputation on the job for having a "wild sense of humor." Although many other BCI investigators participated in the investigation and certainly worked as hard as Streever, he took a personal interest from the start—not for any particular reason other than a child was involved. It made Streever's stomach turn—like other BCI cops—to think that someone, a human being, could abandon or murder a child and toss it in a suitcase like an unwanted, deceased pet.

"We didn't have a case against Dianne Odell," Streever was quick to point out later, "until *she* made it for us."

At six feet, 210 pounds, with brown hair and eyes to match, Streever was known as one of the more experienced investigators BCI had on the force. He had joined the NYSP in 1978 and worked in Sullivan County as a trooper for seven years before becoming part of the BCI in 1986, working out of Middletown, New York, about thirty miles west of Monticello.

Over the years, Streever developed a love for bluegrass music and playing the guitar. The music, he said, helped him forget about the horrors he witnessed every day. Already well into his career, he ended up as one of only a handful of polygraphists the NYSP used. Through that job, he mastered the art of questioning and interrogating suspects.

After interviewing several people who had either known Odell or had somehow been part of her bloodline, Streever finally found her in Hawley, Pennsylvania, where she was living with Mabel, Sauerstein, and her five children. Nobody knew it then, but Odell was four months pregnant, carrying yet another child. She wasn't quite showing yet because she was so overweight.

Odell was upstairs when the BCI knocked at her door.

The house that Sauerstein had found in Hawley was spacious, certainly, but with eight of them—and Mabel, Odell said, insisting on having her own room—it might as well have been a shoe box.

The most bizarre behavior Dianne Odell displayed as she and her family moved around the country would have to been toting the dead babies with her, as if they were nothing more than boxes of old books. Not only because she would have to pick the boxes up and physically move them, knowing what was inside, but what about her living children? Alice was eleven years old; Maryann ten; Doris eight. One can only imagine the horror one of those kids might have faced when opening a box, thinking maybe there were Christmas presents or something else inside, and instead discovering three corpses. The other children, Adam, one, and Clarissa, three, were perhaps too young. But Maryann, Alice, and Doris were certainly old enough—and curious enough—to comprehend what was inside the boxes if they had stumbled upon them.

Odell later claimed she went through great pains to make sure the children or Sauerstein didn't see what was inside the boxes. And, she added, none of them ever did. But the thought of just picking those boxes up so many times, knowing their contents, and moving them around, must have taken an emotional toll on Odell.

"When we moved, *I* moved those boxes," she said. "They were the first things I always took, to be sure I always had them with me. Not for any devious or malicious purpose," she added, "but to make sure when I got to where I was going to settle, and my mother had passed away, I was going to show proof of this and . . . tell my story."

She further claimed she had every intention of going to the police and explaining what had happened. But she couldn't, she insisted, until either Mabel became so incapacitated she couldn't take care of herself, or she dropped dead.

Why?

"I was fearful my mother would harm my children if I ever told the truth about what happened to those dead children. It was always a fear. Always. Always. Always!"

Mabel would prove to Odell at times that she had control over the information in the boxes, and if Odell had ever considered going to police or telling Sauerstein, Mabel would harm her living children, according to Dianne. There was one time when Odell had to go out without the kids and Mabel hid the kids in the house before Odell returned. When Odell walked in and asked where the children were, Mabel said, "See how easily it can happen?" before beckoning the children to come out.

"I knew the real meaning of what was going on. . . . I knew it was directed at me. It was designed to let me know she still had control, still had power. . . ."

In light of this, the questions some asked later were: Why not just leave the house with the children and Sauerstein and the boxes and do the right thing? Why stay? Why tote around Mabel, too, from home to home?

Odell claimed it wasn't that simple. Mabel could have gone to the police herself and lied if she ever left her. She was trapped, in other words.

By the time they settled in Hawley, Odell explained, Mabel, hated Sauerstein.

"She wanted Robert gone. He was never supposed to be anything other than a 'fill-in' to get her over a hump and pay some bills. She knew she couldn't do anything to manipulate Robert. And that tore at her. As a matter of fact, she told my children Robert was not their father, they did not have to listen to him, that he was nothing to them, that he was a bum, that he would never amount to anything, and that he didn't love them and was basically there to see what he could get."

But now there were two of Sauerstein's children in the house and Odell was pregnant with a third.

"You know the Wicked Witch of the West?" Sauerstein said later. "That was Mabel." She was a backstabber. Very angry. With Odell, Mabel was "very domineering. She would only joke around with her and smile at her on payday."

Sauerstein said he didn't find it strange at the time, but later, after he thought about it, he realized it was odd how Odell "always took the children with her whenever she went out. She never wanted to leave them alone with Mabel."

Moreover, it wasn't until many years later that Sauerstein figured out that the three angel ornaments Odell would put on the Christmas tree every year represented the three dead babies.

"She loved those kids," Sauerstein said, referring to Baby Number One, Baby Number Two, and Baby Number Three. "She loved them. She was a great mother."

Odell was upstairs on March 14, 1989, pregnant, in bed resting, when a subtle knock at the door by the BCI was about to send her life into another tailspin. A fetus had been found in the trunk of a car she owned. The BCI needed an explanation.

CHAPTER 12

1

AFTER GRADUATING FROM Brooklyn Law School in 1978, Steve Lungen started his career in law as an assistant district attorney (ADA) in Sullivan County. Four years later, in January 1982, he was elected district attorney for what would be the first of several times. He was born about fifteen hundred feet from the Sullivan County Courthouse, where he eventually would keep an office on the bottom floor. Despite a slight hunch in his walk, at six feet three inches, 185 pounds, weight lifting and running had kept Lungen in excellent physical shape. Lungen was a lifelong resident of Monticello, and his family ran a small garage in town from 1919 until it closed in 1969.

"I grew up in that business working on cars and pushing gas."

After high school, Lungen went to the University of Miami for four years, but never considered law as a career path.

"I always thought I could come back home after college and work in the family business, but the

economy, in the early to late 1960s, dropped greatly
. . . and the business, because of the economy and
the effect it had on Monticello and the Catskills,
changed. Sullivan County went from a credible
tourist county . . . to really economically depressed
for a very long time."

Indeed, the Catskills, during the '50s and '60s,
became a Mecca for top entertainment. Known locally
as the "Borscht Belt," mainly because of its large Jewish
population, the actual mountains are an extension of
the Appalachians, and for anyone making the drive up
Route 17, heading into Sullivan County, they rise
toward the clouds on both sides of the interstate.

Northwest of New York City, the "Jewish Alps," as the
Catskills were once known, drew a plethora of A-list
celebrities: Allen, Amsterdam, Berle, Bishop, Brooks,
Bruce, Buttons, Burns, Caesar, Diller, Davis, Sinatra,
Martin, King, among many others. They had all
worked Catskill Mountain resorts to large crowds
during its heyday in the '50s, '60s and '70s. As it was,
the charming allure and aesthetic brilliance of the
mountains themselves brought in people from all
over the world. For those who lived and worked in the
region—like a young Steve Lungen—business was
great. Restaurants, diners, motels and hotels, gas stations, and five-and-dimes thrived on the tourist money
being pumped in.

Today, the Catskills suffer from the same economic
effects much of America has learned to cope with. Popular entertainment acts stopped flocking to the region
in the late '70s and early '80s as Atlantic City, in nearby
New Jersey, and New York City, in the south, underwent
infrastructure overhauls and began drawing the bulk
of the crowds and big names. Some say a revival has
hit the region recently, but one might be hard-pressed
to see immediate results. Indian casinos are going

up, but the windfall of cash and star power that once dominated the region is gone forever.

One of the only reasons Lungen decided to go to the University of Miami was because he had developed a severe case of mononucleosis during his senior year in high school and doctors suggested he head south, where the weather was generally warmer.

"Let's say it like it was: I was a bad student in high school," Lungen recalled. "I had relatives down in Florida, and when I got sick, it seemed like the place to go. I actually wasn't a bad student in Florida, however. I realized when I got down there, and began studying, that, hey, I can do this."

During Lungen's senior year in college, 1966 to 1967, the war in Vietnam started heating up—and that's when his life changed.

"Being a resident of Sullivan County," Lungen said, "a rural county, the draft quotas were never met. I was really expecting to be drafted. Something came out where they said if anyone had gone to graduate school, anyone who graduated in '67 and decided on graduate school, would get a one-year reprieve from the draft. So I applied to law school at the last minute, and to my own shock, I got in."

But his intentions hadn't included law school. It had never entered his mind until the skirmish in Vietnam broke out, and, like many kids throughout the country, he began looking for a way to avoid the hell of war.

At the time, Lungen began dating a woman he had known since he was a child. Near the end of his first year in law school, he and Eileen got married. Life seemed to be going well. But about a week after Lungen and Eileen returned from their honeymoon, he went to the mailbox and was shocked to learn that he hadn't escaped the draft, after all. It was time to pack his bags and head off to boot camp . . . then on to Vietnam, a place that would change his entire outlook on life and law.

2

The BCI cops knocking on Dianne Odell's door on March 14, 1989, had a few simple questions for her, the most important: Did you own a gold Volkswagen?

They knew she had, but her answer would tell them if it was going to be a productive interview, or a conversation with a liar.

With Odell in her bedroom resting, Sauerstein ran upstairs and calmly said, "The police are downstairs. They want to talk to you."

Odell was advised, according to a police report detailing the interview, of her "constitutional rights and waived them. . . ." Further, "Odell acknowledged her rights and *did not* want an attorney present while she talked."

She later said the investigators asked her "to get dressed and come down to the police station to answer some questions.

"So I went back upstairs, got dressed, and went with them."

When asked about the Volkswagen, Odell confirmed she was the last owner. She also admitted the picture frame found inside the blue suitcase was hers. The blue suitcase—inscribed with her initials, DGI, Dianne Gail Ingalls, her first married name—was hers, too, she said, but she had no idea how it ended up in the trunk of the Volkswagen.

"Do you recall placing the suitcase in the trunk of the car?" one of the BCI investigators asked.

"No," Odell said. Then she denied having any knowledge of the fetus found inside the suitcase. "I have five children and they were all born at hospitals. If I ever have vaginal bleeding or discharge," she then added for no apparent reason, "I immediately seek a doctor."

"What about the blanket in the suitcase?"

"I have no recollection of the bedspread. The initials on the suitcase—DGI—are also unfamiliar to me."

Further, she told the cops how she had moved from one apartment to the next while living at the lake and finally ended up in Pennsylvania after abandoning the Volkswagen.

With her voice cracking, Odell later recalled that day in vivid detail, and had no trouble admitting why she decided to lie to police.

"You have to understand one thing: my mother is alive and living in that house with me and my children at the time. Okay, so they come and they talk to me and they tell me what they find in the VW. And I then turn around and tell them I don't know *anything* about it. I had to do that, because I had to go back and talk to my mother and ask her what she wanted me to tell them. *She* knew the truth and *I* knew the truth.

"I *wanted* to tell the truth," she continued. "I wanted to tell *everything* that had happened—but she told me no." Mabel, according to Odell, didn't want to get involved. "It will involve me, and I don't want to be involved," Mabel said that day after Odell spoke to the police.

"And so, you tell them the truth," Mabel further insisted, "but you just leave me out of it!"

3

First thing Monday morning, May 19, 2003, Sullivan County DA Steve Lungen, along with Thomas Scileppi, NYSP senior investigator for the BCI, Troop F, in Liberty, New York, and one of Lungen's investigators, Paul Hans, a former cop himself, took off for Wilkes-Barre, Pennsylvania. On Sunday night, after he spoke to Rick Sauer a few more times and learned a bit more about the Odell case, Lungen set up a meeting with members of the PSP.

On hand for the meeting, which started at about 11:00 A.M., were Diane Thomas and Bruce Weddle, the two cops who probably knew more about the case at this point than anybody else.

The meeting in Wilkes-Barre lasted about two hours. By the end, one thing was clear: the case was Steve Lungen's. It may have ended in a self-storage unit in Safford, Arizona, but it started in Monticello, New York, back some twenty years prior.

"When we left that meeting," Lungen recalled, "we went outside and began strategizing about what we were going to do."

How were Lungen and his investigators going to, as he put it, "pick this case up and run with it?" They were certain, after speaking with Weddle and Thomas, that Odell had had something to do with the demise of the children.

The PSP had allowed Odell to leave the barracks the previous day. She hadn't been read her Miranda rights or arrested because nobody was all that certain a crime had been committed. Thus, how was Lungen and his team going to approach Odell? Would she continue talking? Had she retained a lawyer? Did he even have a case?

4

The one part of the puzzle the BCI had to complete before they could truly focus on Odell in 1989 as a possible suspect in the death of the fetus found inside her Volkswagen was finding out how the baby had died and how long it had been dead. On March 15, 1989, the fetus was transported from a morgue in Harris, New York, where it had been, to the Albany County Medical Center, in the state's capital city. The county medical examiner, Dr. Michael Baden, would do his best to find out what had happened to Baby Doe, as law enforcement were now calling the child.

In years hence, Dr. Baden would become one of the most recognizable forensic pathologists in the world— the Jack Nicklaus of his field. With a hit television show, *Autopsy*, Baden was the coauthor of two reputable books on forensics. He appeared frequently on the Fox News Channel, commenting on everything from the Laci Peterson murder to the Natalee Holloway case in Aruba to just about anything having to do with high-profile murder and crime.

"In 1965," Baden said later, "I finished my training at Bellevue Hospital [and] I became a full-time medical examiner for the city of New York, and have remained over the years in that one position or another as a full-time medical examiner/forensic pathologist."

Pathology has always been Baden's calling, from that first day he walked into an autopsy suite and tried to understand through the process of death how a person had lived and died.

Near the end of World War II, a system in medicine was developed so a physician could qualify himself as a "specialist" in any number of the twenty-four different fields that make up "medicine": internal medicine, obstetrics, oncology, radiology, pathology, and so on. Meeting criteria designed for each field and having "successfully completed a residency," Baden said, "in that specialty in a recognized hospital," allowed doctors to become "board certified," a term that, one could argue, has been thrown around rather loosely over the years by radio and television doctors.

At 2:30 P.M., on March 15, 1989, Dr. Baden, along with pathology assistant Herman Thomas and criminalist

Cathy Oakes, conducted the first autopsy on Baby Doe. The fetus had been sitting in a blue suitcase for sixteen years. Although it had mummified some, for the most part it was not in the condition a medical examiner might have preferred. As fragile and dry as a decades-old beehive, musty and leathery, Baby Doe looked more like a prop out of a science-fiction movie than a newborn child. To think a cause of death could be determined after so many years had passed, or even blood-typing or analyzing DNA (which hadn't materialized into the dependable science it would later become) seemed nearly impossible. Too much time had elapsed. The environment the baby had been kept in, being moved from place to place, bounced around inside a suitcase for so long, would have an effect on any type of actual testing that would help Baden make his determinations.

Despite all that, however, one thing Baden could say for certain, as he concluded his autopsy at 4:30 P.M. that same day, was that the baby ". . . was a full-term Caucasian female."

Female? Odell would later refer to the baby as "Matthew."

"My belief? It was a male!" Odell said later when faced with the discrepancy. "How they came up with female, I don't know. Somebody twisted it around and said that the last baby [Baby Number Three] was a little boy. I don't know how that got twisted, but there is a lot of information that's twisted."

A forensic pathologist, though, would have a hard time "twisting" medical facts—and Baden was certain Baby Doe was female because he had scientific testing on the child to prove such. Furthermore, in those police reports taken in 1989, Odell herself even agreed.

"You know," Odell said later, "I'm going to be very honest here. A lot of the stuff that I remember is in bits and pieces, because it's not a full memory, umm, oh, a lot of it comes back in flashbacks. And, since my mother was such a *loving* woman," she added sarcastically, "you know, it's very possible that even *I* have it all backwards. There were two male children"—she paused for a moment to collect her thoughts—"and, I believe, two female children. It's very easy to mix them up. The only difference in their births was the fact that my mother was there—and my mother took them first before I had the opportunity to be with them. If I could sit down and rattle off . . . this happened and that happened in chronological order, it would make me a pretty harsh person. . . . That would make me, even to myself, seem calculating."

Baden concluded the baby "had been dead for years," but couldn't pin down exactly how long. "It could be upwards to thirty years," he reported, ". . . before the legalized abortion era, since the birth cord was torn near the placenta instead of cut." It was clear, too, that it was a "spontaneous birth, but I could not determine . . . if the baby was born alive or not."

He said he would submit DNA samples to a local lab to see if it could come up with a death date.

By March 24, word had spread throughout the Kauneonga Lake region that a baby had been recovered from a blue suitcase inside the trunk of a Volkswagen. Hearing about it, one of James Odell's sisters, *Madeline*, got hold of the state police with some rather interesting information.

"Contact George and Marie Hess," Madeline told police. "They may have possible knowledge of the baby you guys found."

The BCI sent an investigator out to talk to Madeline. Maybe she knew more?

"Rumor has it," Madeline said, "that the Hesses discovered a suitcase in the attic of the house they had rented to Dianne Odell and her mother, Mabel

Molina. It was blue. The Hesses called Mabel and told her to come pick it up and they did."

This sent the BCI straight to the Hesses, who, in turn, confirmed the story. It was about eight to ten years ago, George Hess explained. "Yes. There was a fetus inside the suitcase. And yes, Mabel picked it up."

By this time, the DNA had come back, but "an insufficient amount of human DNA was obtained from the evidence materials." The lab, in effect, didn't have the resources or the DNA to draw any conclusions.

Lungen still had every reason to believe either Odell or her mother had had something to do with the baby's death and urged the BCI to continue investigating.

"Question Dianne Odell *again*. See what you can come up with," Lungen urged.

5

At 1:00 p.m., on Monday, May 19, 2003, after a productive meeting in Wilkes-Barre with Diane Thomas, Bruce Weddle, and several other investigators involved in a strange case that had begun in Arizona a week prior, Steve Lungen and his team left to drive back to New York. The case was now officially his. That much was clear. But he really didn't have a clue as to what Odell had admitted to, or if he even had enough evidence to consider arresting her. He hadn't heard the interviews Thomas and Weddle had conducted with Odell, nor had he reviewed the transcripts.

"We decided to drive back to the DA's office," Lungen recalled, "and discuss what we had."

In the interim, as Odell, Sauerstein, and their children were at home in Rome, the media descended upon Odell's house as if she had announced she were giving a press conference. Several satellite trucks, local news vans, newspaper reporters, and a reporter from the Associated Press had finally figured out what had happened in Pima, Arizona, and tracked Odell down. From inside her home, Odell looked out the window to see the media hovering around the house, waiting for her to emerge. News of a mother killing her children was lead story material. Throughout the past two decades, several high-profile cases had made headlines: Mary Beth Tinning, a Schenectady, New York, woman, who, between 1972 and 1985, murdered nine of her children; Susan Smith, a South Carolina woman, who drowned her two boys by "driving her auto into a lake while the children slept in their car seats" and then blamed their "abductions" on a "black man"; more recently, Andrea Yates, a Texas woman, who drowned five of her kids in the family's bathtub.

In the eyes of the media, Odell was possibly part of that group—a mother who had killed not one or two of her kids, but several. Anytime a frightened teenager, pregnant and alone, went to her prom and left a baby in a toilet, the media whipped itself into a frenzy and ran with the story: WHY DO MOTHERS KILL THEIR CHILDREN? Radio and television talk shows, soon after the crimes were reported, were usually inundated with callers looking to try, convict, and sentence these women. It was a social topic that stirred heated debate among Americans—and heated debate, for good or bad, meant ratings. But a mother who could have killed several of her children? Now, that was a story.

"The media was banging on the door, driving my dog crazy," Odell recalled.

As Odell tried to figure out what to do, Sauerstein, knowing the situation would only escalate as the day progressed, began to think of a way to get Odell out of the house without anyone seeing her. Additionally, the kids would be coming home from school soon, and reporters would question them as they got off the bus.

"I told Robert, 'I'm going to have to get out of here and see if I can drag them (the media) with me.' I wanted to sit down and talk to my family as a whole and explain everything that had happened from beginning to end. I didn't want them reading about me in the newspaper."

For a prosecutor, the media was, generally, an annoyance early on in any potential murder case, waiting, hovering, looking for information. Prosecutors were good at molding media contacts and putting out information to assist their cases, but Lungen, at this point, likely knew less than the media. He was convinced they were only going to get in the way and make matters worse. Yet, little did anyone know at the time, but the frenzied gathering outside of Odell's home would, in the coming hours, be an asset to Lungen and his team as they headed back to New York to discuss how to proceed with the case.

As 2:00 P.M. approached, Thomas Scileppi, senior investigator for the BCI in Liberty, drove with his partner in one vehicle from Wilkes-Barre, while Lungen, Paul Hans, and Robert Rowan—Lungen's investigators—drove in a second vehicle behind them. It was a two-hour trip back to Monticello. Although the trip was perhaps long, it would encourage the opportunity for the four men to discuss the case via two-way radios and cell phones.

There was a lot to do.

The first "holy shit" moment of the day, as Lungen and Hans later described it, became the case itself.

"This is a twenty-five-year-old case," Lungen explained, "three dead babies, a fourth dead baby some thirty years ago! How can a legal case of murder be made out of *this*? That's what we were looking at in the beginning. From my perspective as the DA, when we left [Pennsylvania], I knew we needed to get a game plan together quickly. For one, Odell wasn't under arrest; she was out walking around."

There was one problem that worried Lungen at that moment more than anything else, however. "What if she gets a lawyer?" Another problem—at least it seemed like a problem to Lungen as they began to make their way back to Monticello—was the "national media," who were calling Lungen's office looking for information and also calling the PSP in Towanda, the closest barracks to Odell's home in Rome. As a prosecutor, Lungen had become accustomed to telling the media to take a hike. The last thing a competent DA would have done was release pertinent information to the public as a case developed. The less information a suspect had as investigators began digging into his or her life, the better off the DA's office was. The media—nine times out of ten—hampered this process and made it difficult for everyone to do their jobs.

Even more important was that a pathologist in Pima, Arizona, who had autopsied the three babies, hadn't yet come up with a cause of death. Everyone was still waiting. Lungen had called Dr. Baden—who vaguely recalled the 1989 case of Baby Doe he had been involved in—and told him to call Arizona to see what he could find out. Baden said he would.

"Were they stillborn babies?" Lungen recalled later, talking about those early moments of the case as it unfolded. "Were they alive babies? Were they dead babies? We needed to know all of this."

Heading north on Interstate 81, about an hour into their two-hour trip, Lungen, after talking to Scileppi several times over his cell phone, made a decision to meet at Lungen's office to figure how best to approach the case.

Strategize! Toss out ideas. Gather the troops and decide on a first move.

Odell held most of the answers. Lungen needed his people to talk to her. Yet, how could he approach her? She was in Pennsylvania; they were on their way to New York.

"There was no way in hell," Lungen said, "Odell was going to drive herself to New York to be questioned by us."

No suspect in her right mind would. It was a matter of extradition and legal maneuvering. How was Lungen going to get an arrest warrant together? How were they going to get Odell to New York State? Once she spoke to a lawyer, she was all finished talking. But as Lungen and Scileppi continued to discuss the case over the phone, "all hell broke loose," Lungen said, "when we received a phone call that changed everything."

CHAPTER 13

1

WHEN ROY STREEVER went back and spoke to Odell in March 1989 for a second time regarding the fetus found in the blue suitcase, she was prepared, she said, to explain fully what had happened to the child. It wasn't that Streever radiated some sort of magical charm, making Odell feel comfortable about opening up; instead, Streever did what any cop in his position might have done: he presented Odell with the facts in the case as the BCI had uncovered them thus far. And as soon as he mentioned the interview the BCI had done with George and Marie Hess, along with a few more details the BCI had since found out, Odell, in what would be a recurring theme throughout her life later on, "recanted," a police report described, "her original story. . . ."

Odell said, "Let me explain what happened," as Streever and his partner walked into her home.

"Please, ma'am, we're all ears here," Streever said smartly.

Odell admitted the "fetus was hers." It was "still-borned about seventeen years ago," she said. As to whom the father was, Odell claimed the pregnancy was from "a one-night stand." Then, "Around the eighth month of the pregnancy, I visited my father, John Molina, in Jamaica, Queens. After I told him I was pregnant, he became abusive and struck me about the body with a cat-o'-nine tails about fifteen times." Additionally, "I started vaginal bleeding during the night and it continued during the ride back to the lake the next day." Returning home, Odell said, she "bed rested, telling her mother she had a cold."

Later on that night, Odell further explained—as Streever took notes and his partner looked on—"I felt like a bowel movement and I sat on the toilet only to have the fetus come out. . . . The fetus was not breathing and my attempts to get the female baby to do so were to no avail."

"Did the baby move?" Streever asked.

Odell said, "The baby did not move, nor was their any warmth to her."

There it was: *her.* Odell had it said twice. Only later would she change her story and call the baby "Matthew."

By the time Streever and his partner were finished, they learned Odell had, after realizing the child was dead, stuffed it into a "blue suitcase" and "kept it underneath her bed." Whenever she and her mother moved, she said, she would take the suitcase and store it in the closet. In 1981, she put the suitcase in her Volkswagen—and for the next eight years there it stayed.

What was interesting to Streever later—and just about everyone else involved in the case on the prosecution's side—was the fact that as Streever and his partner stood in Odell's living room, talking to her that day in 1989, there, just to the left of where they stood, not five feet away, were three boxes containing three more dead babies, which wouldn't be discovered for nearly fifteen years.

"I've pondered that one myself," Streever said later. "Almost makes you feel like you screwed up because you didn't figure that out. We were concerned about one baby. But who the hell knew there were three more . . . ?

"We were pleased she finally came around and admitted Baby Doe was hers," Streever added. "Whether or not she told the true version of the events, we were at least happy to be able to close the case out and have a statement from her that she had, in fact, given birth."

A few days later, BCI investigators interviewed Mabel. Beyond admitting she had retrieved a blue suitcase from George and Marie Hess's home, Mabel kept quiet about what she knew, if indeed she knew anything. She said she recalled taking the suitcase from the Hesses', but said she never looked inside it and, in turn, gave it to Odell to do with it as she wished.

The case against Odell in 1989 was at best manslaughter, yet it all hinged on what Dr. Baden could find.

"Dr. Michael Baden was on board," Streever remembered, "and he was telling us he was going to be able to pinpoint pretty close to the time of death, whether the baby ever lived, et cetera. So we were kind of banking on him. But when the autopsy report finally came out, he narrowed it down to about a thirty-year span. He could not determine whether it was born alive or stillborn."

With no forensics and no real hard evidence against Odell, the BCI was left with only the two statements from Odell, which contradicted each other. Most important, John Molina, who had allegedly beaten Odell and killed the baby, had died in 1981. It was Odell's word against his. She was young, single at the time, living with her mother. Now she had six living children. Was there a jury that would convict her?

On March 25, 1989, senior BCI investigator Edward McKenna "conferred with DA Lungen" regarding the case against Odell. Lungen was "satisfied," he said during the meeting, with Odell's explanation of the events and the legal fact that "no homicide or self-abortion had occurred." Even more interesting was the idea that Lungen considered prosecuting John Molina "for manslaughter and for causing the miscarriage of an almost full-term baby. . . ."

Seeing that John Molina was pushing up dirt in a Queens cemetery, Lungen concluded the "manslaughter case will be adopted and closed by exceptional clearance. . . ." Lungen even took it a step further, promising in writing how he "would not seek criminal action against any of the other actors involved: Dianne Odell, her mother, Mabel Molina, or the Hesses, for their improper handling of the remains. . . ."

One of the reasons—the main reason, actually—Odell repeatedly gave for toting around the corpses of her many dead babies was to be able to bury them at or near a location where she would eventually pitch her tent for good. On numerous occasions, she later said she wanted the babies close to her so she could one day give them a proper burial.

On March 26, 1989, she had that opportunity. Because BCI investigators went to Odell and, seeing that the case was now closed, asked her what she wanted to do with the remains of Baby Doe.

"She does not wish to bury the fetus," the investigator who spoke to Odell that day wrote in his report, "but wants Sullivan County Social Services to do so."

On the receipt, Odell released the remains of Baby Doe to the "State of New York."

"Further, that on this . . . date, I relinquish all claims to said fetus, and turn her remains over to the Sullivan County Department of Social Services . . . for proper burial."

In the end, the state of New York would bury the baby at a place and time of its choice.

2

Robert McKee, a PSP trooper who had been involved with Detectives Thomas and Weddle and their investigation into the three dead babies found in Arizona, had met with Lungen and his team on May 19 in Wilkes-Barre. McKee was heading back to Towanda later that afternoon as Lungen and his investigators headed toward New York, when he received a call from the Towanda barracks eventually turning the investigation entirely upside down for Lungen.

"We received calls from the Sauersteins saying they are being inundated with news media from around the country," the dispatcher told McKee over the radio.

For a brief moment, McKee paused. Then, "Go ahead, base, what else?"

"Well, they are basically asking us if we can send a trooper over there to help them (or handle) the news media. . . . I don't know what to tell them?"

"Listen," McKee said, "tell her that if she has someplace to go or could get to someplace else, and if she could leave without being seen, to please attempt to do that."

"Ten-four."

About five minutes went by. Then McKee, still traveling back to Towanda, received a second call.

"Go ahead. What's going on now? What did she say?"

"She said she's going to be coming to the [Towanda] barracks."

Odell was in a state of panic. The media was bearing down on her home and wouldn't take no for an answer. Knocks at the door. Phone calls. Reporters hovering around the road leading up to her home. Odell was inside, running from window to window, paranoid, staring, watching, wondering how the hell to get rid of them. She was worried mainly, she said later, for her children's well-being and what word about what had happened in Arizona would do to the kids at school. *Your mommy is a baby killer.* Some kids could be cruel. The jokes. The jarring. Odell was terrified that if any of the major news media outlets got hold of the story and twisted it into something it wasn't, no one in her family would be able to leave the house.

Trooper McKee had been with the state police for ten years. He was a smart, well-liked cop and, with the gut instincts of a fox, knew what he had to do. As he waited to hear from dispatch to see what time Odell would be arriving at the barracks, he phoned Scileppi to inform him what was going on.

The problem Lungen had faced—getting Odell out of her house and into the barracks—seemed, at that moment, to have taken care of itself. Odell was actually voluntarily driving herself to the Towanda barracks. What more could Lungen ask for?

Born in Queens, New York, senior BCI investigator Thomas Scileppi was fifty-one years old in May 2003 when he became actively involved in the Odell investigation. At five feet ten inches, 170 pounds, the white-and gray-haired, brown-eyed investigator had joined the navy after graduating high school in the late '60s—and for the next four years spent his days and nights inside the belly of a submarine. His law enforcement career began on February 21, 1977, when he decided to apply to the NYSP. From there, he spent the next six months banging it out with other wanna-be cops at the NYSP Academy in Albany.

"At the time," Scileppi recalled, "I took an eight-thousand-dollar cut in pay and nobody could believe I would leave the navy. I had always wanted to be a trooper and considered state police troopers to be 'the elite.' I had several friends that were New York City, Nassau and Suffolk County police officers. I had taken all those tests, too, and passed. But my heart was set on being a trooper."

Scileppi got lucky. There had been a four-year hiring freeze on state cops, but he scored "extremely well on the entrance test and was among the first class hired" after the freeze.

"At the time, I was married to my first wife and had one son, who was only two. I was sworn in—the cut in pay really hurt—had another child with my first wife, and then got divorced."

Eventually Scileppi remarried; she was a local woman, Diane, a teacher, who had one daughter, Jessica, from a previous marriage.

Like most cops, Scileppi had seen it all. Rising up through the ranks to become senior investigator in Liberty had not always been easy, but Scileppi said he would not trade his experiences for anything.

"One of the worst days that I'll never forget, one that had an immense impact on me, happened in November 1988."

Scileppi had been working with Roy Streever at the time. They were attempting to locate a "subject" with an outstanding warrant against him.

"We were in Middletown, New York, that day and the weather was terrible: stormy, extremely windy, and heavy, heavy rain. We had heard several radio transmissions and a large request for emergency fire and rescue and police units to respond to the Coldenham Elementary School, nearby in Middletown. So we responded."

When Streever and Scileppi arrived on scene, they were amazed. A tornado had quickly touched down in the area near the elementary school and subsequently hit the wall where the school cafeteria had been. Kids were eating lunch at the time. The upper portion of the wall was made of glass and cinder blocks.

"Several children were buried under the mess,"

Scileppi remembered. "It was terrible. Parents were naturally arriving, having heard what had happened. It was chaos. Numerous deaths. I'll never forget escorting the parents into the emergency room to identify their deceased children. It still bothers me to this day."

When McKee got Scileppi on the phone, after hearing Odell was on her way to the Towanda barracks, Scileppi couldn't believe it. He had just gotten off the phone with Lungen, and they had discussed that very situation. Now Odell was being delivered to them, all they had to do was change course and head for Towanda.

"We're heading to Towanda now," Scileppi said. "We'd like to interview her tonight, if we can."

The situation still posed a problem for Lungen: they weren't going to be interviewing Odell in New York, where the case would, he knew, end up eventually. Pennsylvania would suffice for now, but the goal was to get Odell into the state of New York, where the case, if it came down to it, would eventually be prosecuted.

As Scileppi and Lungen changed course, still about an hour and a half outside of Towanda, they discussed how to go about questioning Odell out of their jurisdiction. If it came down to a trial, perhaps anything they got from Odell in Pennsylvania would not be admissible in New York. Was it something Lungen wanted to take a chance at?

Yet, there was still one other major dilemma. . . .

"Before she got lawyered up," Scileppi said, "we wanted to interview her. But we needed to go back to Towanda and listen to those tapes between Odell and Diane Thomas and Bruce Weddle before we spoke to her."

The tapes were the core of the case. Lungen and

Scileppi had no idea of the substance of those tapes. They had been told Odell had contradicted herself several times and even changed her story on numerous occasions. But they still needed factual information. The last thing a cop wanted to do was go into an interview without any knowledge of the case.

"We were at a disadvantage without listening to those tapes," Scileppi said.

The original plan had been to drive back to Monticello and, along with several other investigators from the Major Crimes Unit in Liberty (Scileppi's team), sit down and listen to what amounted to five hours of taped interviews between Odell, Thomas, and Weddle. If there was any information of any value on the tapes, they were going to set up an interview with Odell for Tuesday morning and question her further.

But all that had changed now that Odell was on her way to Towanda.

3

After Odell made it through the horror of being accused of murdering her firstborn child, Baby Doe, she tried to settle into life as best she could. Not only did she have five children to raise with her paramour, Robert Sauerstein, but she was five months into her tenth pregnancy. The stress alone of the past few days was enough, she certainly knew, to potentially cause problems.

By April 1989, Odell could add one more problem to what was now a growing list: how to explain to her family—who knew nothing about Baby Doe—that she'd had a stillborn child when she was in her late teens and had carried the fetus around with her in a suitcase for nearly seventeen years? She didn't even broach the idea of explaining the additional three dead babies she had stored in the house in boxes. But since the cops had brought Baby Doe to light, there was a good chance everyone in the family knew about it.

When Odell returned from the police station after being interviewed the first time, she said later, Sauerstein went to her and asked, "What the hell is going on here? You didn't have anything to do with that, did you?"

The cops had never spoken to Sauerstein. He knew there was a dead baby involved, but he had no idea to the extent of Odell's involvement.

"No," Odell said when Sauerstein asked her if she knew what was going on.

Roy Streever and his partner returned later that same week to ask Odell more questions. When they left, Sauerstein asked Odell again what the problem was.

"They were just following up on some things, Robert. It's nothing."

Subsequently the subject of Baby Doe was then dropped, according to Odell. No one in the house, at the time, save for Mabel, really knew what happened.

"You know," Odell said later, "I could *not* tell Robert with my mother there. Everybody does not understand the tenuous situation I lived with every day."

For now, she was safe. The case had never made the newspapers, and Odell was never brought up on charges. The cops had come, asked a few questions, and closed the case.

"Actually," Odell said, "it wasn't easy to lie to Robert. It was more . . . of, now I have five kids . . . and God forbid if I do something out of the way, or I go against her in any way, I am going to have five children at risk. Not three. Not two. But five! And she already hated Robert with a passion. So she hated his children as well."

Sauerstein never pressured Odell. He went about his

business of trying to take care of five kids, a "wife" and "mother-in-law."

"I'm sure he had questions, and I'm certain he always knew there was something. Because he would always ask me, 'What does she have on you? What is she holding over you?'"

Brendon Sauerstein, Odell's sixth living child, tenth overall, was born on August 30, 1989. Like each child she had given birth to previously when there was a man in her life, Brendon was born at a hospital, Wayne Memorial, in Honesdale, Pennsylvania. In July 1990, nearly a year after Brendon was born, it became apparent the construction business Sauerstein was involved in was heading for a collapse. The late '80s and early '90s weren't exactly peak periods for construction in and around Pennsylvania. Work was hard to come by. Odell was home, taking care of the children, raising the kids with her mom lurking and creeping around the house, not sure of what she was going to do next. According to Odell later, this was when she truly began living in a constant state of fear. If her mom had killed three of her kids already, as Odell so assertively claimed later, what would stop her from killing another?

So, Odell and Sauerstein faced a decision: look for work in the immediate area, or head west, where Robert had heard he could find work.

"There was no way I was moving back to New York, not under any circumstances," Odell said later.

Odell and Sauerstein sat down one day and talked about moving. What did they have, really, in Pennsylvania? Thus, with nothing standing in their way, they decided to move. Not just to Scranton or Wilkes-

Barre, larger towns in the same state, but all the way across country.

4

Steve Lungen had made it clear to the PSP, he said later, that they were not "to make any more decisions. We are making all the decisions now. It's not your case."

That said, McKee had done the right thing when he called Scileppi with news of Odell's wanting to get away from the media.

"You have to picture the situation," Scileppi recalled. "Odell decided to force our hand."

After he spoke to McKee and found out Odell was going to be driving herself to the Towanda barracks, Scileppi called "his people" in New York and explained what was going on. Several investigators from the BCI in Liberty were then dispatched to drive to Towanda and meet Scileppi and Lungen. They would all meet at Towanda, interview Odell, and see what came of it.

But as Scileppi and Lungen approached Towanda, about an hour outside of town, Scileppi received another call from McKee, who was now at the Towanda barracks with Odell. The media, sensing something was going on, had started calling Towanda for information.

"Unbeknownst to us," Lungen said, "this was a huge story in Arizona and out west. We had no idea how big it was or how big it was about to become."

Seeing they were an hour or so outside of Towanda, Scileppi asked McKee if there was a closer location where they could meet with Odell.

"Well, I grew up around Waverly, New York," McKee said. "I'm familiar with that location. How 'bout Waverly?"

"Waverly's fine with us," Scileppi said. He couldn't

show his excitement—Waverly being in New York—but one would have to imagine that upon hearing where they were possibly going to meet, Scileppi was elated.

McKee said, "Hold on." Scileppi heard McKee take the phone from his ear and ask Odell, who was standing next to him, "Listen, they're still an hour outside of Towanda. . . . We want to expedite this matter quickly. Would you mind driving to Waverly, New York, and meeting them?"

"Sure," Scileppi heard Odell say.

No sooner had they hung up, did Odell get in her car and follow McKee to Waverly.

"Extradition by your own vehicle," Investigator Paul Hans, who was riding with Lungen, said later, laughing.

Scileppi and Lungen agreed. Odell literally was handing herself over to them, in their own jurisdiction. Not only had she agreed to talk, but she was driving herself to some Andy Griffith police precinct in Waverly in what was, at least from a prosecutor's standpoint, a "too good to be true" situation.

"We were in a jam," Lungen said later. "She's the only one who knows what happened to those babies."

Truth be told, Odell was the only person who could tighten (or loosen) the noose around her neck—and she was more than willing to continue to talk about the events. Some suggested later that she *needed* to talk— to get it all "off her chest—" that the guilt, perhaps, had been eating away at her for decades and was too much to take. She already had opened a vein talking to Weddle and Thomas and it perhaps felt liberating. Why not finish what she had started?

According to Odell, she felt she hadn't done anything criminal and wanted to explain herself. She believed she'd sit and talk for a few hours and the matter, like it had in 1989, would go away.

From where Lungen sat, however, it wasn't a case of

manslaughter, stillborn babies, or a simple explanation. One child, maybe. Two, well, it was suspect. But three, or four, counting Baby Doe? There was no way that that many babies could end up dead without something criminal having taken place. It was impossible.

Still, Lungen and Scileppi faced a terrible quandary heading to Waverly: they hadn't heard the tapes that Detectives Thomas and Weddle had made with Odell on May 17 and 18; thus, they had no idea how to question Odell.

"As professionals," Lungen recalled, "you really don't want to conduct an interview with a suspect until you have all the details. We were pushed into this. What if we interviewed her and she needed to be arrested? We couldn't arrest her in Pennsylvania; she would have to be extradited back to New York. There was a whole host of legal issues regarding dealing with her in Pennsylvania. . . . And all of a sudden, we find out that she's *willing* to drive to New York and meet us at a little police station?"

But it wasn't time to celebrate. In effect, Lungen and Scileppi were forced to prepare for an interview with a subject they knew very little about.

"In New York, the law is different than in any other state," Lungen explained. "In New York, with respect to right to counsel, if she exercises her right to counsel, her ability to waive that right is essentially restricted. She can't. In other states, you can change your mind. But if she's deemed to be in custody, she *can't* change her mind. The only way she can waive counsel is in the presence of counsel. Which would mean arrest, appointment of lawyer . . . no one would let us talk to her."

The cards were stacked against them, suffice it to say if Odell had chosen to bring a lawyer with her—but she hadn't. She was alone. She had even left Sauerstein behind.

"If she would have gotten an attorney," Lungen said, "it would have had a major impact on our ability to investigate. So we were in a rush—just like Odell was in a rush to get away from the media—to try to meet with her before any of that happened."

Essentially, a twenty-five-year-old cold case became a race.

"We thought the media would turn into our worst nightmare," Lungen added, "and that they would screw up the investigation. They were camped on her doorstep. We were thinking they were going to force everything . . . force it to go the wrong way. But as it turned out, the media pressure was one of the best things that ever happened in this case for us."

With Odell sitting, waiting in Waverly, willing to talk, the legal extradition issues had, in effect, resolved themselves. It was one less hassle Scileppi and Lungen had to worry about going into the interview. Now they could focus on finding out the facts of the case, which, they both said later, was all that concerned them.

As they walked into the Waverly station, they discussed how to go about the interview. "What should I begin with, Steve?" Scileppi wanted to know.

"Just go in and see what she'll tell us."

Because Lungen ultimately would be the lead prosecutor, if the case ever went to trial, he couldn't be present for the interview. If he had, he effectively would make himself a witness.

So Lungen decided to work in the background, coaching Scileppi on legal issues as questions came up.

"Just begin by talking to her and see what happens from there."

Dressed in his usual attire—blue suit, silk tie, white shirt—Scileppi presented himself as a clean-cut cop. Calming in his demeanor, he spoke with a soft Queens, New "Yok," accent.

Any experienced cop will admit that building a rapport with a suspect is key to getting that person to open up during an interview. Scileppi didn't know much about Odell as he prepared to head into the room where she sat waiting. But as luck would have it, he had grown up not too far from the neighborhood where Odell had spent a better part of her childhood. Would this seemingly inconsequential connection between them end up being a building block for a foundation that, by the end of the day, would send Odell to jail for the first time in her life?

Scileppi, fixing his tie, brushing the shoulders of his jacket with his hand, was about to find out as he approached the door to where Odell waited.

CHAPTER 14

1

DURING THE SUMMER of 1990, Odell made contact with her former sister-in-law, who had lived in Ogden, Utah, for years. "Robert had lost his job in Pennsylvania," Odell recalled. "There really wasn't anything holding us in New York. There was work out west for Robert."

Sauerstein and Odell were in need of income. Once again, Odell was pregnant—the eleventh time. She was thirty-eight years old.

Ogden, the sixth largest city in Utah, offers some of the most dazzling landscape in the country. The Rocky Mountains, seemingly kissing the clouds, with their snowcapped peaks as sharp and defined as beach coral, surround a gravelly base of bright green valleys and two-lane roadways that ostensibly go on forever. Just thirty-five miles north of Salt Lake City, Ogden is, surprisingly, only twenty-seven square miles, yet its elevation rises between four thousand and five thousand feet above sea level. Known for its striking outdoor scenery, one can expect to see wildlife that might fill the pages of *National Geographic* magazine: deer, moose, elks, ducks, geese, swans, even mountain lions. When Americans think of Utah today, though, most associate it with the Mormon community, which reportedly makes up about 70 percent of the population.

For Odell and Sauerstein, Ogden didn't offer much, but it did present a new outlook, a different way of life, not to mention fresh surroundings that spoke of rejuvenation and clarity. One couldn't wake up in the morning in Ogden and believe there wasn't some sort of Higher Power calling the shots. The mere aesthetics of the land alone were enough to make a believer out of even the most ardent skeptic.

Mabel hadn't made the cross-country trip. Not that Odell had left her behind, but she and Sauerstein wanted to get settled first. So, about a month after they found a place, enrolled the kids in school, and Sauerstein began working, Mabel took a train and subsequently moved into the trailer Odell and Sauerstein were now calling home.

The cache of items Odell had brought with her to Ogden included everything she owned. No one, save for maybe Mabel, knew it, but inside the U-Haul, which she and Sauerstein had packed as tight as cordwood and trekked west, were the three dead babies, carefully packaged inside three separate boxes.

By January 1991, Odell had given birth to her eleventh child, seventh living child. *Toby* Sauerstein, a healthy eight-pound eleven-ounce baby boy with dark eyes, was born at Saint Benedict's Hospital in Ogden. Sauerstein was there again for the birth.

Alice, Odell's oldest daughter at thirteen, had not adjusted well to life in Mormon country. But she, like the rest of the children, did the best she could to accept her new lifestyle. In June 1991, merely days after Alice had turned thirteen, she was the victim of an alleged statutory rape by someone, Odell said later, Alice had been dating.

"We reported the rape to the police out there, or whatever they are called," Odell recalled.

As one might expect, the rape had frightened Alice and the family. One might think that with all the Christianity in the air out there, one would be a bit more respectful of their fellow human beings. But it hadn't turned out that way. As Odell and Sauerstein—not to mention Alice—learned, sexual abusers know no bounds.

"I wanted to—and would have—killed the guy," Robert Sauerstein said later.

"A month later, I took Alice and got out of there," Odell explained.

It wasn't a hard sell. The rape and the culture had weighed heavily on everyone. With Odell, Sauerstein, Mabel, and the seven kids living in a trailer, to say they were crowded would be an understatement—they lived on top of each other.

"The kids slept in the bedroom with me. Absolutely, it was cramped," Odell said. Adjusting to Mormon life was also rough. "They preach to you about one thing and they are absolutely devilish in the other half of their lives."

Pima, Arizona, was one thousand miles away, a fifteen-hour drive, but the climate was much warmer during winter months and there seemed to be a construction boom taking place in the region. It was July 1991. Odell and Sauerstein had been in Ogden about a year—a year too long. So, they packed it in and headed south to Pima.

When Odell arrived, she immediately applied for food stamps. She and Sauerstein moved into a motel in town while Mabel took the children and moved into an efficiency apartment nearby. Odell kept Toby, Brendon, and Adam with her in the motel, while her mom took the girls, Clarissa, Doris, Maryann, and Alice. Certainly, in some respects, Doris, Maryann, and Alice could fend for themselves; they were between ten and thirteen years old. But Clarissa was only five. If Odell was worried about the welfare of her children around Mabel, especially Sauerstein's children, why would she allow Mabel to care for them until she could find a place big enough for all of them?

"I was trying to find a place for my mother by herself to put a separation between us," Odell said. "Not make her think I wanted her to leave, because I knew if I told her flat out that I wanted her to leave, it was going to be devastating and somebody was going to end up getting hurt. But I wanted her to be separate from the rest of us. But it never quite happened. Every time I would get her—even out there when we found housing— there was a trailer right next to the house we were living in, she took the trailer and we took the house next door, and she would always have one or two of the kids staying with her there. So I was never able to pull away from that and get the kids completely away from her. . . . I knew every day, looking in her face, into her eyes, the threat was there of hurting the children or taking them away, doing something unspeakable."

Either way, after they arrived in late summer 1991, living arrangements in Pima didn't change.

Not long after settling down, with nowhere to store their worldly possessions, Odell and Sauerstein rented a self-storage unit at a facility in Safford. They chose two units big enough to hold most of the belongings that wouldn't fit in the motel room—including the three boxes of dead babies. The babies had been dead now for about ten years. The boxes were starting to show signs of their age, appearing oily and pungent from the body fluids leaking from the babies. But there they sat, tucked inside a self-storage unit, among old family photos, record albums, an old computer, cards, and letters. Just one more piece of Odell's history packed away.

No sooner had they gotten established in Pima, did Odell have another announcement to make. Yes, she was pregnant once again. Yet, this child, too—everyone was about to learn—would meet an early death.

2

Odell seemed quiet and composed as she sat in Waverly at 5:45 P.M. on May 19, 2003, waiting for BCI senior investigator Thomas Scileppi. As she sipped water from a white Styrofoam cup, she felt she was doing the right thing. She wanted to clear up the matter of the three dead babies, explain what had happened, and move on with her life. The babies were secrets she had kept buried in her soul for over twenty years. It was time to come clean.

But as the interview got under way, Odell claimed later, she realized immediately it wasn't going to be as easy as telling the truth.

"When they walked in to interview me," Odell said, "they had the 1989 case in their hands," referring to Baby Doe. According to her, Scileppi was "waving" the case in front of her face, as if to say, "We know about the first baby!"

Scileppi later disagreed with Odell's recollection. Of course, they had a look at the 1989 case. Cops need to know everything they can about a suspect before an interview. Odell had given birth to a child in 1972 and it, too, ended up dead. They were investigating the deaths of three additional children she had possibly given birth to who had turned up dead. Why wouldn't they want to talk to her about the 1989 case?

But that wasn't Odell's worry, she insisted—that they were flaunting the 1989 case in front of her. Her major concern, at least initially, was that they knew her father had beaten her and essentially killed the child. It was there in her statement.

"Knowing that," she said, "why didn't they seek some kind of professional help for me? Why didn't they have somebody else, who had a little more compassion, talk to me? They came in with the idea they were going to put away this mass murderer."

Regarding the early part of the interview, Steve Lungen later said: "She was cooperative. She spoke freely, somewhat guarded about information she was going to give. She was not under duress or in custody. . . . She drove herself there. She expected the New York State Police to be there and she agreed to talk. . . ."

If there had been one dead child, well, it wouldn't have been an issue. Two? Okay, something might be going on. But four? Lungen and his team were investigating three homicides on top of another death, all possibly connected to the same woman. It was not about getting a shrink in to see her. That was not their obligation, Lungen said. It was about finding out the facts surrounding the deaths of three children.

Because he had been involved in the 1989 case, Roy Streever was called in to assist Scileppi. Together they would see if they could get to the bottom of what had happened to the three babies and figure out if Lungen had a case to pursue.

"I wouldn't say she looked scared," Scileppi said, recalling seeing Odell for the first time. "I would say she looked depressed, concerned. For the first hour and a half, I was just getting to know her. Nothing was said about the babies. I had to feel her out and build a rapport, so I could figure out how to take a shot. How to start this."

Trooper McKee had been there waiting, but he didn't stick around long after Scileppi and Lungen arrived.

"She was very receptive," Lungen said. "Very at ease

to being talked to. And she's not someone you have to pull words out of. Very verbal. Very talkative."

By the time Scileppi and Streever were prepared to talk to Odell, Lungen had spoken to the pathologist in Arizona, and had been given a preliminary report regarding the autopsies on the three babies.

"We found out the babies were full-term," Lungen said, "but they couldn't tell us if they were born alive or not. Still, they were full-term babies, they *weren't* premature, and there didn't appear to be any initial appearance of any kind of disease."

The idea was to "arm" Scileppi, Lungen added, with some sort of information to talk about with Odell. This would be an entirely different interview from the two Diane Thomas and Bruce Weddle had conducted previously. It would be more refined and detailed. There would come a time when Scileppi wanted answers from Odell.

"The key to me, at the time," Lungen said, "was only one question: if we can't prove the babies breathed life, we can't prove they were murdered."

It was that simple. Were the children murdered or left to die? Big difference in the eyes of the law. Interestingly enough, there was only one person who could provide those answers.

For a time, Scileppi and Odell spoke about inconsequential theatrics that make up everyday life: where she grew up, background, family. After an hour or so of chitchat, Scileppi stepped out of the room to confer with Lungen about where to take the interview next.

"We need to establish that the three babies were alive. Finding three babies was great, but if we can't establish that, at some point, the babies were alive . . . that's the only question," Lungen told Scileppi.

Scileppi shook his head. He understood. If Odell said they were stillborn and maintained that fact, there was no case. In other words, all she had to do was say the children were stillborn and, essentially, the case was over.

Trooper Rick Sauer, who had made the original call to Lungen on Sunday night regarding Odell and the three babies, had been on hand for much of the early part of the interview. He sat and listened while Scileppi asked most of the questions. Scileppi later said Odell knew exactly why she was there and had even expressed interest in talking the situation through. Sauer later backed it up.

"She was very open to participating in the interview," Scileppi remembered.

Furthermore, Odell was advised several times that she wasn't under arrest or in custody. She was free, in fact, to leave at any time. Additionally, on numerous occasions, Scileppi, Streever, and Sauer offered Odell food and drink. Anytime she needed to excuse herself to use the bathroom, Scileppi said, she was free to do so. It wasn't like she had been thrown into a closet-size room with a light perched on her face, and cops swarming around her like CIA interrogators. It was relaxed, laid-back. They were, Scileppi said, just talking.

After they went through Odell's life—where she lived, how old her children were, and how many lovers she'd had throughout the years—Scileppi brought up the point that out of her twelve children, eight of which had been born in hospitals, four had not. Out of the eight born in hospitals, all had lived. The other four were dead. Those circumstances alone, Scileppi urged, needed further explanation.

Several times throughout the interview, Odell would stop the conversation and ask, "What is going to happen to me?"

"We don't know what's going to happen to you, Dianne," Scileppi said more than once. "Why would you ask a question like that?"

Odell shrugged.

"Let me ask you this, then," Scileppi said after Odell continually badgered him about what was going to happen to her. "What do you *think* should happen to you?"

Odell looked down at the table, fidgeting with a tissue in her hand. The tea-bag-colored puffiness under her eyes seemed like an indication of some sort of private inner battle she had waged for the past two decades. She was obviously debating what she wanted to say. Finally, looking up at Scileppi, she said, "I should probably go to jail."

"For what, Dianne? Why would you say that?"

Odell didn't answer. But it was apparent, Scileppi said later, that "she clearly was feeling guilty of things or expressing guilt of things. . . ."

At times, Odell would break down and sob, even tremble, Scileppi recalled. But she would ultimately talk her way through it and compose herself.

The conversation fluctuated between Baby Doe, Baby Number One (1982), Baby Number Two (1983), and Baby Number Three (1985). It was confusing for Scileppi, to say the least. But Odell would trudge on, talking about several of the children at the same time. At one point, she began talking about Baby Number Three, born, by her estimation, in February or March 1985.

"As I woke up," Odell said, "I cuddled the baby, held the baby close, and crawled next to the bed with the baby."

This was significant, Scileppi explained later. "The more I spoke to her about it . . . she broke down and said the baby had 'gasped or cried upon its birth.'"

It was the first indication, as far as Scileppi could tell, that one of the babies had been born alive, as opposed to stillborn. It meant—at least in theory—that something other than the birthing process had ended the child's life.

With that comment, the nature of the interview took on a more serious undertone for Scileppi and, more important, Steve Lungen.

After spending a few more minutes with Odell after she admitted, basically, that the third child had been born alive and she had even held it, Scileppi stayed with her for a time because she had become so distraught.

When he felt she was okay by herself, he stepped out of the room. "I'll be right back, Dianne."

For the next ten minutes or so, Scileppi conferred with Lungen about what to do. They felt they had evidence of one of the babies being born alive. That meant, at least on the surface, that a homicide had occurred.

Lungen gave Scileppi direction and sent him back in to talk with Odell.

Walking into the room, Scileppi didn't say anything at first. Instead, he stared at Odell for a time. She was okay, but still a bit shaky. The act of purging herself of this secret had unleashed a torrent of emotion. She appeared calm, but also disturbed.

"Miss Odell," Scileppi finally said, "listen . . . you okay?"

"Yes, thank you."

"Listen, Miss Odell . . ."

"What . . . what is it?" Odell asked. She seemed frazzled.

"I need to do this before we go any further," Scileppi said, reaching into the side pocket of his sport coat and taking out a small card. "You have the right to remain silent," he began, looking down at the card one moment, looking up at Odell the next. It was a fragile situation. Continuing slowly, "Anything you say can and will be used against you in a court of law. You have the right to a lawyer and have a lawyer present with you when you're being questioned. If you cannot afford to hire a lawyer . . ."

When Scileppi finished, he asked, "Do you understand each of these rights I've explained to you?"

"Yes, I do," Odell said, again tearing up.

"Having these rights in mind, do you wish to talk to us now?"

"Yes."

It was pushing midnight. They had been talking for close to six hours. Inside of the next two hours, though, Odell would talk further about what had happened to the three babies, giving Scileppi and Streever, who had been in and out of the room, a written statement that included some of the most shocking details about the life and death of the three babies to date— details, in fact, Scileppi later said, he thought he'd *never* get out of Odell.

3

On September 22, 1991, living in Arizona only about two months, Odell was rushed to Mt. Graham Community Hospital emergency room. She was hemorrhaging.

"I was sitting on the bed in the house," she said, "and I had Toby, he was sitting on my lap. I had no idea I was even pregnant. Well, I was sitting there bouncing him up and down and I felt like a *pull* on the inside. And I got up and went into the bathroom, and when I got into the bathroom, there was blood all over the toilet tissue. It was like somebody had turned on a faucet."

Sauerstein and Mabel were in the kitchen. When she saw the blood, Odell burst out of the bathroom, she claimed, and said, "You have to send somebody for an ambulance. . . . I'm bleeding and it won't stop."

Mabel looked at her without saying anything.

Sauerstein, quite speechless himself for the moment, had one of the kids run across the street to a neighbor's house, saying hurriedly, "Go, go . . . call 911 right now!"

By the end of the day, Odell found out she had lost the child.

Over the course of the next year, life in Arizona became rather mundane and automatic. Odell and Sauerstein went to work, came home, and tended to their daily affairs. Mabel was living in the house, but getting on in years, meddling in her daughter's life less and less each day. She still continued to assault Odell and the kids mentally, Odell later insisted.

In all the years they were together, Odell said, the older children, James Odell's kids, had had problems getting along with Sauerstein. Odell said it was Mabel who had poisoned their minds, repeatedly telling them Sauerstein wasn't their father and didn't care about them. Whatever the case may be, between December 1991 and March 1992, Sauerstein was charged by Arizona authorities with aggravated assault against Doris, who was ten at the time. Several months after the charges were lodged, they were dismissed. Yet a month later, he was charged with aggravated assault against Alice, and the charges against Doris were reopened.

"I had asked the children what happened," Odell said, "and Alice had given me her story. I had asked Maryann [who was there and had seen what had happened] what took place and she said Robert never touched her sister. Because of what I had gone through with people not believing me, I believed her."

Throughout this entire time, with chaos seemingly running rampant in the house, unpaid bills piling up, no phone, the lights turned on and off, Odell kept up payments on the self-storage unit in Safford. After all, what choice did she have? Many of their belongings were inside the unit—not to mention three dead babies.

With all that was going on, it seemed as if the ebb and flow of daily life still revolved around Mabel. When was the woman going to drop dead? Odell said she was waiting for Mabel to die. With Mabel gone, the pressure would be off. She could go to the police and tell them what happened. What had become a dark "secret" she had been harboring for twenty years could be set free finally.

CHAPTER 15

1

ACCORDING TO SCILEPPI, by midnight, he had gotten Odell to admit that her third baby, born in 1985, had been brought into the world alive. Odell didn't say how the baby had died. But if Scileppi had his way, by the early-morning hours of May 20, he was going to find out.

Odell later explained the night in a different way. She claimed Scileppi and Streever "coerced" a confession out of her—that they badgered her until she told them what they wanted to hear.

"I kept saying to them, 'Look, in the state I was in, I did not hear these children. I mean, how many more ways am I going to have to explain it to you?'" After she said that, she claimed, Scileppi got up from his chair and walked out of the room, and after being gone for five minutes, he returned and sat down next to her. Pausing for a moment, he grabbed hold of her shoulder and began "like, you know, rubbing my back.

"Inside, I starting freaking out," Odell said. "I don't

really want to jump out of my chair and start screaming, because I have never done that."

As Scileppi rubbed her shoulders, Odell insisted, he began saying, "Are you sure a towel didn't end up in the baby's mouth? Are you sure? Or a leg over the baby's face, or a sheet in the baby's mouth?"

Odell said that's when, under pressure, she told them yes. But her actions later on that night would lead one to believe her memory has become clouded over the years and she recalled the interview years later the way she might have *wished* it had happened.

Scileppi and Streever assertively denied Odell's version of the events. Like a lot of things, Scileppi and Streever later said, Odell was twisting the truth to make it fit an agenda she would later begin pushing.

Roy Streever had been involved in the interview with Odell at certain times throughout the night. Streever had investigated Odell back in 1989, and while Scileppi questioned Odell throughout the evening, Streever reviewed the reports from the 1989 case, refreshing his memory.

At various times, Streever would go in and question Odell about the stories she was now telling. Odell found herself backed into a corner, she said. She had been Mirandized. She was going to be charged with murder. Inside of twenty-four hours, the stakes, she realized, had changed remarkably. At one point, she claimed, it occurred to her that she wasn't going home. And that, alone, scared her into saying things that weren't entirely true.

"She's stuck on the story that each time she gave birth," Streever recalled, speaking about Babies Number One, Two, and Three, "it was at home, she passed out during the deliveries, and when she came to, the child was dead. I was trying to get across to her that it just doesn't happen that way—especially because of what she knows; she's had *eight* living children," three of whom born *before* the three dead babies. "It's not like a child could have died because you didn't do anything to sustain its life. At the same time, though, we were trying to give her something she could cling to. A way out, essentially. Like, 'I didn't murder these babies.'"

Once Odell admitted that one of the children had breathed life, the interview flipped from, Scileppi recalled, casual conversation to an *interrogation*.

Big difference.

As Streever and Scileppi interrogated Odell further as the night wore on, her mantra, Streever said, became "*I had passed out during birth, and if they died, it was because of my negligence.*" Malicious intent was never part of Odell's argument, at least according to her on that night. No one had murdered the children, she was saying; they had died because she had passed out and they essentially had been smothered in the process.

Where was Mabel in all of it? Why wasn't Odell giving up her mom? Mabel had been dead for many years. Odell had always trumpeted the notion that as soon as Mabel died, she was going to run to the police and tell them what happened.

Here was her chance.

"The only mention of her mother," Streever recalled, "was that Dianne was 'in fear' of her mother. That she would get beaten by her. This was her opportunity to get [her] mom involved in the picture. Mabel Molina was dead. She couldn't deny it!"

Point in fact, Odell had even told Scileppi and Streever she had "concealed" the pregnancies from Mabel, which she had also told Thomas and Weddle.

"You know, maybe for the average person on the street," Streever recalled, "a woman could conceal a pregnancy, maybe even from one of your coworkers, if you're a person who doesn't really show a lot. It's kind of tough for me to relate to, but I know of cases where females have concealed their pregnancies. But from your *mother*, who is there every day? That's bullshit. Wouldn't her mother, at some point, ask, 'Dianne, didn't you get your period for the last six months?'"

Streever was fixated in his quest to get Odell to tell them what had happened to the babies. At one point, he asked, "You know, Dianne, you said you gave birth to those babies on the floor of the bathroom. Okay, you're emotional; you're blacking out; you got blankets and towels down on the floor. Maybe, just maybe, one of these kids got a towel caught up in its face somehow and choked to death, smothered?"

It was a fair question, from a competent, experienced investigator who was having a hard time believing the babies had died on their own.

Odell looked up, Streever said later, and said, "Yeah, in fact, one time I woke up and there was a towel stuck in the baby's mouth."

"Really," Streever said. "How much of the towel?"

"Oh, about eight inches."

Okay, sure, Streever thought, staring at her, unconvinced, *and a newborn baby just sucked in eight inches of a towel?*

At best, a newborn baby's throat is a bit larger than a pencil. The baby Odell was talking about was fewer than twenty inches long. A newborn, on top of that, has a hard enough time finding its mother's nipple. How could, Streever wondered, a newborn "suck in" eight inches of a towel without any help? It wasn't possible. It was a lie.

"If I had any doubts before that statement," Streever said, "I was sure she had killed these babies after she made that statement."

While Scileppi stayed in the room with Odell, shortly after Streever had gotten the towel statement, Streever stepped out to confer with Lungen regarding what Odell had just said.

* * *

There are key differences between first- and second-degree murder. By legal definition, first-degree murder, although the legalities vary from state to state, "is generally a killing which is deliberate and premeditated (planned, after lying in wait, by poison or as part of a scheme), in conjunction with felonies such as rape, burglary, arson, or involving multiple deaths, the killing of certain types of people (such as a child, a police officer, a prison guard, a fellow prisoner), or certain weapons, particularly a gun."

Second-degree murder, for which Odell was now facing multiple charges, involves "a nonpremeditated killing, resulting from an assault in which death of the victim was a distinct possibility."

Steve Lungen now understood that the babies were born alive and had died under Odell's care. That alone qualified Odell for second-degree murder charges.

Forty-nine-year-old Dianne Odell was sitting in Waverly, New York, essentially, giving Lungen and the BCI exactly what they needed to charge her with murder. If she wanted a lawyer, she could have asked for one at any time. But she never did, at least according to the BCI and an elected district attorney who had been prosecuting criminals in Sullivan County, New York, for the past thirty years.

Lungen needed Scileppi to obtain a complete written statement from Odell, signed and dated—a permanent record of what she had said.

At about 11:50 P.M., after Odell took a trip to the bathroom and got herself a fresh cup of coffee, Streever, Scileppi, and Odell sat down and began working out what, precisely, Odell wanted to say in her statement.

By morning, Odell's statement would be replete with contradictions, lies, truths, and the most bizarre set of circumstances surrounding the short life and untimely deaths of the three babies that anyone involved in the case had heard thus far.

2

In 1882, John T. Lytle, a common rancher, established what he called "Lytle Station" along the Texas route of the United States International Great Northern Railroad, making the little ranch town just southeast of Dallas, in the northern portion of central Texas, the only place in the county with a railway station at the time. When Lytle opened the station, the town bearing his name had a population of fifty. Not much in Lytle would change in 110 years, but as April 1992 approached, Odell and Sauerstein would be among Lytle's twenty-two hundred residents.

Pima, Arizona, like Ogden, Utah, turned out to be nothing but problems and letdowns for Odell and Sauerstein. But that wasn't what necessarily drove Sauerstein to move to Texas so suddenly. There were charges pending in Pima regarding an assault incident he had gotten into with one of Odell's children.

"To hell with this," Sauerstein said later, after he and one of Odell's daughters had gotten into the scuffle, "I am *not* going to jail for something I didn't do!"

So Sauerstein "booked," he said, to Texas, and Odell soon followed.

Loading their vehicles with everything they could fit from their apartment, Odell and Sauerstein didn't leave much behind. Yet most of what was inside the self-storage unit in Safford was abandoned. There just wasn't room. Of course, inside the storage unit were the musty corpses of three dead babies—and as long as Odell continued paying the bill, no one would ever know. As soon as they got settled in a town they could call home and Mabel died, Odell kept telling herself, she would return to Safford, pick up the boxes, and give the children a proper burial. Until then, her secret was safe as long as she could afford to pay the bill and had a stamped envelope to send it.

Life in Texas would not be cowboy sunrises and romantic rides on horseback for Odell and Sauerstein. In early 1993, as soon as they got settled, Mabel became severely ill. She began moving slower. Talked less. Had trouble breathing and walking. It was her heart. Her body, Odell said, was shutting down. After Mabel was "diagnosed with congestive heart failure, we decided to move back to New York so she could get treatment."

So, after being in Texas less than a year, the Odell-Sauerstein train was once again packed. Because Mabel was so ill, Odell and Sauerstein decided to drive across country. Their destination? Endicott, New York. It was close to where Mabel had lived for most of her life. She could, Odell said, get better treatment "back home."

"She had said to me one day, 'I don't want to get sick and die here (in Texas).'"

"Well, this is where we're living," Odell replied. "I'm not sure [that] going back to New York and living there is what I want to do."

"Well," Mabel said, "it's what *I* want to do. So you talk to *him* (Robert) and tell *him* I want to go home."

Around the same time, Sauerstein had lost another job. Bills were piling up.

"I had her grinding in my ear, demanding to go home. I finally said to Robert, 'Let's just go! Let's go back. At least we know we can find work there.'"

Before they left Texas, Odell began having problems with her gallbladder. She said she had suffered unbearable pain for "two years" before being diagnosed with gallstones. Nonetheless, they were determined to leave Texas as planned. So by the beginning of July 1993, despite Mabel's and Odell's blossoming health problems, they took off.

During the trip back home, their car broke down in Virginia. With no money to speak of and nowhere to stay, they took up in a mission. Missions generally offered free food and shelter, as long as one abided by the rules. Odell and Sauerstein had been on food stamps. They had collected welfare and used government assistance for electric bills. Staying at a mission for a few nights wasn't going to bruise anyone's ego; in fact, it might be good for the family to be around a bit of godly righteousness.

For the first few days, Odell, Sauerstein, Mabel, and the kids stayed out of everybody's way and went about their business. But Odell's gallstones, she said, began acting up; going to the hospital one night after suffering an attack, Odell had surgery to have her gallbladder removed.

The surgery would be the least of Odell's problems as she returned to the mission after her operation. Within a week, she, Sauerstein, Mabel, and the kids would leave, but one of the children would not make the trip back home—and, in fact, Odell would never see the child again.

3

Scileppi and Streever sat across from Odell during the early-morning hours of May 20 and began to go over what she had said earlier, so a formal statement could be typed up. Odell had admitted already that she had heard one of the babies "cry" and "gasp" for air, according to Scileppi. But was she willing to put that admission in writing and sign the statement?

As Odell spoke, Streever typed. Scileppi, with his soothing demeanor and soft-spokenness, helped Odell sort through what she wanted to say. For the most part, he was working from notes he and other members of the BCI had taken throughout the past six hours of conversations with her.

She talked about all the places she had lived, worked, and where she had given birth to each one of her living children. When it came to Baby Number One, born in 1982, Scileppi asked Odell who the father was.

"I had been the victim of a sexual assault, which occurred [at the lake]," Odell said as Streever typed. "I did not report the rape to the police, nor did I tell anyone that it had occurred. However, I became pregnant. Because I had a relationship with my mother that included verbal and physical abuse by her, I made a decision to try and conceal the pregnancy from her, as well as from everyone else. I was successfully able to do this."

If Odell wanted to pin the death of the child on Mabel, this was her chance; but she never mentioned Mabel in light of her actions pertaining to killing any of the children. In truth, when it came to giving an explanation of what actually happened on the night Baby Number One had died, Odell said, "When it came time for me to have this child, I remember that my children were with my mother overnight."

So, Mabel was nowhere in sight?

With intense certitude, Streever later recalled the night he and Scileppi questioned Odell. He remembered Odell as being cold, callous, and reserved: "Not showing much emotion at all." But when it came time to talk about the actual moment Baby Number One had died, that's when she began trembling and crying, he said.

"That was the only time that I could say she really

broke down. There was maybe five or ten minutes of crying and hugging. She got it out. It was a bit of a purge. And then it was right back to the same demeanor: quiet, just sitting there. It was like she confessed. It was all we were going to get in terms of a confession out of her."

As they continued going through the entire story of what had happened, Odell would read each paragraph for accuracy after Streever typed it and gave him input regarding those areas where she believed the statement needed more or less information.

"As I began to have contractions and experienced a 'bloody show,'" Odell continued, still speaking about Baby Number One, "I realized it was time to deliver the baby, and I began to make preparations. I brought blankets and towels into the bathroom and situated myself on the bathroom floor. When I felt that the time was right, I began to push the baby out. As I was doing this, I began to hear [a] loud ringing sound in my head. At the same time, I began to black out. Above the ringing sound that I was hearing"—to Streever and Scileppi, this was one of the most important statements she would make all night—"I heard the baby's first muffled cry."

Streever asked Odell to look at the typewritten page so she could verify that what she had said and what he had written were one in the same.

She gazed at the page for a few moments, then shrugged her head an assertive yes.

"Great," Streever said, "continue."

"It was at this time that I believe that I lost consciousness. As I began to come to, I looked down and saw the baby. Several inches of one of the towels was inside of the baby's mouth. I removed the towel from the baby's mouth to clean it up."

Then came another clear moment where Odell could have implicated Mabel if she chose, but instead, she said, "It had been my intention to tell my mother that someone had left the newborn baby on my doorstep and that we would then take the baby to the hospital."

Scileppi and Streever remembered later that in almost a calculated and cold inflection, Odell then said she wrapped the baby up in blankets and, a few days later when she had gotten her strength back, "placed the baby in a box and put the box in an [un]inhabitable bungalow behind the apartment house where [she] stored some of [her] other belongings."

Thus, the baby now had a resting place.

Perhaps even more chilling was how, with an eerie sense of simplicity, Odell explained those few days while she slept on the couch: "During this time [that] the baby was in the closet, I did not hear any more sounds from the baby."

As the night progressed and Streever continued to type and Scileppi kept Odell focused on what she wanted to say, the conversation shifted to Baby Number Two, born in 1983.

"About a year [after giving birth to Baby Number One], I became pregnant again. I was not dating any one person exclusively at the time and I do not know who the father was."

Once again, Odell decided not to seek prenatal care, she said. Then she explained how she didn't "tell anyone [she] was pregnant—especially my mother. Throughout this and the previous pregnancy, I had a significant fear that if my mother found out I was pregnant, there would be hell to pay."

Her kids, she continued, would often sleep over her mother's, who, she said, lived in a separate apartment on the same property.

"It was during one of these sleepover nights that I went into labor."

Contradictory to what she would say later, Odell

Thomas Bright purchased the contents of this self-storage unit at an auction in Safford, Arizona. *(Photo courtesy of Graham County Sheriff's Office, Safford, Arizona.)*

To his shock, Bright found the remains of three dead babies in one of these boxes. *(Photo courtesy of Graham County Sheriff's Office, Safford, Arizona.)*

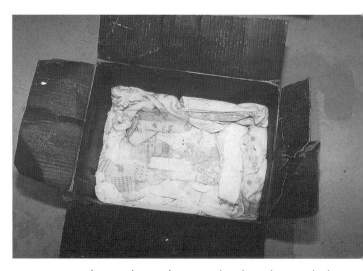

Among Bright's purchases: this tattered and torn box, soaked in bodily fluids. *(Photo courtesy of Graham County Sheriff's Office, Safford, Arizona.)*

The Graham County Sheriff's Office found the remains of a second baby in this box on May 12, 2003. *(Photo courtesy of Graham County Sheriff's Office, Safford, Arizona.)*

Inside these boxes were the mummified remains of one baby and the bones of two others, all murdered more than twenty years before. *(Photo courtesy of Graham County Sheriff's Office, Safford, Arizona.)*

These blankets and a lone bone fragment were culled from the boxes containing the bodies. *(Photo courtesy of Graham County Sheriff's Office, Safford, Arizona.)*

DNA extracted from these blankets would provide clues to the brief lives and untimely deaths of the three babies. *(Photo courtesy of Graham County Sheriff's Office, Safford, Arizona.)*

Residents of Safford, Arizona, set up a memorial outside the storage unit. *(Photo courtesy of Graham County Sheriff's Office, Safford, Arizona.)*

This box, sealed with black electrical tape, contained the remains of one of the babies. *(Author photo.)*

Another baby was wrapped in blankets and bound in plastic, then stuffed inside this cardboard box. *(Author photo.)*

The Graham County Sheriff's Office was the hub of the initial investigation into the lives and deaths of the three babies.
(Photo courtesy of Diane Thomas.)

Graham County Sheriff's Office Detective Diane Thomas flew from Arizona to Towanda, Pennsylvania, to investigate the babies' deaths. *(Photo courtesy of Martha Hendrix.)*

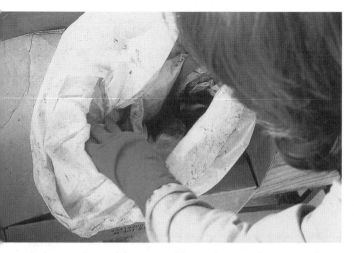

Diane Thomas dons a lab coat and latex gloves and examines the remains of a third dead child. *(Photo courtesy of Graham County Sheriff's Office, Safford, Arizona.)*

The box that Diane Thomas opened and searched contained two smaller boxes with the remains of one of the babies. *(Author photo.)*

This x-ray shows the skeletal remains of two of the babies.
(Author photo.)

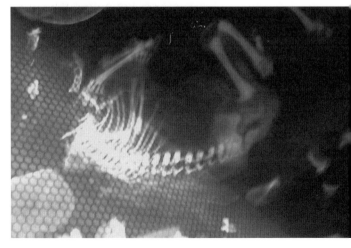

This x-ray shows the curled up skeleton of one baby, which, when found, appeared to be nothing more than a pile of dust and bones. *(Author photo.)*

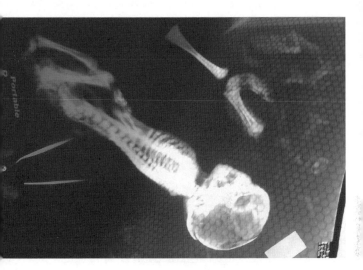

This x-ray proves that the mummified remains of one baby were those of a full-term infant. *(Author photo.)*

Graham County Sheriff's Office Detective Bruce Weddle, who flew to Towanda, Pennsylvania, with Diane Thomas, was instrumental in getting the babies' mother to admit that the babies were hers. *(Photo courtesy of Martha Hendrix.)*

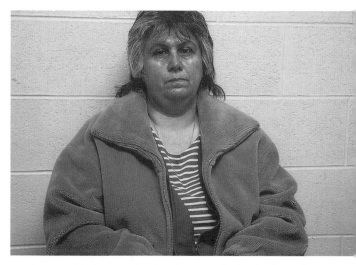

Dianne Odell posed for this photograph shortly after talking to
Diane Thomas and Bruce Weddle on May 18, 2003.
(Photo courtesy of Pennsylvania State Police; Towanda Barracks.)

Odell was still wearing
her Rite-Aid uniform
when Pennsylvania State
Police took her photo on
May 18, 2003.
*(Photo courtesy of
Pennsylvania State Police;
Towanda Barracks.)*

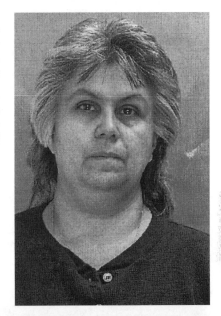

This mug shot of Dianne Odell was taken shortly after she admitted to her role in the deaths of three of her children. *(Photo courtesy of New York State Police; Liberty Barracks.)*

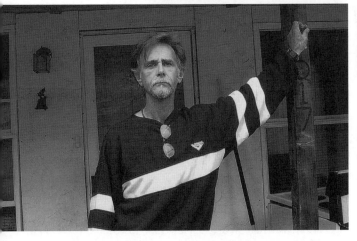

Diane Thomas snapped this photograph of Robert Sauerstein, Dianne Odell's paramour, before questioning him. *(Photo courtesy of Graham County Sheriff's Office, Safford, Arizona.)*

These photographs were taken by a New York State Police trooper after a junk dealer in Bethel, New York, discovered the remains of a fetus inside a blue suitcase—a fourth dead baby that would eventually be tied to Dianne Odell.
(Photo courtesy of New York State Police; Liberty Barracks.)

Investigator Paul Hans, of the Sullivan County, New York District Attorney's Office, worked closely with veteran District Attorney Steve Lungen to secure evidence in the Odell case. *(Author photo.)*

Sullivan County District Attorney's Office Investigator Robert Rowan was also instrumental in putting together evidence in the Odell case. *(Author photo.)*

New York State Police Senior Investigator Thomas Scileppi got Dianne Odell to admit that three of her dead children had made sounds, which meant they were alive when they were born. *(Author photo.)*

These two excerpts from a statement Investigator Scileppi took from Odell on May 19, 2003, clearly show her signature next to his. *(Author photo.)*

I have read the above statement consisting of three pages and it is true and accurate to the best of my recollect. This statoint was given of my own free will and I have been treated fairly. I have been offered food and drinks and have been permitted to use the bathroom as needed. THIS STATEMENT WAS BEGUN at 11:50 p.m. on May 19, 2003 and cmpleted at 3:15 a.m. on May 20, 2003.

WITNESS   SIGNATURE

OF THE _____ NEW YORK STATE POLICE _____ , OF THE FOLLOWING:

I HAVE THE RIGHT TO REMAIN SILENT, AND I DO NOT HAVE TO MAKE ANY STATEMENT IF I DON'T WANT TO.

IF I GIVE UP THAT RIGHT, ANYTHING I DO SAY CAN AND WILL BE USED AGAINST ME IN A COURT OF LAW.

I HAVE THE RIGHT TO HAVE A LAWYER PRESENT BEFORE MAKING ANY STATEMENT OR AT ANY TIME DURING THIS STATEMENT.

IF I SHOULD DECIDE I DO WANT A LAWYER, AND I CANNOT AFFORD TO HIRE ONE, A LAWYER WILL BE APPOINTED FOR ME FREE OF CHARGE AND I MAY HAVE THAT LAWYER PRESENT BEFORE MAKING ANY STATEMENT.

I ALSO UNDERSTAND THAT I HAVE THE RIGHT TO STOP AT ANY TIME DURING THIS STATEMENT AND REMAIN SILENT AND HAVE A LAWYER PRESENT.

I FULLY UNDERSTAND THESE RIGHTS, AND AT THIS TIME I AGREE TO GIVE UP MY RIGHTS AND MAKE THE FOLLOWING STATEMENT:

SIGNATURE

WITNESS

Roy Streever was the first New York State Police investigator to interview Odell. *(Courtesy of Corinne Streever.)*

Sullivan County District Attorney Steve Lungen and the courthouse where he prosecuted Odell. *(Lungen photo courtesy of Susan L. Parks; author photo of courthouse.)*

Court TV set up cameras inside this Sullivan County, New York courtroom to broadcast the Odell trial in December 2003.
(Author photo.)

claimed time and again she was alone during each of the three births.

As for what happened during the birth of Baby Number Two, she blacked out and heard loud ringing noises, then passed out and fell against "some fixtures" in the bathroom, and "struck my head on the wall, or one of the fixtures."

Important to Scileppi and Streever (perhaps more important to Lungen, who was still in a separate room, monitoring the conversation), Odell then said, "I can also recall hearing a noise coming from the baby, which is hard to describe, but somewhere between a cry and a cough."

Further, Odell said that when she passed out, she must have fallen on top of the baby. Because when she woke up later, "I felt something under my leg. . . . The baby was under the thigh part of my leg. I worked myself into a position where I could check on the baby.

"There were no signs of life."

After that, she wrapped the baby in blankets, stuffed it into a cardboard box, and put it "into the same shed behind the apartment house" as Baby Number One.

"To my knowledge, no one was aware I had given birth or discovered the contents of the box."

Next, Scileppi and Streever asked Odell to describe what happened to Baby Number Three, whereby her most chilling confession of the night would emerge.

4

The Staunton, Virginia, mission that Odell, Sauerstein, Mabel, and the kids were staying at during the latter part of July 1993 appeared to be a godsend. There was no hurry getting back to New York. Mabel was ill, but she was holding up fairly well considering the circumstances. It was Odell, just out of the hospital after gallbladder surgery, who was in worse shape, but at the same time recovering quite quickly. As soon as she was well enough to travel, they would be on the road again heading for Endicott, New York.

Things would take an unexpected turn, however.

"When we lived in this mission," Odell said later, "I did not realize my daughter Alice (the oldest, at fifteen) was telling all of the other people in the mission stories about me. They weren't true. She was doing it to get attention."

Unbeknownst to Odell, while she was in the hospital, Alice had gotten involved with a twenty-one-year-old man who was also staying at the mission.

"She had decided she wanted to do what she wanted to do. So, she was getting romantically involved with him, and when I came back from the hospital, the people who were running the mission took me into the conference room."

"If you do not put an *end* to the relationship that is developing," one of the board members said rather sternly, looking at Odell as she sat listening, nursing her stitches, "we are going to ask you to leave. We cannot have this type of relationship going on underneath our roof."

Odell said she understood that it was a religious organization and an inappropriate relationship between a twenty-one-year-old *man* and a fifteen-year-old *minor* was not something God would have approved of.

Leaving the meeting, Odell went straight to Alice.

"I tried to sit down and explain to her what was going on." The day before the ball had dropped on Alice's new love interest, as Odell was in the hospital, Alice had "punched a wall and blamed Robert for it, because [he] told her that she couldn't get involved with [the man]. I guess he knew . . . or had heard rumors."

As she and Alice talked the situation through, the

conversation became heated. They started arguing loudly, screaming back and forth.

"I was on medication, because I was in a lot of pain, and I was supposed to be resting. But, my God, Alice wouldn't have it."

So as they argued, Odell said, Alice, who was holding Toby in her arms, Odell's youngest child, "threw him on the floor in a fit of rage."

As she went for Toby, who was on the floor crying, Odell said, "You go sit out on that cot in the hallway."

While Alice walked into the hallway, Odell checked on Toby, who appeared to be fine. She had a hard time leaning down to pick him up because, she said, her stitches went from her right breast all the way down to her waist.

After picking Toby up and making sure he was all right, Odell then took the "leg of a toy" on the floor next to her and walked out to where Alice was sitting on a cot.

"She sat on the cot and I went out with the stick, and I was so angry with her I hit the cot and, accidentally, hit her arm."

The woman who ran the mission had since come out and taken Alice away to talk to her, to find out what had happened. According to Odell, Alice made up several stories: among them was that Odell had been driving while drunk, and she deliberately had hit her with the stick.

The woman then called Child Protective Services.

Here was where things got really ugly, Odell explained. The woman from Child Protective Services showed up and conducted a brief investigation. Afterward, according to Odell, the woman said, "I want permission to take your daughter."

"At this point in time, I was so overwrought," Odell

said, explaining herself, "I just said to her, 'Go ahead and take her! Go ahead and take her!'"

Alice was immediately taken away and placed in foster care. Odell was subsequently charged with assault and summoned to appear in court a day or so later.

Eventually, after three court dates, Odell said she was released on her own signature, pending a future court date.

The court later reported that Odell "never returned to court" and thus a "warrant," which had been issued for her, was "vacated [after] three years."

CHAPTER 16

1

SCILEPPI AND STREEVER had one more bit of business to take care of before they could present Steve Lungen with Odell's statement: Baby Number Three.

"We went back and forth, back and forth with her," Scileppi recalled, "and she started to open up more and more. Once again, it was never a question of: she didn't want to talk to us."

To the contrary, Scileppi insisted, Odell was openly discussing the birth and death of each child, as if she were getting some sort of self-gratification from revealing such dark secrets. Streever and Scileppi, sitting, listening, felt Odell *needed* to talk.

Later, Odell's version of the night would differ substantially. She said she felt intimidated and pushed into confessing, not to mention scared of implicating her mother or father. But her statement didn't refer to her dad or mom being involved in the deaths of the babies. The only references to her parents refer to the abuse Odell had suffered from them. She never stated that either one had had anything to do with the deaths of the babies.

"About six months [after Baby Number Two was born], I was dating a man whose first name began with an *H,* although I'm not totally sure of his first name," Odell said as Streever typed.

It was pushing 2:00 A.M. and Scileppi and Streever were exhausted. Odell was showing signs of breaking down, Streever and Scileppi recalled, but demanded they finish what they started.

"We dated for about six weeks. During this time, I became pregnant again."

When she found out she was pregnant, Odell said, she was no longer dating the man she now called "H."

"Due to the same circumstances of fear of my mother's reaction and lack of financial or emotional support, I elected to have the child at home and without medical assistance."

For Scileppi and Streever, the same pattern that had been present throughout her previous two pregnancies presented itself again: whenever there wasn't a male figure in Odell's life and she became pregnant, the baby ended up being wrapped in plastic and put in a cardboard box.

She further explained how she had carried the child full-term without anyone realizing she was pregnant, including Mabel. By this time, she and Mabel were living together in the same apartment, along with her three living children. Yet, she said, Mabel and the kids lived on one side of the apartment and she lived on the opposite side.

Each side, she claimed, had its own bathroom.

The day of the birth, she said, started out with explosive "lower-back pain," which, to Odell, meant labor. She had given birth six times previously, so she knew by then when labor began. It was later that night, in February or March 1985, she couldn't recall exactly which month, when she went into full-fledged labor. In fact, she remembered, she had been sleeping and the labor pains were so severe, they woke her out of a deep sleep.

"After getting on the toilet, my water broke. Within a short period of time, I was in full labor and situated myself on the bathroom floor. . . . As had happened with my previous two births at home, I began to hear ringing and to black out as I began pushing. I lost consciousness at some point and I recall waking up to see the baby lying on the floor before me. Although there was no apparent obstruction in the baby's mouth, nor was I on top of him as in the previous instances, there were still no signs of life."

She then wrapped the baby in a towel, but this time made sure not to obstruct the baby's face.

Again, these were remarkable details—but details, in effect, that seemed to remove some of the blame from Odell.

"I crawled with the baby to the floor next to the bed and lay there holding the baby close to me. I don't know how long I was there, but it was beginning to get light out, so I laid the baby in the closet and climbed into bed."

"So I laid the baby in the closet and climbed into bed"—as if it were just another day in her life. Streever and Scileppi couldn't believe how common she made it sound.

At no point during any one of the three births—that eventually would end in the deaths of three babies—did Odell ever consider, according to her statements then or later, calling 911 herself to, perhaps, save the child's life.

The remainder of her statement consisted of Odell explaining how she had met Robert Sauerstein and moved throughout the country, the entire time toting the three dead babies around with them. That is, until she moved to Pima, Arizona, and—like she later would

do with her fifteen-year-old daughter—abandoned
them.

Finally: "In the third and final unsuccessful birth that
I described above, I recall just before losing consciousness that the baby made a brief cry of a second or less.
Also, I would like to add that I know now the decisions
I made to do the things the way I did was wrong, but
I now realize I was motivated to do this because of the
terror I always felt from my mother and my father. This
in no way excuses my decisions, but today I would do
things differently."

Perhaps the most telling statement Odell would
make during the course of the entire interview came
at the end. It spoke of someone who was ready and willing to accept the consequences and responsibility of
her actions, and, in Steve Lungen's view, could have
been made only by someone who was guilty.

"I have read the above statement consisting of three
pages"—single-spaced pages of text at that—"and it is
true and accurate to the best of my recollection. This
statement was given of my own free will and I have
been treated fairly. I have been offered food and
drinks and have been permitted to use the bathroom
as needed."

Odell signed the statement next to Scileppi's signature.

Lungen had exactly what he needed to prosecute
Odell for the murder of her three children. All that
was left to do now was arrest her and process her in
Liberty, New York. Once that was done, she would sit
in jail until her arraignment.

If Scileppi had intimidated Odell into saying she had
killed her children, as she later claimed, why would she
sign such a statement? After all, one of the final sentences was very clear: "This statement was given of my
own free will and I have been treated fairly."

"From my point of view," Odell said, "I had been talking to police," and she stumbled a bit with her words here, taking long breaks to collect her thoughts before continuing, ". . . how can I explain this so you'll understand . . . for three days. I was absolutely exhausted. But that was not something *they* were concerned about. The reason I signed it was I didn't know I could *refuse* to sign it! I'm surprised I wasn't sitting on a mushroom the way they fairy-taled this thing out."

Odell went on to say she believed, at the moment she signed the statement, that she had no support from her family. She felt, essentially, alone. Moreover, she was convinced, she added, that Sauerstein was going to take off with the kids, which scared her into doing many things she didn't want to do.

"The reason I signed the statement was because I thought Robert was taking off with the children, and the best thing for me to do was to sign the statement and disappear into the penal system for the rest of my life. Because if I lose them, I have nothing anyway."

Although the ride back to Liberty took only two hours, it seemed much longer. It was late. The sun was rising. Odell was beyond tired. Still, the things she would tell Investigator Robert Lane, one of Scileppi's investigators from the BCI in Liberty, who was in charge of booking her, would implicate her further in the deaths of her children. But perhaps more important, it would give law enforcement a taste of the motive behind the murders, which was something Scileppi and Streever hadn't touched on during their interview with Odell.

2

According to Odell, during one of her court appearances in July 1993, before she left Staunton, Virginia, she had a conversation with Alice regarding the situation between them that had escalated to the point where Odell had allegedly struck Alice with a child's toy.

"I said to Alice in the courthouse that day, 'We need to sit down and talk. We need to start bridging this gap.' She stood in the courtroom hallway . . . while I said, 'Come on, we need to try to bring this back together,' and she said, 'I am *not* coming back to live with *you*! I will do whatever I have to do so that I do not have to come back and live with you.'"

Odell walked away from Alice that afternoon, she said. She felt Alice would cause her "big trouble down the road." Outside the courthouse, she explained further, she stood for a moment and contemplated the future: *If I continue to stay here and try to make her do something she doesn't want to do, the stories are going to continue, they are going to get worse. I'm going to end up going to jail for something I didn't do . . . and my mother is going to have these kids.*

Facing the difficulties of parenting a troubled child was apparently too much for Odell to swallow—because she left Alice in Staunton, in foster care, didn't fight to get her back, and never saw her again.

By September 1993, Odell, Sauerstein, Mabel, and the six kids, minus Alice, were living in Endicott, New York. Odell had tried to make payments on the self-storage unit in Safford, where the dead babies were stored, but she couldn't keep up with them. By June 1994, she had stopped paying the bill altogether.

Knowing what Odell knew, why in the world would she stop paying the bill, certainly aware that someday, most definitely, the contents of the unit would be auctioned off and the three dead children, she had kept hidden from the world, would be revealed? Did she want to get caught? Was it some sort of unintentional way of allowing the situation to resolve itself?

"You know what?" Odell said later. "When you don't have the money to pay, where do you get it from? It wasn't a conscious thought to stop paying the bill. I had also made every conscious effort to get money to [pay the bill] as soon as I had it . . . but my mother had gotten really, really sick as soon as we settled in Endicott."

Indeed, throughout the next year, Mabel got sicker and sicker. It was all she could do to move around the house they were now living in. She stopped talking and walking. She seemed to be preparing for death.

At home one day in 1995, Mabel "dropped," as Odell later put it, and never got up.

"I called the ambulance and they took her to the hospital."

By the early-morning hours of the following day, the woman who had become Odell's emotional ball and chain was gone. The same woman who had caused her daughter so much pain, so much tragedy and dysfunction throughout their lives together, was finally dead. Odell wouldn't have to worry any longer about what Mabel would do to her kids. She wouldn't have to stress over Mabel running to the cops, telling them she had three dead babies in boxes in Arizona. It was all over. The burden of a lifetime gone for good.

One might suspect Odell would have thrown a party the night Mabel died, jumping for joy at the mere thought that the woman (and all of her problems) was finally out of her life.

"There was a portion of me that was terrified. She had told me she was never going to let me go. She was coming back to get me after she died. After she died, I kind of looked around every corner, and had a hard time going to sleep."

At Mabel's request, Odell had her cremated. She took care of all the arrangements. There was no memorial. No funeral. Mabel died, her body was cremated, and that was the end of it. Odell notified her brothers and went on with life.

* * *

One of Odell's brothers, Richard Molina, wasn't shocked by his mother's death when Odell called. He knew Mabel had been sick. And although they hadn't spoken in many, many years, and hadn't gotten along well, it was still comforting to Richard to get the news. He could, he said, finally let Mabel go.

Fifty-seven-year-old Richard Molina later remembered his life in the Molina household back in Jamaica, Queens, during the early '50s and '60s, very differently than his sister. Soft-spoken, with an obvious Queens accent, Richard later spoke of his life with Mabel, his dad, his two half brothers, and Dianne Odell as though he had grown up in another house entirely. For example, Richard felt it his duty to "speak up for his father," whom he loved dearly, and misses immensely, to this day. He didn't want his father's name, he said, besmirched by a woman—Dianne Odell—he claimed has "lied about everything her whole life."

"We were a family," Richard said, "of all boys until Dianne was born." Admittedly, Richard "divorced himself from the family" in 1981 after John died.

"My father was a hard worker all his life." Mabel, on the other hand, was a "schemer, a liar, a con artist. She did whatever she could to con people."

He remembered a time when his father had been saving money in a bank account to start his own automotive-repair business. He had thousands of dollars stowed away—that is, until Mabel found the bankbook and pillaged it, leaving John with nothing more than enough money to buy a few tools and proceed with "side jobs."

His dad did drink, Richard confessed without hesitation, and would get belligerent when drunk, but that was the extent of it, he insisted. It was hard for

Richard to call his dad an alcoholic, because, he said, "he drank, but he got up every morning and did what he had to do." Violence or anger wasn't part of John's behavior when he drank, Richard claimed. When he was "on the sauce, he'd walk around the house and stress that he was the boss, the one in charge, the breadwinner." But his torments were directed at Mabel, Richard said, not Dianne or any of the other children.

During the early '60s, it was only Richard and Dianne in the house with Mabel and John. Six years older than his baby sister, Richard said Dianne was always viewed as the "spoiled one. To my father, you must understand, she was the only girl."

Richard recalled, "She was the flower of my father's life. She could do no wrong! He had four sons, but they didn't matter like his 'little girl' did. She didn't have to do *anything*."

While Richard remembered having to wash and wax floors, scrub toilets, paint and help his dad at work (which he didn't mind), he said Dianne never had to do anything. She might have swept a floor once in a while, but she never did any physical, hard labor. Quite a different story from the one Odell would later tell of living under the sword of dear old dad— mopping, sweeping, and scrubbing floors on all fours—as if she were Cinderella.

According to Richard, any notion of his dad physically abusing Odell was "not true at all."

"Dianne always had a problem: she couldn't very well get along with people." She had no social skills, he said. "There were some nice girls in the neighborhood, Dianne's age, but Dianne just couldn't get along with any of them. . . . My guess is, Dianne wanted to always be in charge and they kind of rebelled against that."

Dianne Odell repeatedly painted Mabel as an evil person, laying much of the blame for what happened in her life on Mabel.

"I won't totally disagree with that," Richard said. "The one thing my mother was, was diabolical. Definitely! Meaning, some of the things she did—not alone, mind you—some of what she did, she did with Dianne and the other kids."

One story Richard told explained perfectly this rather odd dynamic between Dianne and Mabel. It was nighttime in the Molina household when John came home from work stupidly drunk, staggering all over the place. Noticing this, Richard claimed, Mabel and Dianne waited for him to pass out. Once John was in a stupor, sleeping off his bender on the floor, Dianne and Mabel "cleaned him out," as if he were a hobo on the street being rolled by two hoodlums.

But that wasn't the end of it.

The following day, after John failed to realize he had been ripped off, and Dianne and Mabel felt they had gotten away with it, they laughed about it together, rejoicing in having made a successful "score."

"Those were the kinds of things they did."

Odell and Mabel, Richard went on to say, "bonded" in a strange way. They were "connected." Odell, he added, "always had a way of making things up." Whether it was something that had happened at school, on the way home from school, or with a kid in the neighborhood, she was always "concocting stories about how [people] mistreated her."

She played the role of victim, according to Richard, congenially, absorbing sympathy people showered on her, learning how to use it to her advantage.

It was in junior high school that Dianne became known as "loose," Richard opined. She started hanging out in other neighborhoods, he said, with other kids. In Queens, during the '60s, neighborhood was everything to a kid. One stayed in his or her neighborhood or risked invading someone else's property. Turf wars weren't something invented in S. E. Hinton's novel

The Outsiders; it was a mortal sin to be caught in another neighborhood. Dianne, apparently, fell in with other kids, from different neighborhoods, and Richard recalled adamantly, "God knows, she would never open a book and do any homework. . . . I don't recollect her doing it at all. It was in those years that she became close to my mother. She recognized that being the only other female in the house, that that's who she should bond with the most."

Richard joined the navy in 1965. Dianne was 11 years old. Soon after, about midway through his tour, Dianne and Mabel moved out of the Jamaica, Queens, house and into Kew Gardens. However, whereas Odell would tell stories of being forced into prostitution by Mabel and living under the reign of a dungeon master—not being able to leave the apartment and having to answer to Mabel's every whim—Richard saw it differently.

Even more interesting was that Richard swore that his father stopped drinking around this same time.

"First of all, he had a very bad back; he'd had a heart attack, so it was kind of detrimental to his own health to continue drinking. . . . He may have had a drink of wine or something like that, but he wasn't drinking anywhere near the way he used to."

As for Odell's claim that one of her half brothers had raped her when she was six years old, Richard said "absolutely not. No way. My father would have killed anyone who touched her. That was *his* little girl. As much as I dislike my half brothers, they weren't that type of people. I'm not saying we were the *Leave It to Beaver* family, by any means. We had our hard times, but we saw them through."

Halfway through Richard's tour, he was allowed to go home for a visit. Dianne and Mabel were living in Kew Gardens by then, by themselves, having little contact with his dad.

"I went there to visit them when I came home for a break. I would talk to my mother, and Dianne was there, and they would fight and argue in front of me. She would accuse my mother of lying about things . . . and my mother would complain that Dianne didn't want to go to school. She wanted to stay home all day. She didn't want to work. And, you know, Dianne would be saying different: 'No, she won't let me get a job. I want to go to school and work part-time and you won't let me because you want me to do the chores you should be doing in the house.'"

Typical teen angst. Dianne was rebelling against authority. Richard called it "nonsense."

As for Mabel allegedly putting Odell to work on the street, Richard said it couldn't have been possible.

"I don't think my mother would even know how to start something like that . . . you know, set it up," he said, laughing. "She wasn't the brightest person in the world. Okay, if that were the case, I would have found out while I was there."

If his sister was living this unspeakable life of a teenage prostitute, living in fear of Mabel, Richard believed she would have mentioned something—anything— to him when he visited.

"When I went to visit, you must understand, they are both looking at me as someone who they want to get on their side."

Fighting for position, in other words: *"Mom did this. Richard, help me."*

"Dianne is not going to school. Richard, she doesn't want to listen. Do something!"

"They were both telling me different tales, hoping I would take one side or the other. If what Dianne says today is true, regarding the prostitution, I would have heard that from her then. She would have pleaded: 'Save me, help me, get me the hell out of here.'

"That was *not* the case."

Furthermore, while he was there, Richard made a point of telling Odell, "If you're not happy here with Mom, why don't you go back to live with Pop?"

Later, Odell claimed the reason she didn't want to go live with her dad was because he was abusive, both sexually and physically, and she feared for her life. Instead of indicating this to Richard while he was there, however, she told him, he claimed: "No, no, no! I'm not going back with Pop. He's going to try to run my life. He's going to try to rule me. He won't give me any kind of freedom at all."

Was this positive proof that Odell *wasn't* involved in a life of prostitution and frequent abuse from her mom and dad, as she later claimed? Absolutely not. But it was at least another view of her life from someone who was there.

One of the stories Richard laughed at and said was totally outrageous was the story of Odell's brother, along with John, setting her up and scaring her. Her father had told her to answer the door if anyone knocked. When she went to the door, Odell said, there was a man with a stocking over his head who came at her with a knife. After brandishing the knife and grabbing her by the throat, the man took off the stocking, as her dad looked on, and revealed himself to be one of her half brothers.

According to Richard, it was one more in a series of falsified stories that seemed to fuel Odell's deep-seated hatred for her mother and father and allow her to, perhaps, live with the way her life had turned out. The half brother in question, Richard recalled, was a troublemaker. He had gotten into a few problems with the law and John Molina had bailed him out of jail, but "[he] would never, *never* condescend or demean himself to do something like that."

Furthermore, "Why would my dad, who viewed Dianne as his princess, do that? He and my brother

weren't close in that way. They would have not conspired to do that. No way."

As far as Odell's children were concerned—even the
dead children—Richard saw them as fixtures she
could latch onto. Security blankets.

Could Mabel or Odell have murdered the children?

"I don't see my mother killing babies," Richard said.
"She was a schemer, don't get me wrong. But I don't see
her as a murderer. If there was no benefit, financially,
for her, I just don't see her doing it. If there was money
involved, maybe she might entertain it; but if there
was no monetary benefit to it, no way. Dianne, well, I
don't see her . . . Dianne, you see, was many things, but
I don't see her . . . I don't think she's the type to put
her hands around a child's neck and kill it. But in des-
peration, in order to save herself, she would say, 'I have
to get rid of this baby.' I can see that! . . . She was definitely naive enough to think that she could pull off
hiding three or four dead babies. With Mom dead,
unable to defend herself, Dianne sees her as the easi-
est one to blame for *everything*. I can see her filling
that role. It's easy for her to blame all of her problems
on my parents."

When his dad died in 1981, Richard took care of all
the arrangements, and buried the old man. Admittedly, he hadn't spoken to anyone in the family since.
Whereas Odell later said she was basically dragged
down to her father's funeral by Mabel, Richard didn't
remember the day like that.

"When my father died, I was the executor of the
estate, in charge of selling off the house and fulfilling
my father's final wishes." Those wishes, Richard continued, included selling the Jamaica, Queens, house
and splitting the money among Mabel, Odell, and
Richard. The other two children, who were from an
earlier marriage of Mabel's, were totally left out.

Richard phoned Mabel at the lake the day John died.

"Crocodile tears," Richard insisted, came first. Odell and Mabel began crying as if they had loved John all their lives. But what happened next showed their true colors, he said. After they cried and "acted" as if they cared, Mabel abruptly stopped crying and asked about the money.

"At that time, I had hardened myself to their behavior. Through all the things that went on throughout the '70s and '80s, Dianne was the type of person who would not call my father for six, twelve, eighteen months. Then, suddenly, she'd call and start crying, saying she needed this or that, needed money. He would send her money or she would come and get it. My father, whenever Dianne needed help, would help her. She was his little girl."

Not only did Odell and Mabel drive to Queens after hearing about John's death, Richard said, but they "rushed down and left the kids in New York with someone, I don't know who."

Odell later said she took the children with her.

The first thing Richard noticed when he saw his sister was the size of her stomach. "What are you doing?" he asked, looking at Odell, her stomach bulging out of her dress. She looked uncomfortable and overweight.

"Well," Odell said, "Dad's dead and I want to be here to help."

"To what end?" Richard wanted to know. "You don't see him for eighteen to twenty months at a time and *now* you want to help? Why is it imperative that you see him now? There's no reason for you to be here! It's going to be a small, quiet thing. Then he'll be buried."

"Well . . . well, I want to be here because, well, because . . . I want to pick some things up."

With that, Richard thought, *Yeah, I know why you're here: you're trying to figure out what you can scam.*

Mabel, sitting, listening, then chimed in: "What about the will, Richard? Where's the will?"

"I'm going to take care of the estate. Don't worry, Ma, you'll get yours."

Richard then explained what the will stipulated.

"They were only interested in the money. They were getting a third—and a third of *anything* was a lot to them."

"Dianne, you're pregnant, you need to take care of yourself. I'll take care of everything. You and Ma will get your money, don't worry. Go home."

Richard was devastated by his father's death. He was up to his neck in making funeral arrangements, paperwork, calling people, not to mention the emotional toll of actually burying him. He said he didn't need any more stress brought on by his sister and mother beating him up for money when his dad's corpse wasn't even in the ground yet.

Richard finally said, "Here's the deal: you don't have to worry yourselves about getting anything that's coming to you." He was talking to both Mabel and Odell as they sat, looking at him. As he spoke, he showed them the will. "I'll sell the house and send you a check. That's his last will and testament. I'm going to be honest with you: I don't agree with it, but I am going to fulfill his final wishes."

After Richard finished, Mabel and Odell, apparently confident Richard would keep his word, left. They did not, Richard insisted, go to the funeral or wake. They clearly had heard what they wanted and had driven back up to the lake the same day.

"After the funeral, I sold the house, cut them their checks, and, knowing they both had problems, wrote them off and never heard from them again."

Odell later said she lost touch with Richard over the

years because "for one reason, he can't stand me. He thinks the sun rose and set in my father's eyes and that he would believe my father could do no wrong. He had no clue about what went on after he left [to go into the navy]. . . ."

Richard lives today near the same neighborhood in Queens where he grew up. He has been married for decades and has several children, all of whom speak very highly of his character, as a man, husband, father. Richard, incidentally, has never been in any trouble and served his country in the navy with honors.

CHAPTER 17

1

AS ODELL RESTED her head against the window in the backseat of BCI investigator Robert Lane's unmarked cruiser, en route from Waverly to Liberty, she perhaps didn't fully understand the gravity of the situation. She was going to be booked, fingerprinted, photographed, and placed in a jail cell, where she would sit until she was arraigned.

Investigator Lane later said Odell slept that morning during much of the ride. Odell, however, said she was faking it.

"No, they *thought* I was sleeping!" She had her eyes closed, but she was listening to what Lane was saying to the cop he took along for the ride, sort of eavesdropping on the conversation she believed they were having about her in whispers. "There was a part of me that raged," Odell explained, "because, even from the very beginning, in 1972, I wanted to make my father pay for what he did to me, and I got shamed out of it by my mother."

Among other things, it was that rage fueling her desire to stay awake.

Nevertheless, Odell was on her way to jail, possibly even prison—all for something, she maintained, she didn't do. Furthermore, she honestly believed the entire process was some sort of vendetta Steve Lungen had conspired against her because he couldn't prosecute her for the death of Baby Doe in 1989.

"Steve Lungen," Odell said, "doesn't like to lose. And he couldn't prosecute me in 1989—but he was *definitely* going to find a way to do it this time."

This was a ridiculous theory, considering the circumstances surrounding how the babies were found and what Odell had told police during the three days in which they interviewed her. She had lied on several occasions when she had the opportunity to tell the truth about what she later claimed happened—that her mom had killed the children. But she didn't. Moreover, she had signed a statement implicating herself in the deaths of the children. When Steve Lungen first heard about the babies found in Arizona, he had a hard time recalling the 1989 case related to Odell.

All the same, Odell claimed that as they drove to Liberty that morning she overheard Investigator Lane, on numerous occasions, talking about how the "Arizona authorities were going to file charges against her if they [the BCI] couldn't come up with anything to hold her there."

Again, this later memory of that morning was in stark contrast with the actual facts of the case. Odell had already made an admission of guilt by the time she took off for Liberty with Lane. In addition, why would Lane, or anyone else, say something like that at that point? The BCI and Lungen didn't need any more evidence to prosecute. She had given them enough herself already.

Lane, who later denied having said anything about the case during the car ride with Odell, had been an investigator with the BCI for the past four years, with the NYSP since 1984. He spoke with candor and integrity. Other cops respected him. He had been one of Scileppi's top investigators since joining the BCI. With his slicked-back black hair, shiny suit, and expensive tie, he embodied, perhaps, the image of what many might view as a television cop: flashy, crass, direct. But his record spoke for itself. Lane was a clean cop all the way. He had made countless arrests that had led to convictions. There was nothing Hollywood about Robert Lane and his determination to put criminals behind bars with good, solid evidence.

In the early-morning hours of May 20, Lane's job was to transport Odell back to Liberty so she could be processed. The hard part was over; the case, seemingly, a slam dunk. Odell had confessed. For Lane, it was a matter of paperwork and processing.

Or was it?

They arrived in Liberty, Lane recalled, at 5:40 A.M. Investigator Linda Paul was waiting at the station for them and greeted Odell and Lane as they entered the building. Incidentally, Odell later said Linda Paul rode with her and Lane from Waverly to Liberty; so her memory of that day, even of the most basic facts, was cloudy at best.

"Do you need to use the bathroom, Miss Odell?" Paul asked cordially upon greeting Odell.

"Yes, that would be nice."

When Odell returned, Lane led her into the interview suite at the end of a long hallway. As she sat, sipping coffee, Lane went back to his office, he later said, to "prepare the accusatory instruments charging her with murder second."

About a half hour later, Lane and Paul walked into the room where Odell was waiting.

"Miss Odell," Lane explained, handing her copies of the accusatory instruments, "you're being charged with three counts of murder in the second degree."

She took a brief look at the paperwork. "Well, I expected that I would be charged with something like this."

Odell seemed unaffected by the mere significance of what was transpiring, as if she still expected to get out of it somehow. The weight, perhaps, of what was actually happening had not yet settled on her. Maybe she thought she still could, with the right words, explain everything away. Perhaps she was in shock? Who knows?

In any event, Lane had read the statement Streever and Scileppi had prepared the previous night, so he was familiar with the particulars of the case.

While sitting across from Odell at the table in the interview room as Odell went through the paperwork, Lane began shaking his head.

"What is it?" Odell asked.

"I just find it unbelievable that you do not know what the sex of the infants were and who the fathers were? You must know the father of the children, or the fathers of the children?"

For a brief period, Odell and Lane discussed who the fathers "could" possibly be. Odell kept changing her mind. She couldn't recall if one man, whom she described as a "poultry inspector," was the father of Baby Number One or Baby Number Two.

"The father of the first child," she said, "is the brother of my ex-husband."

Eventually Lane began mapping out the brief history of each child on a piece of paper, who the fathers might be, and what year each child had been born and died. It was hard, because Odell couldn't remember exact dates, times, or sexes of the children. Selective memory, perhaps. As for Baby Doe, Odell said, as Lane noted it on his map, that child was fathered by a "young kid." Again, here was one more opportunity for Odell to implicate her father and say that he had raped her and fathered the child, but she didn't. As for the next baby, Baby Number One (1982), Odell claimed it was her brother-in-law's child. Baby Number Two had been, according to her, fathered by a "washing-machine guy." Baby Number Three had been fathered by a "poultry inspector . . . David something," she finally said, but couldn't recall his last name.

The man's name, David Dandignac, hadn't resonated with Odell as she sat talking to Lane on May 20, but Dandignac later would remember his relationship with Odell quite remarkably.

Dandignac wasn't just some common poultry inspector, as one might have gathered from what Odell said; he worked for the Department of Agriculture as a poultry *grader*, whose job it was to make sure New York residents could depend on the Grade A insignia slapped on the front of turkey packaging. He had also worked for the U.S. Department of Agriculture for sixteen years. In 2003, when members of the BCI caught up with him, Dandignac was married for a second time, had two boys from a previous marriage, and was living with his wife and her children, making him, in effect, a father of five.

Dandignac met Odell when he lived on White Lake next door to where she and Mabel and the three kids from her marriage to James Odell had lived. It was 1983. At twenty-three years old, seven years younger than Odell, he was inspecting eggs at the time for the state of New York. They struck up a friendship one day, he explained, that soon turned into an intimate relationship.

"We just started talking now and then and would visit on occasion or something, and I would stop over. . . ."

At some point during the spring of 1984, after being friends, they became "romantically involved." As the affair heated up, living next door to Odell wouldn't suffice—by June of that same year, Dandignac said, he was living with Odell, Mabel, and the kids inside their bungalow on the lake.

Three months later, however, in August, "things started to not go well and we just didn't . . . we just didn't mesh well as a . . . as a couple, or as a family."

Dandignac had just turned twenty-four years old. Odell was thirty. He was doing well at work and saw the opportunity for his future. Odell was working as a secretary and having a tough time making ends meet.

Odell said she never really wanted anything more from Dandignac than to be "friends with benefits." Again, she claimed, it was Mabel who had pushed for the relationship.

"David was a very, very nice guy," Odell recalled. "I had nothing against David, ever. I liked him as a friend. When I sent David away, it was to make sure he was not going to be plundered by my mother."

It was Mabel, Odell added, who had asked Dandignac to move in (although he later recalled it differently).

"My mother said to him one day, 'You can move in here with us. . . .' And I looked at her and said to David, 'Could you give us a minute?'"

A private, whispered talk with Mabel did nothing. Dandignac was moving in and that was the end of it. The problem for Odell was not that he wasn't a nice person, or that she didn't trust him—she just wasn't attracted to him. He lived right near their bungalow. She could see him anytime she wanted. She'd had sex with the guy. It didn't mean she wanted to marry him—or have his child.

"Actually, I would have preferred not to see him at all. It's not that I didn't like him. I just wasn't *interested* in him. He was a friend when I [lived down the road], and when I left there, I assumed the friendship would stay there. Not once did I ever consider he would visit my mother and, better yet, be in my house when I came home from work."

After it was clear they didn't, as Dandignac later put it, "mesh well," instead of moving out of the house, he agreed to stay until he could find and afford a place of his own. All the same, they "slept in the same bed, but nothing," he said, "was happening." They weren't having sex.

By September, Odell went to Dandignac and said, "Let's just end the relationship. . . . You need to move out."

He didn't argue.

With little money of his own, Dandignac, who was paying part of Odell and Mabel's rent, talked Odell into allowing him to move into a different section of the house. It was spacey enough for them all. He could sleep in the front room, where the kids had been sleeping, and the kids could move into Odell's room.

Through October, November, and December 1984, he stayed in another room, all the while proclaiming that he was going to move as soon as he had enough money. But by the time January 1985 came around, he was still there. There were no hard feelings to speak of, Dandignac said later. He and Odell were finished. Furthermore, he got along well with Mabel, Odell, and the kids. He said Mabel was a normal old person. There was nothing strange about her. She could be overbearing, sure, but he liked her.

Nonetheless, there was something else between Dandignac and Odell that wasn't being discussed—a secret, perhaps, that lingered as fall turned to winter and it became more apparent he was going to have to leave as soon as possible.

Back in July, Odell had gone to Dandignac and told him she had missed her period.

"I'm pregnant," he later remembered Odell saying.

"What?" he responded. *"Pregnant?"* He was in his twenties. He had worked hard. Gone to college. He was planning a career in agriculture.

"Do you want me to get an abortion?" Odell asked.

"I don't know. . . . I can't give you an answer. I don't know what to do."

Dandignac was confused. No one wanted to end a life with one breath and a simple yes to an abortion. It had to be thought out. Planned. Time would tell.

A while went by and David decided, he said later, that he wanted Odell to have the child. They could work it all out. He'd support the child, even if she didn't want to be involved romantically.

Months went by. It was well into January 1985 and the matter of whether Odell would get an abortion or have the child hadn't been resolved. It reality, though, it was too late, anyway. She was, by January 1985, seven months pregnant. No doctor would grant her an abortion at such a late stage. Still, Dandignac was behind having the child and kept insisting he'd support her. Whenever they would discuss his moving out of the house, he'd assure Odell, "I will give you money toward the child."

"I don't want it," Odell said one day, Dandignac recalled later.

"You don't want my money?"

"No! I don't want you paying me any money."

Odell wanted to raise the child herself, she said later. "It wasn't that I wanted to *deny* him that child," she recalled. "I was trying to get him out of the house to stand on his own. . . . What I was afraid was going to happen is, if I accepted money from him, then he would end up staying. And if he stayed there, my mother would, you know, the dollar signs would have just popped right up in her eyes . . . and she would have thought, 'Even if they are not sharing the same bedroom together, with the baby coming, he's going to want to do everything in his power.' She's going to need this and that . . . and we're going to be able to do this and that. . . . I could hear it going over and over in my head because I had heard it all before."

Odell, then, wasn't hiding the pregnancy from Mabel, as she later told police she would rather chop off one of her arms than tell Mabel she was pregnant.

During the time she was pregnant, Dandignac said later, he never knew of a time where she had told Mabel about it. "She was fairly stocky," he added, explaining how Odell looked when she wasn't pregnant, "large, very large-boned."

They had talked about adoption as time went on, but again, a particular plan was never resolved or put in motion. The subjects of abortion, adoption, and Dandignac financially taking care of Odell and the child were always left in limbo.

By late January 1985, however, Dandignac was finished talking. He moved to Monticello. Any decision about the baby would fall now on Odell's shoulders. He'd done all he could.

A few weeks later, he returned to the house to pick up an item he had left behind. Mabel answered the door. "I forgot a kitchen utensil," he said.

"Wait here. I'll get it."

Dandignac walked into the foyer area. Odell was standing there as he walked by.

"Hello" was all she said.

Dandignac said hello back, grabbed the kitchen utensil from Mabel, and walked out. It was the last time he would see or hear from Odell for nearly eighteen years. As far as how Odell and Mabel got along, David said they had a "good relationship. . . ." Mabel was a "nice lady." As far as what happened to the baby, he said he never knew or found out.

After the BCI tracked him down during the summer of 2003, Dandignac agreed to give a DNA sample.

Baby Number Three, born sometime in 1985, was indeed fathered by Dandignac, DNA subsequently proved.

"I kept waiting to see," Odell said later, "if he would show up at the door or, you know, call." When he left, that was it. Odell expected a knock on the door one day after she had the baby, she claimed, or at least a phone call from him—but it never happened. "I know he had the phone number. He didn't want to show up. He never did. He never picked up the phone and said, 'Are you all right? Do you need anything?' It was like a hole opened up in the ground and swallowed him."

If Dandignac would have shown up or called, no one can say what Odell would have told him, but he would have never seen his child—because by then, it had been murdered, wrapped in plastic, placed in a box, and stored in the closet along with two others.

2

As Odell sat across from Investigator Lane on the morning of May 20, she admitted for a second time that the babies were alive at some point after she gave birth. "'Felt child move against my thigh,'" Lane wrote as Odell spoke. "'Heard noise.'"

Although quite subtle, those two words—"move" and "noise"—meant perhaps more than anything else Odell had said during the past three days. Those children were given life by Odell, both life *and* death, Lungen and his team of investigators were now entirely convinced.

The conversation shifted to Mabel at some point. Lane asked Odell "repeatedly whether her mother knew about the pregnancies. . . ."

"Absolutely not!" Odell said firmly, again and again.

"I was in a subordinate relationship with my mother and fearful of what she would think or what she would do if she found out I was pregnant."

Odell said she had even kept the relationships she had with the fathers of the children secret from Mabel, with the exception of the "poultry inspector," David Dandignac, whom, Odell said, she had been forced to stay in a relationship with because he was "supporting the family monetarily."

"What about the storage locker," Lane asked. "Why stop paying the bill?"

This, too, baffled investigators. *Why stop paying the one bill that could expose the dark secrets of your life?* It made no sense—unless, of course, you *wanted* to get caught.

"My intention was to go back and retrieve the boxes, but I couldn't afford to travel out to Arizona."

Lane soon found out that after Mabel died in 1995, Odell called the owner of the storage locker and asked if she could get her belongings, but the owner said he had sold everything to pay her overdue bills.

"I felt quite a bit of trepidation," Odell explained, "that there would be a knock on the door [after that], but then nothing happened and I kind of thought he had not told me the truth and that he *didn't* sell everything."

"Why didn't you throw the boxes out?" Lane asked.

This was also a mystery. Why hadn't Odell discarded the boxes? No one would have likely ever found the remains.

"I wanted to give them a proper burial. And I wanted to have evidence when I went to the authorities, so they didn't think I was some sort of wacko."

Evidence of what? Here, once again, was Odell's chance to involve Mabel, but she never mentioned Mabel as being connected to the deaths of the children.

Investigator Linda Paul had stepped out of the room at one point to get Odell a glass of water. When she opened the door and returned, Odell leaned in toward Lane and whispered, "Can she remain outside?"

"Sure," Lane said.

Paul looked at Lane as she handed Odell the water. Lane motioned for her to leave.

"Okay," Lane continued as Paul left the room, "you have eight living, healthy children, all born in hospitals. You have these children that are in boxes that no one knew of. . . . Why is that, Miss Odell?"

Odell took a break for a moment, possibly to collect her thoughts. She had been, when it came down to it, interviewed for the past three days, under the light for nearly twenty hours. It was the first time anyone had asked this type of question. Here, perhaps without Odell even realizing it, Lane was getting to the motive behind the murders.

"The reason I hid the pregnancies," Odell said quietly, according to Lane's report, "is that they were bastard children, born out of wedlock. I was afraid of what my mother would think."

Lane wrote down part of the statement on the piece of paper in front of him: "bastard children." Next to that, he signed his name. Then he slid the piece of paper across the table and placed it in front of Odell.

"Would you be willing to sign that?"

"Sure," Odell said as she grabbed Lane's pen.

3

With Mabel dead, Odell and Sauerstein began spending their time in Endicott, New York, during fall 1995, concentrating on providing for their rather large family. They finally had found, it seemed, a place to settle. At least for the time being.

While in Endicott, though, they moved around quite a bit. From one end of town to the other, they packed it in and relocated several times over the period of a year or more. By the end of 1996, Sauerstein decided he wanted to go back to Lytle, Texas. He had heard there was work available, Odell said later, work he wasn't finding in Endicott. A friend had even offered him a job. Yet, Odell and the kids weren't going because they couldn't afford to pack everything up and move across country all over again.

Nevertheless, after four months in Lytle, Sauerstein returned after not finding work. Odell was now living in Johnson City, a five-minute ride from Endicott. She had a hard time recalling exactly where she lived and when, but she was certain about having moved around quite a bit while in Endicott and Johnson City.

"A lot of this comes to me and a lot of this stuff is blended," Odell said, speaking about her life in general during that period. "I asked my therapist [later] why it comes to me this way, and she said it is my way of dealing with the trauma and my way of trying to block it out."

Regardless of how she remembered her life, a paper trail left behind pointed to a gypsy's life of getting into trouble with Child Protective Services at times, running from bill collectors at others, abandoning apartments under the cloak of darkness, and changing jobs as often as three and four times a year.

In June 1998, Odell became a grandmother. Her daughter Doris, unmarried then, gave birth to a healthy baby boy.

By the end of 1998, near Christmas, Odell wasn't feeling well. She was forty-five years old. She'd stopped menstruating around Christmas and thought perhaps she was experiencing early signs of menopause. Yet as the new year dawned, it became apparent she would have another announcement to make to the family.

CHAPTER 18

1

HEATHER YAKIN, A reporter with the *Times Herald-Record,* a local newspaper in Sullivan County, was sitting at her computer on the morning of May 20, skimming the Associated Press wire, checking for any national stories that might have a local angle. It was part of her morning ritual to check the wire, she said, and plan her day.

As she read, Yakin was struck by a story slugged with a rather bizarre headline: INFANT REMAINS. Being a crime reporter, it was a story Yakin knew she had to check out further. So, as she sipped her first cup of coffee of the day, she continued reading.

"Dianne Odell, now living in Rome, PA," the AP story began, "told investigators she gave birth to four babies that died in New York state between the late 1960s and 1984, including three found last week in boxes abandoned in a storage shed in Safford, Arizona, said Graham County Sheriff Frank Hughes."

The words "New York" jumped off the computer screen at Yakin. *A local connection!*

Obviously, the AP had gotten a few of its facts wrong,

but that was the nature of the daily news business. Either way, Yakin knew her day was going to be consumed with tracking down as much information as she could about the story.

Part of her daily routine included calling local police stations in the Monticello region to see what was brewing. Like any reporter well-entrenched in the political infrastructure of a small town, Yakin had contacts and sources that fed her information. When she called the NYSP Liberty barracks moments later and asked about the Odell story, all the trooper would say was "Go to the press conference this afternoon."

"Is someone dead?" It was one of Yakin's standard questions.

"No comment," the trooper said.

No comment, of course, was as good as a yes. Trick questions. Reporters, at least good reporters, were masters at spinning words to get the information they wanted.

Yakin asked the trooper where the case was being investigated.

"Sullivan County."

Another great answer. She had contacts in the Sullivan County court.

After hanging up, Yakin phoned Steve Lungen's office. It took her a while, but she got Lungen on the phone. "[He] wouldn't say anything beyond, 'This is [going to be] a big case,'" Yakin recalled.

With that, she hit Lungen with: "Is someone dead?"

Lungen hesitated. Then, "The case is out of Bethel. It's not a recent case. It happened over a period of years. . . . The defendant was living in Pennsylvania and Arizona . . . and the case involves the deaths of three babies."

Oh God! Yakin said to herself. *The babies they found in the storage shed in Arizona. . . .* It all made sense now. The AP story and Lungen's information; it was connected.

With the press conference only hours away, Yakin realized she had to move quickly.

Big case. *Big* story.

Later that morning, more stories were published around the country. For the most part, the AP was updating its original stories as information flowed in and reporters backed up bits and pieces of information.

One story ran with the headline WOMAN CHARGED WITH MURDERING THREE CHILDREN. The brief accompanying article began by outlining the criminal case against Odell, but focused more on the bizarre nature of what amounted to a woman toting around the mummified and decomposed remains of her three children for over twenty years.

"Think about carrying around three corpses, your own children . . . ," NYSP major Alan Martin, who worked out of Troop F, Scileppi's troop, in Liberty, told the AP. "It's very hard to comprehend. Why? That's the sixty-four-thousand-dollar question."

By midday, the story had sparked media interest from all over. It was, by most standards, a slow news day, anyway. A mother killing her children was surely a crime story that could offer the talking heads on the nightly cable tragedy-TV shows something to discuss. Without a doubt, the mummified corpses of Odell's children were going to be talking points in the days and months to come for anyone in the business of broadcast media.

Quite persistent now in getting to the core of the story, Yakin started calling more of her contacts. She had been working at the *Herald-Record* since 1997. One of her professors at SUNY, New Paltz, a rather popular local college, back in 1996, who had himself worked at the *Herald-Record* at one time, let Yakin know the "night cops beat" was open. She was interested. So he put in a "good word" for her, and the next thing she knew she had the job.

Heather Yakin had covered just about everything as a crime reporter—except a story like the one unfolding on the morning of May 20.

"I was hooked [on covering crime] from the moment I first had to ask a cop what kind of knife some guy . . . had used to stab his wife," Yakin said. "That was my second night on the job. I worked 'night cops' part-time for seven months."

This, mind you, while keeping a full course load in college at the same time. Then, "In August 1997, eager to put in the time in hopes of a full-time job," Yakin said she worked every day of the month.

The effort paid off, because she was offered a full-time job. And in March 1998, she became a full-fledged reporter working the Sullivan County crime-and-justice beat.

The Odell story had the potential for Heather Yakin to make her mark at the *Herald-Record*. It had the juicy details that make Lifetime Television movies and Court TV trials so popular among those audiences today who have enormous appetites for crime and forensic entertainment. It was, in retrospect, Yakin's chance to follow a day-by-day crime story, do some investigating—which she loved—and write about it. Many of the stories about Odell would likely end up on the front page. Everyone in town, by now, was talking about what had become the "Babies in Boxes" murder case.

Her sources inside the Sullivan County Courthouse were talking. She was going to run Odell and Sauerstein's names in the electronic library at the *Herald-Record* and see what popped. Her gut was telling her the story was going to get bigger. In addition, as she began to learn more about Odell's life, she realized it was her own bloodline that could potentially be the pot of gold as far as getting an exclusive story.

Yakin's roots went back to the town of Bethel, where Odell had spent a better part of her early life and, more important, the location where the babies had been born.

"My family," Yakin said, "on my maternal grandfather's side, has been in the town of Bethel for at least one hundred years. When I was six years old, [in late 1973], my parents, brother, sister, and I moved into [a] farmhouse there that had been my great-grandmother's. . . . We kids rode the school bus each morning with Max Shapiro's kids, and we were friends with them."

Max Shapiro was the junk dealer who had found the blue suitcase containing the remains of Baby Doe back in 1989.

Yakin's mother was elected to the Bethel Town Board when Heather was nine.

"My sister and I used to run around downtown Kauneonga Lake in the summer while the board met. Town Hall was located behind the post office," which was a side step from one of the bungalows where Odell and Mabel had once lived.

The Yakin family then moved to Monticello in 1982 after Heather's mother ran an unsuccessful campaign to head the board. After graduating high school, Heather found herself at the University of Chicago for the next two years. Then came a stint, she laughingly added, at trying to be a "rock star" and going to Orange County Community College.

"This [was] when I was trying to decide what to do with my life. I quit . . . [a few jobs]. . . . After a couple of months, I picked up day shifts bartending. My mom, who had gone back to school to get a bachelor's and her CPA license, actually came up with the idea of journalism."

The Odell story was, perhaps, a stepping-stone for Heather Yakin. She already had written about many different aspects of crime—murder, rape, sex abuse, arson, larceny, contractor fraud, elder abuse, Internet crime, burglary, robbery, drug crime—when she came upon the AP story about Odell. But none could match the drama of a mother involved in the deaths of her children some twenty years ago. No, this was different. Not your typical, run-of-the-mill murder story tucked away somewhere on page A8. It had titillating elements and a hometown connection.

Front-page all the way.

"You name it," Yakin said, "Sullivan County has got a bit of a reputation for having lots of sex offense cases. I think much of that comes from the DA's office and the police, including the Family Violence Response Team formed in 1999. They've learned how to build cases, including how to get confessions."

Indeed, an important element in the Odell case that would come into play later on: how to obtain confessions. Had Odell been coerced into an admission?

"The DA is aggressive about prosecutions," Yakin added, but "the same officials [also] go after people who file false reports of rape or sexual abuse."

For that reason alone, Heather Yakin said, she believed the scales of justice are balanced in Sullivan County.

2

For the past three days, Odell had been questioned about her dead babies. She had told several different versions of what amounted to one common story: because of her actions, three of her children were dead. There was no confession of malicious intent, where she explained how she snapped and strangled them; and there were no wild stories of her going crazy and murdering the children in some ritualistic act. If anything, she had told police exactly, she said, what she remembered.

And where had it gotten her? In a Sullivan County jail cell, in downtown Monticello, awaiting arraignment on several counts of murder.

For Robert Sauerstein, he was at home tending to his and Odell's five children, one of whom was not even four years old. In many ways, the events of the past week were surreal. One moment, Sauerstein and Odell were raising a family, moving around the country, trying to find a place to settle, and the next, well, she was in a jail cell looking at life behind bars.

Had it really all happened this way?

On Thursday, May 22, 2003, one of the guards in the holding area at the Sullivan County Jail, where Odell was being held, rattled the bars of her cell with his keys and said, "Get dressed, Odell. You have a visitor."

"Who is it?"

"I don't know, Odell, just get up!"

"Is it a legal visit?"

"No, no. It's no legal visit."

Odell had been trying to sleep. The past week had been a blur. Time hadn't passed; instead, the days and nights, she said, had all run together. On Tuesday and Wednesday, she spoke to her court-appointed defense attorney, Stephan Schick. But Odell insisted later she hadn't really gotten any information out of Schick that was useful. Their first meeting was more or less a "get acquainted" conference. In her view, a good attorney—not that Schick wasn't—would have gotten her out on bond by Wednesday. Scared and lonely, sitting in jail, she was wondering what the hell was taking so long.

"I'm in jail on Tuesday and Wednesday," Odell said, "and I did not receive a visitor. You know, no communication with my family whatsoever."

When she didn't hear from Sauerstein or Maryann, who was twenty-three years old now, or anyone else from her family, she assumed Sauerstein had "taken off with the kids to make sure they were safe and okay."

As Odell walked out into the visiting area of the jail, she was startled to see Sauerstein and a woman named Danielle, a neighbor with whom she had been friends ever since living in Rome. Odell and Sauerstein lived next door to a general store in Rome and Odell had worked at the store from time to time, where she met Danielle.

Odell sat across from Sauerstein and her friend. At first, they looked at her and couldn't believe where they were. Odell appeared beaten down, tired. The bags under her eyes were more pronounced than they had ever been, her face devoid of any real energy or life. She had been crying, of course, on and off, wondering how she had managed to land herself in jail for the murder of her own children.

Almost simultaneously Sauerstein and Danielle said, "What happened?"

Odell shrugged her shoulders and looked down at the graffiti-laden table. So many initials carved in the tabletop, representing so many women who had come and gone before her through what was a revolving door. Now she, too, was a notch in a table.

After thinking about it for a moment, Odell looked at Sauerstein and said, "My mother was involved."

It would be a recurring mantra in the weeks and months to come. Odell would place all the blame on Mabel. Yet she'd had her chance—multiple chances, really—to tell police about Mabel's responsibility in the crimes, but thus far had chosen not to say anything.

When she explained to Sauerstein that Mabel had been involved, he said, "I knew it! I knew it! I knew it! I *knew* you were hiding something."

At that moment, Odell believed that Sauerstein was having trouble coming to terms with the situation. Not what had happened to the babies, she was quick to point out, but what had happened to her.

"I don't think Robert wanted to deal with [the issues regarding the police] at that point. But I think he was having problems about him not coming to my rescue . . . not barging in on a white horse, but you know, showing up with a lawyer and doing all of those things."

Sauerstein was a man with a strong moral character, Odell insisted. He was from the old school, where a man took care of his wife, no matter what the circumstances were.

Nothing came out of the visit other than the fact that Odell now knew her husband was going to be there for her. The visit was his way, she believed, of showing support.

What started out five days ago on a Sunday afternoon as answering a few routine questions for the Graham County (Arizona) Sheriff's Office had turned into the worst possible situation imaginable. Odell believed then that all she had to do was answer a few questions about the babies and the situation would work itself out. After all, in her mind she hadn't done anything criminal.

"That was what I thought at the start. The first thing I wanted to do was, I wanted to sit down and I wanted to talk to my family and I wanted to let them know everything that had happened and everything that went on. From the very beginning to the very end, which included what had happened with my father and everything else."

Furthermore, she said Thomas Scileppi, Diane Thomas, Bruce Weddle, and the Sullivan County DA's Office all lied to her when they told her the media was chasing the story on a national level.

"On the first day when I spoke to the police, at the end of that conversation that had included me in the media, they (Thomas and Weddle) are telling me this story is going across the nation and all of this other *shit*. It's on TV. It's here. It's there. It's everywhere. And I'm thinking to myself, 'Okay, this is the way this is going to go if you tell them the truth. You're going to tell them that your mother was there, your father raped you, all the way down the line. From beginning to end: you were raped by your [half] brother when you were five, your father took his turn, and after you turned fourteen, your mother put you into prostitution. . . . My God,' I'm thinking to myself, 'my kids are going to have to live with this?'"

Because of that pressure, Odell insisted, she began lying on that first day to protect her family, mainly her living children.

From what?

The fallout from everything that came with being branded a baby killer.

"No matter what happens to me, my kids are going to have to live with this. So I kept my mouth shut."

Wasn't a mother's place with her children? If Odell had chosen to lie for the sake of protecting her children, she now realized where those lies had gotten her. All she needed to do was look around at the steel bars and stainless-steel toilets and hear the screams and foul language and smell the wretched odors coming from her surroundings to know that her kids were not better off with her in jail. Why not come clean and get it over with? Why not tell the truth and go home to your kids?

3

It wasn't planned, Odell claimed later. It was something that just "happened." And for the first four months of her latest pregnancy, she said, she never knew she was pregnant. When she stopped menstruating, she thought she was experiencing early signs of menopause.

But with the birth of the baby came one of the best surprises of her life. On August 7, 1999, Odell celebrated her forty-sixth birthday with labor pains. The following day, August 8, merely six hours after the day she was born, she was given what she later described as "the best birthday present I could have ever given myself."

Seth Sauerstein, a healthy, vibrant, feisty little boy, was born at Tyler Memorial Hospital, in Tunkhannock, Pennsylvania. Odell and Sauerstein, after moving to Harpersville, New York—or, according to police later, running from Child Protective Services in February 1999, telling them they were moving to Albany but instead fled to Pennsylvania, eluding them—welcomed their fifth child together.

Child Protective Services had been alerted because Odell and Sauerstein's children, police found out later, were reported to have "excessive absenteeism from school."

Odell claimed they had never run from Child Protective Services, but admitted she had kept her children out of school.

Why?

"When we got to Harpersville, the place just brought us all down. The kids there were mean. I don't know how to put this, but as delicately as possible, but . . . it [Harpersville] was like the trash heap of the world."

She was scared, she said, for the well-being of her children.

"My son went out to play one day and some kid threw a two-by-four at him and split his head open. . . . It got to the point where we didn't allow the children to even go outside."

Thus, because she feared her children would be hurt, she kept them home from school.

"I didn't want anything to happen to them."

At the time, she and Sauerstein worked thirty miles from home.

"God forbid if anything happened to them while I was at work, it would take me an hour to get home, or an hour to get to the nearest hospital."

Apparently, being at home by themselves, missing out on an education and being around the potential dangers that lurk in any unsupervised home, was a risk she was more willing to take.

None of that trouble mattered much to Odell after they moved from Harpersville later that spring to Pennsylvania and she had her eighth living child. She now had another life to take care of. And no criminal charges were ever filed against her for neglect.

"I would do it all over again to protect my children if I had to."

The pregnancy, she recalled, and the circumstances surrounding it, were a gift from God.

"I'm walking around one day and I felt this flutter in my stomach." She was months into the pregnancy at the time. "I didn't have any other discomforts; I didn't have any nausea."

Odell had never experienced morning sickness, she claimed, with any of her kids. And one would have to imagine that after being pregnant for the better part of nine years, her body was used to it by 1999.

"I was thinking, 'Okay, well, it's about time [for my period],' and then I feel this flutter, this movement—this feeling of life. And I said, 'Oh, my, God.'"

When she realized she was pregnant, she went to Sauerstein with the news.

"You better sit down. . . ."

"Why?" he asked.

"Well, you better sit down . . . and I'll tell you why." She paused for a moment. Sauerstein took a seat. "We're going to have another baby."

Silence.

Then he looked at her and laughed. "You're kidding, right?"

"No, I'm not."

"You're crazy."

At that moment, Odell said, the baby moved, so she put Sauerstein's hand on her stomach. "See."

"Okay."

"He seemed to be happy," she recalled. "What, really, was he going to do?"

They were excited and scared. Her age had a little to do with it, but it was more that she had grandchildren by then and knew she wasn't going to be able to work all the way through her latest pregnancy, like she had with most of her pregnancies.

When she realized she was pregnant, she sat down and thought, *Was this given to me for a reason? You know what, yeah, you were given this gift for a reason.*

In terms of the law, Odell had eight "gifts" that had been given life—and four "bastards" that hadn't.

What would a jury think of it all?

4

Between 2000 and the time she latched onto the Odell case in 2003, *Times Herald-Record* reporter Heather Yakin said, "There [was] a rise in more white-collar [crime], contractor fraud, big larcenies" in Sullivan County. So she was always busy. But the Odell case offered her something more than the usual drug-related shooting, theft, or embezzlement case. It had elements that fueled a good story.

By May 26, 2003, a Monday, more facts were made public. Yakin had been beating up her sources for information. The press conference held days before had been the typical "all we can say at this point" nonsense that police spokespeople, forced by white shirts to stand in front of a garrulous bunch of reporters, had to promulgate.

Before the press conference, Yakin had found the Graham County Sheriff's Office Web site on the Internet and had gotten hold of Frank Hughes, the sheriff.

"Nice guy," she recalled. "Filled me in on their end of the investigation, how the babies were found, described the boxes, gave me rough dates on when the babies were born, when Odell and Sauerstein lived in Safford, and how many living kids Odell had."

After she spoke to Frank Hughes, Yakin grabbed a copy of *Death Investigator's Handbook* by Louis N. Eliopulos, one of the many reference books she kept on the windowsill by her desk.

"I checked the sections on decomposed remains, child death, injuries associated with child abuse, and abandoned newborn/stillborn/fetus."

Doing that, she said, "refreshed" her memory regarding investigative concerns, and helped her formulate questions for law enforcement.

A good reporter should always stay objective: get a sense of the story, report the facts, but leave her own opinions about the case with the bartender, a spouse, a friend. One might imagine that Heather Yakin, being a female, had developed personal feelings about Odell and the case in general. If what police were saying turned out to be true, Odell had murdered four of her children. In the eyes of many, she would be considered a monster.

"Well," Yakin said, "I don't have kids, and, frankly, I've never wanted them. I'm pretty much devoid of maternal instinct. I really didn't have a frame of reference on dead newborns. And I'd been doing this job for a few years at that point, covering sex abuse, child abuse—including child abuse fatalities—robbery, assault. Honestly, I'm bothered less by quick deaths than by lingering deaths. . . . [But] although I have no maternal instinct, I tend to feel rather protective of crime victims, especially murder victims and their families. So my primary reaction to Odell was as a reporter."

Still, the case had flooded Heather Yakin with what she described later as "sense-memories," which, she would soon learn, would be substantially encouraging to where her reporting was heading. Memories, she said, of "being a kid, running around those safe, quiet rural streets in the half dark of summer, playing on the shore of White Lake . . . riding on the school bus, passing those buildings and those streets every morning and every afternoon."

Odell had once lived in one of those buildings. It was the bungalow she and Mabel rented after Max Shapiro found the remains of Baby Doe in her Volkswagen.

If Odell had gone to school up here, Yakin was thinking as she began plotting her next move, *she'd have gone to school with my aunts and uncles.*

Without hesitation, she began making calls. Maybe somebody she knew would remember Odell? If so, she had the scoop of her career.

5

In their view, Steve Lungen and his team of investigators had gotten Odell to admit she had killed three of her babies. Odell had been arraigned, where she pleaded not guilty, in what amounted to a five-minute court appearance. For Lungen, the case against Odell was just beginning. There was no doubt, he believed, she would either present an insanity defense or try to explain the deaths of the three babies as accidental, with the hope of reaching one juror. So, for starters,

Lungen had to prepare to prove Odell had, in fact, *murdered* the children—that they hadn't died of natural causes or by accident. And, secondly, Odell knew what she was doing at the time.

None of this would be easy. The condition of the babies' remains, Lungen was about to find out, was going to be his first major hurdle.

Investigator Bill Maloney had been with the NYSP for eighteen years. For the past eight, Maloney had worked in the Crime Scene Unit out of Middletown, New York. Unlike television, where actor William Petersen's character, Grissom, on the CBS hit show *CSI*, arrives at a crime scene and figures out a murder in sixty minutes, Maloney spent hours, days, and weeks processing crime scenes and evidence, which could aid in a successful, later prosecution. A lot of that time is spent documenting the scene and preparing evidence for later analysis. Troop F, where Maloney worked, is responsible for five separate counties. Forensic work is tedious and time-consuming. With all the theatrics displayed on television and crime scene classes at colleges filling up, one might be more inclined to believe that being part of a crime scene unit is a glamorous job, replete with fame, fortune, and earth-shattering discoveries. For those who work the job, day in and day out, however, scouring crime scenes on their hands and knees with magnifying glasses and other high-tech gadgets, working fifteen- to twenty-four-hour shifts in the lab, it's hard, backbreaking work.

Bill Maloney, crime scene technician Theodore LaRuffa, and two investigators from Troop F in Liberty left on Tuesday morning, May 27, and flew to Tucson, Arizona. Their main purpose for the trip was to retrieve the three decomposed bodies of Odell's children and bring them back to Albany so Dr. Michael Baden could have a look and, perhaps, find out what had happened. While they were there, Bill and his crew also were going to "secure" evidence collected by Detective Diane Thomas, Detective Bruce Weddle, the GCSO, and bring it all back. Lungen would be the first to speak highly of the GCSO. Still, he needed to have his own team examine and collect evidence. Furthermore, he didn't want the burden of having to fly in a dozen or so witnesses from Arizona if the case went to trial. The more witnesses he had closer to home base, the better off he was.

"One of the reasons for the three of them to go all way out there was," Lungen said, "we wanted one person to handle all the chain of custody of the evidence and that's what he's trained to do. The other two were there to conduct background investigation with the Arizona people as to what they got. Essentially, we wanted our New York State Police cops to redo what [Arizona] had already done. Go to the scene. Go look at everything. Take all new photographs. I was concerned with how many of the Arizona people would have to come to New York as witnesses. If I could re-create a lot of it and re-photograph it all, I could get away with mostly New York witnesses."

The more local people Lungen had at his disposal, the better off his case preparation would interconnect. Having witnesses fifteen hundred miles away was not what a prosecutor wanted. The expense of travel alone would be enormous—not to mention locating people and finding out information while preparing a case.

Maloney and his team ended up spending five days in Safford, studying every container Odell had stored in the two self-storage units. After that, they met with Dr. David Winston, a pathologist in Tucson who had conducted preliminary autopsies on the children. From there, Maloney photographed and logged each piece of evidence and prepped it for travel back east. It was decided that Dr. Baden would call Dr. Winston and—to maintain the integrity of the evidence Baden was going to be looking at in New York—begin a carefully documented succession of command. That way, Dr. Baden could handle any trial testimony. In turn, Dr. Winston wouldn't have to make the trip.

One of the boxes Maloney collected had a particular waxy, dark-colored character to it; he described it later as a "distinct odor." The entire box had been saturated in some sort of liquid, which had since dried. Looking at it, Maloney knew the odor, accompanied by the waxy, dark color of the box, could mean only one thing: decomposition. One of the babies had decomposed inside the box and leaked bodily fluids, saturating the cardboard.

After a long trip back home, Maloney brought the remains of the children to the Forensic Center in Albany.

On June 4, Dr. Baden conducted the autopsies so he could eventually report his findings to Lungen.

Baden had done tens of thousands of autopsies throughout his career. He had opened up junkies, prostitutes, stockbrokers, homemakers, businessmen and women, teenagers—and, of course, babies.

Hundreds of babies.

The Odell babies were different, however. They had been sitting in boxes for two decades, maybe longer. Doing autopsies on them would be akin to an archaeology dig, a careful examination of the human body in one of its rarest forms. Two of the babies were mere bone fragments and dust. One, though, was in fair condition, having been entombed and preserved in mummified skin, like leather.

A forensic pathologist, Baden explained, "is a doctor who gives testimony in public." The term, he added, was likely born out of Ancient Greece. Part of the forensic pathologist's job, "especially when it comes to deaths, is to make his or her interpretations from all of the history, circumstances, interviews with families and friends and doctors, police, as opposed to the hospital-based pathologist who has a chart."

Professionally speaking, the forensic pathologist opts to rely on *all* the evidence, not just what the body tells him or her later on during the autopsy process; while the hospital-based pathologist, on the other hand, relies on what a nurse might report, what a patient's chart suggests, the time of death, and the health history of the patient.

There is, of course, a major difference between the two.

"When I work as a hospital pathologist and somebody dies," Baden said, "I have a whole chart of everything that happened in the hospital . . . the history and circumstances, and that is all part of medicine." But the forensic pathologist "almost always deals with people who die *out* of hospitals."

It is those out-of-hospital deaths that can be tricky for the forensic pathologist to figure out, especially when it pertains to time of death. Most go by the rigor mortis process, rigidity, and temperature change in the body. But also, perhaps more important, "the forensic pathologist . . . will render opinions and conclusions based upon not just what they see, but also what they can learn from . . . outside sources."

And that would, ultimately, be what the Odell case came down to: outside sources, coupled with what Baden was about to find out while conducting the autopsies.

There are five stages of decomposition: respectively, "fresh, bloat, decay, dry and remains." The Odell babies were, evidently, in the "dry and remains" stage. So, for Baden, the police reports, interviews with Odell, and other sources involved in the case would be indicative to the autopsy process and his ultimate findings.

Still, figuring out an exact time of death from the autopsy alone was going to be nearly impossible—and figuring out a cause of death was, likely, an unrealistic possibility. When it came down to it, this was one of the most important tasks for Lungen to prove as he prepared to indict Odell in front of a grand jury. Because if a grand jury failed to indict Odell, Lungen didn't have a case. None of what Baden was doing would matter.

CHAPTER 19

1

ROBERT SAUERSTEIN AND Dianne Odell found themselves, by early 2000, the parents of a new baby boy. Both were well into their forties, with four other children at home. Although Seth wasn't a burden and they were proud to have him, Odell later said he demanded a lot of her attention.

By late 2000, they were living in Montrose, Pennsylvania; a few months later, they moved again, to Rome, Pennsylvania, where they would end up staying until Detectives Diane Thomas and Bruce Weddle walked into the Rite Aid pharmacy, where Odell was working when she was first questioned in May 2003.

As Odell tried to figure out how she was going to get herself out of jail and back home with her children (one of whom would celebrate his fourth birthday in August) as May turned to June, she felt that if she came clean now and, in her words, explained how her mother had murdered the children, no one would believe her. Moreover, what really scared her, she said, was the fact that her living children would suffer. As she met with Stephan Schick and explained to him that her mother had been the culprit all along, she said Schick told her she should keep her mouth shut. The less she said, the better off she'd be—and that meant with Sauerstein, the kids, anyone.

Part of Odell's strategy not to talk about Mabel's involvement was that if she mentioned it, especially to Sauerstein, the information would end up being used against her later on during trial.

For Sauerstein, when Odell told him on that Thursday in May when he and Danielle visited, that Mabel was involved, "there was anger; there was relief."

Sauerstein knew what she was talking about without her discussing any of the details.

But what really bothered Odell as summer 2003 moved forward was that she had no idea what Schick had planned for a defense. She didn't know, she claimed, because he never told her and rarely went to visit her to explain what he was doing on her part.

This seeming invisibility by Schick would, in the coming months, be the one thing that, Odell said, drove a wedge between them and ultimately caused big problems for her down the road.

Stephan Schick was in his late fifties. Balding, with thinning gray hair, when he wore his glasses, he resembled Vice President Dick Cheney. He spoke confidently, carefully choosing his words, as if each carried the weight of repercussion. Schick grew up on a farm in Ulster County, New York, just northeast of Sullivan County. After graduating from Cornell, he finished his law degree at New York Law School, then did a brief internship at the Sullivan County District Attorney's Office, where he met then assistant district attorney Steve Lungen for the first time. It was 1978. Lungen was well into his career as Schick showed up at the office and began clerking. The two hit it off, Schick said, and became fast friends. Never did they believe they'd be on opposite sides of the legal scale years later.

After leaving the DA's office, Schick went into private practice in Monticello. Because he had worked in the DA's office and familiarized himself with criminal law, he began his career as a criminal lawyer. With a real estate boom going on in the Catskills at the time, however, he quickly merged into real estate law.

In 1985, when work in his private practice became somewhat unfulfilling, Schick went to work for Legal Aid. Although Legal Aid has changed over the years, its core dynamic remains the same: contracted with the county to represent those who cannot afford a lawyer, Legal Aid, staffed with eight to ten lawyers at any given time, is hired by the court to act essentially as a public defender's office. Some rural counties in New York do not have a public defender's office, like the larger communities. Sullivan County is one. Legal Aid makes up for the loss. It is a nonprofit organization run on a budget set by the county.

Schick said qualifying his tenure at Legal Aid as "happy" would be an "interesting view of it."

"I'm happy to the extent that I am [now] the boss in the office. On a day-to-day basis, I have the freedom to exercise my own goals and strategies."

It has been a bit easier since working his way up throughout the years into a position of running the show. There's no one in the office, Schick added with a chuckle, "looking to chop my head off."

Not everything, though, has been roses and chocolate. Fiscal realities, Schick maintained, plague Legal Aid. Like any government-run business, there have been cutbacks and budget constraints that stop him from doing certain things.

"Only a certain amount of local tax resources go into public defense. It's not a popular expenditure. I think in many upstate rural counties, local legislatures and local politicians, reflecting the more conservative view of the population, the constituency, would prefer not to fund or spend any of the taxpayers' money on public defense at all."

Making a valid point, Schick went on to say that it is hard to go to a citizen and say, "You know that guy who just burglarized your home and stole all of your family heirlooms? Well, we have to increase your property taxes to hire a public defender to represent him." Whereas, the opposite argument is much more appealing: "We have to increase your taxes because we want to give the DA's office more money to increase public safety."

While most criminal defense attorneys have a keen understanding for explaining away the obvious regarding a client's culpability, Schick has always had a canny way of currying favor. Instead of trying to dodge the evident and make excuses, he faces the realities of putting on the best defense he can for clients. This strong moral characteristic, which could be construed as detrimental to a defense attorney, would come into play when the Sullivan County court dropped the case of Dianne Odell in Schick's lap in early June 2003. Because he had the most trial experience out of the lawyers in his office, Schick decided to take the case on himself.

Indeed, because he viewed a situation the way it was, dealt with issues, and tried to construct a defense around facts, he and Odell would be at odds, starting with how they were going to approach Mabel's culpability in the babies' deaths.

2

The case for Steve Lungen came down to the fact that whenever there wasn't a male figure present in Odell's life, the children she gave birth to ended up wrapped in plastic bags, decomposing in boxes. It was, he believed, strong circumstantial evidence that pointed to what he understood firmly now to be her motive: bastard children don't deserve life. She had said it herself, in not so many words, to one of his investigators.

"Ultimately," Lungen recalled, "that was the case right there. The babies that ended up dead were babies where she didn't have any relationship with their fathers. They were the products of casual relationships."

Odell was gearing up, of course, to present a different portrait. It was Mabel who didn't want those children. It was Mabel who considered them bastards and murdered them. And it was Mabel who had made her nervous about acquiring prenatal care and denied her access to the hospital when she went into labor and couldn't drive herself.

Mabel. Mabel. Mabel.

The evening when Lungen, Scileppi, and two of Lungen's investigators, Paul Hans and Robert Rowan, drove back from Wilkes-Barre, Pennsylvania, and ended up doing a beeline for Waverly, New York, to interview Odell, had changed the entire scope of Lungen's case.

"The difference of her going home and not going home [that night]," Lungen recalled, was based on decisions made on the spot while driving from Wilkes-Barre to Waverly. "We had to make a decision whether we had enough to arrest her or not. And until she told us the babies were born alive—and if she would—that was the key."

Lungen had Odell's statement, which was, in a sense, telling in its own right. He believed the statement alone was enough to convince a jury she was responsible for the deaths of the children. Yet, fundamentally, the cusp of his case relied heavily, like most murder cases, on circumstantial evidence.

* * *

Most people have a misconception regarding how effective circumstantial evidence can be in the eyes of a competent jury. The term "circumstantial evidence" almost implies by itself that a prosecutor has little else, meaning forensics or an eyewitness, to present to a jury—that perhaps his case isn't as strong as he'd like it to be. But circumstances, when it comes down to it, are what murder cases, most anyway, are built around. The most powerful example of how valuable circumstantial evidence can be is, most prosecutors will admit, "people can lie, but circumstances cannot."

A way to look at it more basically is, if two people walk into an empty room and one exits with blood on his hands and the other ends up dead, an outside observer can determine, vis-à-vis "the circumstances," that the person with blood on his hands had something to do with the death. There can be no other logical explanation.

It's not science, just common sense.

Lungen could prove the babies were alive after birth because he had their mother admitting it. What better witness was there? He could prove the babies died because Odell had kept their remains. The DNA, he was being told, was going to be shaky at best, because of the age and condition of the remains. Still, Lungen had enough circumstantial evidence that when he spread it out for a jury, he believed, would convince them that Odell had not only murdered her children, but kept the pregnancies hidden from her mother—the one person whom she was now preparing to pin the deaths on.

"The people's theory," Lungen said, "[that Odell] will never admit, is that these children were killed because of their illegitimacy and because they were *un-wanted*. They were pregnancies by casual relation-ships, and whether it be her mother's influence or her own, she was not going to keep babies whom she knew she didn't want by fathers who were not around to support them."

When Lungen sat down and read the interviews with Odell by Diane Thomas and Bruce Weddle, along with those conducted by Scileppi, Streever, and Lane, he realized one significant factor that Odell herself had perhaps overlooked as she told one lie after the other during the days after her arrest. Through a careful review of those transcripts, Lungen was convinced, Odell defined her own lies and put them into perspec-tive herself.

"When you analyze those interviews, right up until the last moment, a couple of things are so: One, she never completely told the truth. The whole truth was never out there. There were still plenty of issues and questions unresolved. But, when she changed her stories each time, it was only based upon what the police *knew* or could reasonably *infer* in between each interview."

In other words, as Odell began cracking under the pressure of being interviewed, she started to make up stories based on what she believed the police were un-covering. During her first interview with Thomas and Weddle, for example, she denied knowing whose babies they were. Yet, as soon as she found out the babies were connected to her by documents found inside the boxes, she suddenly admitted, "They're my babies, *but . . .*" From there, she claimed, the babies were the product of rapes. Then, after she learned that DNA could possibly prove who the fathers were, she began to talk about getting pregnant during "casual relationships." After the police learned that DNA was going to be able to prove almost positively who the fathers were, she *then* admitted that *yes*, her brother-in-law had, in fact, fathered one of the babies, and David Dandignac had fathered another.

In effect, Lungen maintained, over the course of three days, she changed her stories to reflect what the police were discovering. Moreover, if she hadn't done anything, why would she lie in the first place? An innocent person isn't afraid of the truth.

"The biggest claim out of all of them, that her mother—which we didn't find out until much later, after trial—was the bad person; well, her mother *liked* David Dandignac," Lungen said later, "the father of Baby Number Three. *She* wanted that relationship to exist. It was *Odell* who canceled out that relationship. And it was *Odell* who told Dandignac to go. And because she didn't want that relationship, it was a *fourth* baby that she *wasn't* going to keep."

That baby's fate, Lungen insisted, had been "preordained. She had already, in my view, intentionally decided, when she kicked Dandignac out of her home, that based upon what she had done to the other three children, Dandignac's baby was going to die."

It was, by the first week of June, easy for Lungen to sit, review the documentation, look at autopsy reports, go over Odell's statements, and call her a murderer. But regardless of what he thought, he still had to prove it to a jury. That was the task at hand. Would Lungen be able to convince a jury with circumstantial evidence that Dianne Odell was a murderer?

His first test would be before a grand jury.

3

Heather Yakin found out that Odell had grown up in Queens, New York, which was probably a good reason why, after making a few calls to some of her relatives in the Kauneonga Lake region, none of them could recall ever meeting her.

The Odell case, for a small-town crime reporter, had the potential to boost her career—and Yakin knew it. All she had to do was score that one exclusive interview, open up a vein in the story no one had poked yet, and it would take on a life of its own.

"I knew it was big," Yakin said later, referring to how the story was beginning to play out in the early part of July 2003. "I knew it was a national story. And I knew I wanted the *real* story—to find out what happened and, to the best of anyone's ability to determine it, *why* it happened. I wanted to find the story's place in the world."

A reporter after the social significance of a mother allegedly murdering four of her children. This was what Heather Yakin's readers would want out of her reporting: what the story meant to society at large. Why was it that so many mothers murdered their children?

Back on May 22, Yakin had published an article that spoke to that part of her curiosity. Headlined WHY DID ODELL ALLOW HER BABIES TO DIE? the story focused on the psychology behind why mothers kill their children. Yakin had interviewed a psychiatrist, Dr. Neil Kaye from Wilmington, Delaware, who had "consulted on more than one hundred infanticide cases."

On average, about "once per day," Yakin wrote, "somewhere in the United States, a newborn baby is killed or discarded." Shocking statistic. Nearly one baby per day didn't make it because of the actions of his or her parent. Yet, a woman who murders "multiple children," Dr. Kaye explained, "and [gets] away with it," was "very rare."

The doctor had a hard time, like many people involved in the case, accepting that no one knew Odell was pregnant four times.

"A lot of people had to not notice . . ." he said.

All Lungen would say on the record for Heather Yakin was that the babies "had died from a criminal agency." Lungen wouldn't commit to how or why.

Dr. Kaye noted in the article that one of the reasons "why" mothers murdered their children was because "[they] don't want to be pregnant. They don't want the baby. They don't form a bond." More bizarrely, though, he added, because Odell had kept the children with her for two decades, "she may have thought they were still alive." It was just "speculation." No one could really tell at that point because, he said, Odell hadn't yet been interviewed by a psychiatrist.

So as the case for Lungen moved forward, Heather Yakin began digging in, tracking down leads, and interviewing as many people involved in the case as she could. With any luck, she'd soon have answers to those important questions.

4

By the end of June, Dr. Baden had conducted the autopsies on the three babies and handed his report to Steve Lungen. He had examined the X rays taken in Arizona of the babies and also X rays taken in Albany more recently.

"The babies were largely skeletonious," Baden said, "some soft, leathery tissue attached." Through those observations, he added, he could, without a doubt, maintain that the babies were full-term, which was important, of course, to Lungen's case. Moreover, the babies "showed no evidence of any disease process, congenital anomalies that can show up in bone." Further, there was no "fractures to any of the bones." The babies were, Baden concluded, newborns. "There was no evidence of [them] having lived for a while."

One of the things that had intrigued Lungen from

the start was how the babies had managed to mummify. A process that originated with the Ancient Egyptians, mummification thousands of years ago was possible because Egyptians generally buried their dead in tombs surrounded by sand, which sped up the process of dehydration because of the dryness and warmth of the sand. Bodies under those conditions can dry out quickly as a tough, leathery outer shell of skin emerges over time and seals in bodily fluids. For years, scientists and archaeologists have been astonished after digging up ancient tombs and, considering the age of the corpse, finding mummies in immaculate condition.

"After death, or after the babies [were] born, the baby," Baden reported, "initially looked like a baby, full-term. . . . Then, depending on weather conditions, temperature, not weather but environmental condition, especially temperature there, if as in a situation the baby being born at home where the temperature is reasonable, then initially be some decomposition caused by bacterial proliferation. Babies can turn greenish and bloat over a period of days or weeks. At some point, these babies were put in a warm environment in which there was loss of fluids and water and drawing out of the baby, and that leads to hardening of whatever tissues are left, which is usually the skin . . . and mummification refers to the drying out of tissues because of loss of fluids and water. In this instance, that process developed after all of the internal organs were destroyed by the decomposition process. The bones themselves remained intact and were presented as normal skeletal remains."

Important to Lungen's case was the fact that the process had taken place on its own; it wasn't as if Odell had intentionally wrapped the children in sheets and blankets to preserve their bodies, like the Egyptians. What happened to the children happened because of how and where the bodies had been stored, which told Lungen several things as he approached the case. For one, it leaned more toward his theory that Odell had killed the children because they were unwanted. She wasn't acting out on some insane notion. She couldn't claim insanity, at least in his view—that maybe she snapped and decided to mummify the children in some sort of ritualistic act of passage. Second, the pre-meditation factor looked more favorable now: carefully wrapping and positioning those babies in boxes meant she *knew* what she was doing.

Baden further explained that the age of the children was easy to tell because of the bone structure. Bones develop in the first twenty years of life only one way, he explained, and it is, for a forensic pathologist, easy to tell how long a set of bones has been growing.

When it came to the manner of death, well, that's where Lungen's problems began. He wasn't going to be able to rely exclusively on Baden's autopsy report. From what Baden could tell from the autopsies alone, he couldn't conclude *how* the children died. He would have to take into consideration police reports and interviews with Odell, along with other factors.

Baden was a pro. A world-renowned pathologist, he had been involved in some of the nation's most high-profile (and historically important) autopsies and ex-humations: Medgar Evers, JFK, Martin Luther King. He had been working in the field, all over the world, for forty-plus years. He was no slouch, coming up with harebrained theories favoring the prosecution's point of view. Likewise, he was no hired gun, determining manner of death and pulling evidence out of the air to support that theory. He was one of the best in the world—and juries, history would prove, respected and valued his "opinions" and medical findings.

Manner of death, Baden said, falls into "five catego-rizations: natural, accident, suicide, homicide, or an undetermined fifth classification.

"The cause of death is the reason for death, the manner—and that is done by the pathologist, the medical examiner, based on examination of bodies." Moreover, medical history and "circumstances of death and crime, the scene of death," are all part of the examination process.

He further clarified how he comes to conclusions regarding manner of death. If a woman, for example, had been found on a sidewalk dead, her injuries, during the autopsy, might prove she had died of multiple fractures and internal injuries. But those findings wouldn't necessarily explain the manner of death, which could be suicide, homicide, or accident.

"A case like that will rule out and will depend on history from friends, neighbors, police. Did somebody see her being pushed out of the window? Did she write a note and jump out? Was she washing windows and, accidentally, the strap broke or something?"

It was that type of information, Baden maintained, gathered from "other sources," that the judgments he and his colleagues made depended on and "is required on death certificates around the country. . . ."

Heading into a crucial stage of his preparation for the grand jury, Lungen was convinced Baden could step into a court of law and, based on his *entire* investigation, say without a doubt that the cause of Odell's babies' deaths was homicide.

CHAPTER 20

1

"MY LAWYER WAS asked two more times . . . in July," Odell recalled, "to submit paperwork for bail, but he never processed a bail application for me."

To Odell, it was just one more careless piece of lawyering on Stephan Schick's part that was keeping her confined behind bars and away from her family. Furthermore, being in the dark about the kind of case Schick was going to present was something Odell later said she came to live with as the summer months dragged on and on. She insisted she never knew what Schick was doing or planning.

Why?

Because, she claimed, he never told her.

As for getting Odell out on bail, it was entirely out of the question, Schick said later. The court wouldn't even consider it. Odell had made it clear she had no money. Sauerstein had no money. Her bail would be $1 million dollars or more, not hundreds of thousands. Why waste the court's time if there was no chance of Odell ever coming up with the money?

"Obviously," Schick added, "with three homicide

charges and her having traveled all over the country, there was no way she was going to make bail." Additionally, Odell lived in Pennsylvania. She had no connection to anyone in New York. "There wasn't going to be bail set on an amount anywhere near what she could afford."

Another key component was the application itself. Filing an application for bail would involve giving a lot of background information regarding Odell's life. In her case, Schick said, that wouldn't be the wisest thing to do.

"You don't want to give away things that may be contradictory to what you want to present to the court later on. You have to be careful. We didn't want to say anything about her background that we would later have a different viewpoint about." They would be stuck, Schick added, explaining away things that they themselves had put on record for the DA's office to chomp on.

It would have been a disaster.

2

When the BCI tracked down David Dandignac and matched his DNA to the DNA extracted from Baby Number Three—the results of which had come in—he was mortified to learn that, for one, Odell had given birth to the child, and two, the child hadn't survived.

Lungen had the BCI running all over the country looking for the fathers of the babies. Roy Streever had gone to Florida to speak with James Odell and his brother; while Scileppi focused on the Kauneonga Lake region, having his investigators bang on doors there. They had found Dandignac. They had spoken to Dianne Odell's brother-in-law and confirmed an intimate relationship. That took care of two of the babies. But Odell herself had claimed one of the children was fathered by a "washing-machine" guy.

Needle in a haystack.

In the end, all the BCI could prove scientifically—and be certain of—was that Dandignac had fathered Baby Number Three. Through interviews, they believed James Odell's brother had fathered one of the other children, but there was no DNA available to prove it conclusively. Still, at least Lungen had Dandignac. Bringing him into court was going to give *all* the babies credibility. With most murder trials, the gallery in the courtroom was split: family and friends of the victim on one side, family and friends of the accused on the other. Both were generally there to show solidarity and support. In this case, Lungen knew, the victims were not going to be represented. It fell on his shoulders entirely, he believed, to represent the babies and make the jury understand they were, in fact, human beings.

"Those babies," Lungen said, "had never had their first day of kindergarten, their first date, the prom—all those things that came with being a human being. I had to represent them in that manner—because there was going to be *no one* else in that courtroom who would or could!"

What the BCI and Lungen learned from Dandignac set off a maelstrom of speculation. Dandignac was under the impression, he said when they interviewed him, that Odell had aborted the child. It was the main reason why he never returned or called.

"Because she didn't want the relationship," Lungen said, "that was just a fourth baby she was not going to keep. The day she kicked Dandignac out," Lungen added, "was the day she decided, based upon what she had done to the three previous babies, that this baby, too, was going to *die*." Lungen believed his case hung in the balance on that note alone.

As the BCI pieced together Odell's life, Lungen began to learn odds and ends that, in his estimation, only further proved Odell's guilt. And more important, it added to his belief that she had planned each death rather heartlessly and coldly.

He knew the case of Baby Doe wouldn't likely be allowed into trial if, of course, Odell was indicted. There would be hearings about the admissibility of the baby, sure. But experience told Lungen it wasn't going to happen. Regardless, the Baby Doe case, as Lungen went back and studied it, spelled out clearly many things about Odell's state of mind as she toted the remains of the three additional babies around with her.

"The key to Baby Doe," Lungen said, "which was always important to me, was that it answered the question of 'Why would a mother take the *other* three babies with her and tote them around from place to place, wherever she moved, keeping them hidden?' It answers that question clearly.

"Because she got *caught* by *not* taking the first baby with her. She was not *now*"—meaning all those years she kept the additional three babies hidden—"going to lose possession of the other three."

One could argue that Odell couldn't let go.

"It was not maternally that she couldn't let go! It was strictly a matter of a crime, a cover-up! If she took them with her, they weren't going to be found. And if they weren't found, well, she wouldn't get caught."

The babies became, in Lungen's view, pieces of evidence. Odell, in other words, learned her lesson back in 1989 when Baby Doe showed up in the trunk of her Volkswagen and the BCI knocked on her door and questioned her about it.

Any emotional ties Odell had to the four babies, Lungen insisted, were "nonexistent, or false.

"You can't have an emotional tie and do what she did, and have *eight* living babies in between. When she didn't want the baby, she simply hid the pregnancy best she could, and when she *did* want the baby, she had the child at a hospital."

For Lungen, it was simple: hospital birth, baby lives; home birth, baby dies.

Lungen further maintained that as he and his colleagues traced backward and began to dig into Odell's life on the road with Sauerstein, based on his decades of experience as a prosecutor, the evidence pointed to one thing: child abuse.

"In Arizona, Robert Sauerstein was arrested," Lungen said, "for abusing Alice Odell. And that's why he took off to Texas. And that's why Odell took the kids and ran off to Texas—to be with him. And that's what ultimately left the three babies in the storage shed in Arizona. She couldn't transport everything by herself at one time. That's why the babies ended up left behind. She *had* to leave the evidence behind. She was forced to, really. Sauerstein left Arizona because he *knew* the cops were looking for him."

Moreover, anytime a family moved from state to state, Lungen added, abruptly picking up and leaving town, like Odell and Sauerstein had done some twenty times over a fifteen-year period, "it is generally a sign that child abuse is occurring in the home."

Throughout the summer of 2003, as the investigation into Odell's life heated up for the BCI, Scileppi started to put a finger on what he and Lungen had suspected all along was repeated child abuse accusations against Odell and Sauerstein. Yet, when it came time to delve into hospital records, the law kept them from going any further. Police station after police station, in some of those towns where Odell and Sauerstein had lived, had complaints of some type of child abuse, the same as Social Services, Lungen and Scileppi found out. All against Odell and Sauerstein.

"We caught the abuse a little bit in 1991 and 1992

as we went through and looked at Social Services records. Aggravated assault by Sauerstein. Twice. On two of the kids."

It was more evidence, in Lungen's view, of bad parenting on Odell's part, allowing her children to grow up in an abusive environment.

Odell viewed Lungen's argument as biased. He had put her life in a box and filled it with circumstances and evidence that conformed to his argument.

"One of the reasons we moved around a lot," Odell explained later, "was because Robert was never happy or satisfied in one particular spot. Every time we moved . . . he would get a job and then something would happen, where he would lose his job. It had always been his dream to own a piece of property in Arizona. He was the reason we moved around a lot, not me! Not because of any specific *child abuse* charges. Because if that made any kind of sense, don't you think Child Protective Services would have had something on record somewhere? I mean, that's kind of an insane thing to say without any kind of documentation. . . ."

But there were, of course, accusations made by Social Services and police regarding assault against two of Odell's children.

"We moved around a lot," Odell concluded, "because Robert was never happy. He had, I guess you could say, a great wanderlust."

3

Heather Yakin kept banging on doors as the case against Odell proceeded, talking to former neighbors and friends of Odell's, hoping to score one interview that could offer a different perspective on the case. Many people in town were shell-shocked. Here was a woman who had, based on the stories being generated and the facts the DA's office was making available, murdered three of her children and carried their mummified remains around with her for twenty years. Public reaction to just how bizarre that behavior was in the face of reality never wavered. Justifiably, people were horrified.

For Yakin, after talking to a few friends and neighbors of Odell's, she didn't find out anything new, but she did develop a professional relationship with Robert Sauerstein, who could become an important source down the road, she knew.

"I struck up a fairly friendly relationship with Mr. Sauerstein," Yakin recalled. "I gave him my card after Dianne's arraignment, [and] the next time he was in town, he stopped by the office to talk. . . ."

Fortunately, Yakin hadn't put Odell's photograph on what she later described as the "Bad Boys" wall in her office. Because if Sauerstein would have seen it, he would have likely turned around and walked out the door.

"My photographer, Michele Haskell, and I," Yakin said, "had set up this half-joking 'Bad Boys' bulletin board. Mostly, it had mug shots and stills of bank robbery suspects and police sketches, plus an Orange County school superintendent who had molested a student, [along with] a mug shot of my editor, one murder suspect—oh, and a picture of Steve Lungen's face superimposed on a Batman costume. Some local guy had bought Batman and Spider-Man costumes stolen off movie sets, and Lungen's office and the state police had recovered them. They gave us photos of the costumes for the caper story, and, well, the mug of Lungen and the Batman picture in the paper were a perfect size match. . . . I faxed a copy to Lungen's office for good measure. Great merriment was had."

Yakin said she spoke to Sauerstein "a few more

times throughout [the summer], [and later as the case progressed], although he didn't want to talk on the record."

In early September, Heather Yakin received a letter from Clarissa Sauerstein, who was now seventeen years old. Clarissa was standing tall behind her mother. She couldn't understand why the community had turned against Odell. In Clarissa's view, her mother wasn't "capable" of murder.

What drove her to this belief?

"If she was capable," Clarissa wrote, ". . . then why would the rest of us still be here . . . ?"

"Great letter," Yakin recalled. "I got permission and wrote a story [about Clarissa's] defense of her mom."

The story ran with the headline ODELL DAUGHTER DEFENDS MOM.

Part of the letter blasted Stephan Schick, who the family insisted wasn't "communicating with them or Odell." Moreover, if he was working hard behind the scenes on Odell's part, he wasn't sharing his strategy with anyone in the family.

"I went to see Dianne fairly often," Schick said, defending himself. "Beginning in early June. You also have to understand that, unlike private attorneys, our office is across the street from the jail, and we have a direct telephone connection. Unlike other attorneys, it's a free call. We don't have to pay for it."

If a suspect has a private attorney, he or she would have to go down to a certain area in the jail and call collect. Legal Aid has a direct line to the jail. Anytime a client wants to, he or she can pick up the phone and call. For Odell, she could have called Schick's office every day if she chose to.

"Anytime she wanted," Schick said, "on any weekday, she could have called me directly."

In July, Schick filed the appropriate paperwork with the court to have Odell examined by a psychiatrist. The court had since agreed and a meeting between Odell and Janet Hooke, a psychiatrist, was scheduled. Schick had also gone to a Drug Court Training Conference in Florida during the first week of September and—lo and behold—Steve Lungen and Judge Frank J. LaBuda, who was presiding over the Odell matter, happened to be there. Schick said he spoke to them about Odell and tried on her behalf to get some sort of offer, but nothing ever came of it.

Schick felt, after speaking with Odell on several occasions, that there were issues regarding her sanity. Those potential conversations, coupled with the fact that she had toted the babies around for twenty years, could possibly make for a strong insanity defense. Furthermore, he wasn't at liberty to discuss intimate details of the case with family members.

The family, however, didn't see it that way. According to the letter Clarissa wrote to Heather, Clarissa was 100 percent behind her mom and couldn't believe she could have done the things people were saying.

But the letter showed, perhaps, how much Clarissa *didn't* know about the case. She said her mother was "scared and alone" at the time the babies had died; she was a "young" woman then, she wrote, "faced with her babies who had passed on. . . ."

4

Enlisting in the army back in the late '60s changed Steve Lungen's life and, he said, instilled in him a passionate personal interest he later took in representing the People of the State of New York.

The Vietnam War turned thousands of boys into men seemingly overnight. Children of seventeen and eighteen years old found themselves working on their dad's farm, hauling hay and plowing fields, or hanging out on street corners one day, and the next huddled down in a foxhole somewhere in an Asian jungle, dodging incoming rounds. For Lungen, his experiences in Vietnam as an infantry officer during the early '70s were defining moments in his brief military career—but also in his life as a prosecutor years later. Serving in Vietnam taught him how fragile life could be, he said. How inescapable death is as a part of life. He had worked at his family's garage for much of his childhood and believed life would consist of changing oil, pumping gas, and following in the footsteps of the family business, which didn't seem all that bad when it came down to it. But when he found himself on the front lines of one of the bloodiest wars in history, he understood how delicate life was, not to mention how things could change in an instant. Moreover, those difficult moments in combat taught him discipline. He learned how to respect authority and live in the shadow of uncertainty. But the sheer horror of it all and the stance the United States took in the face of opposition also infused in Lungen the characteristic of fighting for a cause he believed in and standing up for probity.

In truth, Lungen had served two years and eight months in the military. One of his tours in Vietnam included a role as an infantry leader and commander, which, in turn, became his first taste of leadership.

"The military changed my life and made me understand a lot of things," Lungen said. "I wasn't a good student. I was . . . Well, it put life and all it meant into a different perspective. Clearly. You found yourself. . . . Well, I was in charge first as a platoon leader, then as a company commander, the lives of one hundred thirty, maybe one hundred forty men. I was twenty-four years old."

During the summer of 2003, as the Odell case was headed for the grand jury, Lungen was fifty-seven years old, but he looked much younger. He was at the tail end of what amounted to a stellar career, as an elected prosecutor, some thirty years in the making. He had tried hundreds of cases and generally came out on the winning end of them all. It wasn't that Lungen had never lost a case, but he consistently found himself on the winning side, which was why, perhaps, he had been reelected so often.

Still, it was those years in Vietnam that shrouded the accomplishments in his life. Although quite proud of what he had been able to achieve as a prosecutor, Vietnam was a point in his life, he insisted, that marked everything afterward; whatever hurdles he faced in the courtroom paled in comparison. He had been married for twenty-seven months, had a five-week-old child—a boy, Richard—when he shipped out to Vietnam. That first tour, he said, while his new family waited for him back home, taught him a sense of "responsibility." But also a sense of "life" and—more important to his work later as a prosecutor—an "understanding of death."

"I was in a combat unit," Lungen said with resounding respect in his voice for the red, white, and blue he represented, "so I saw *things* and did *things*, and have a clear understanding of how important those *things* are. And clearly, there's a maturing and growing that takes place on foreign soil during wartime."

When he returned from Vietnam and reenrolled in law school, the curriculum, which had given him trouble before he left, now seemed easy. His peers were three years younger. But, Lungen added, it was "three years and a world away.

"Law school was like, shit, 'this is easy. This is *not* life or death.'"

Furthermore, the idea of being a lawyer, better yet a prosecutor or trial attorney, was never a vocation Lungen had taken seriously back then. The last job he could have ever seen himself in as an adult some thirty years previously would have involved standing in front of people talking. He was terrified of public speaking. Fighting in Vietnam was one thing. Seeing his fellow soldiers die, the enemy terrorizing villages and destroying people's lives, seemed like a cinch compared to standing in front of a body of people and giving speeches.

While still in law school, in 1973, Lungen found a job in the Sullivan County District Attorney's Office. One of his best friends was an assistant, part-time district attorney and had a law partnership with the district attorney. Lungen's friend called him one day when he spied a vacancy in the DA's office and told him he had spoken to the DA on his behalf, and just like that, Lungen found himself working in the DA's office.

By June 1973, he graduated from law school. It was a good thing, he explained, because he now had a second mouth to feed, another son, Matthew. "I had from my military experience a really good understanding and appreciation of how to work with cops."

From the moment Lungen began investigating bad guys and got involved in the prosecution side of the law, he "loved it." So much so, he would often go out on drug raids with investigators to fulfill an urge for action and a hunger for hands-on knowledge. He wanted to know everything he could about the prosecutorial side of cases. He yearned to have that field experience to go along with what later would be part of his job of standing in front of juries discussing cases. He wanted to live his work, in other words. He didn't want to talk to juries about experiences he had not been a part of himself.

Over the years, Lungen said, he became friends with many cops—some of those same cops would later end up working for him on cases. Paul Hans was one of those young cops Lungen struck up a friendship with early on when Lungen first joined the Sullivan County team of prosecutors. Hans was a state trooper. In June 2003, as Lungen prepared to bring the Odell matter in front of a grand jury, Hans was there by his side, working now as a special investigator for the Sullivan County District Attorney's Office. Investigators like Paul Hans and his partner, Robert Rowan, who worked behind the scenes tracking down some of the more complex and ostensibly unreachable facts used during trial, were key players, Lungen said. This was done, of course, without soaking up any of the credit or glory that went along with high-profile murder cases.

CHAPTER 21

1

INDICTING A WOMAN suspected in the deaths of three of her children in relation to a grand jury proceeding might seem like an undertaking that should take weeks, if not months: witnesses, testimony, evidence. To present it all to an audience of twenty-three people and allow them to vote to indict or not, in theory, should be a process mimicking a trial. And indeed, some grand jury proceedings have taken years and involved dozens of witnesses and thousands of pages of documents and other evidence.

In the reality of justice, though, a grand jury is nothing like a trial. It is a one-sided presentation of the facts by a prosecutor who is, by moral and legal obligation, bound to present conflicting evidence but, in some states, also act as judge. It is almost a certainty that if one is brought before a grand jury—in most cases, the accused doesn't even know a grand jury is meeting to discuss his or her fate—his or her fate has been sealed. Some prosecutors claim it is the people's burden to present facts to see if, indeed, there is sufficient evidence to later present to a jury during trial, where the accused then has a chance to defend himself or herself. Arguably, a grand jury is the most efficient and adequate way to reach that goal. Yet, many defense lawyers claim a grand jury is akin to a public lynching.

In New York, in order to proceed with a trial by jury against a charge of murder, a felony, the people must proceed with a grand jury. It is the law. In Odell's case, it took only a few days' worth of testimony to convince a grand jury she should face trial. By June 25, a grand jury had indicted Odell on six counts of murder, two counts for each baby.

Lungen had presented witnesses in front of a secretly impaneled grand jury of twenty-three people who had sat and heard evidence against Odell. Based on that evidence and the law, they voted on whether a crime had been committed, by whom, and the charges Odell should face at trial. In short, the grand jury's indictment was an accusation of felony murder: the case against Odell was headed to trial.

"They voted to indict Odell," Lungen said, "on two theories of murder for each baby. One legal theory being intentional murder, and one legal theory being depraved-indifference murder."

Essentially, what the grand jury had said with its decision amounted to quite a job for the people. Lungen would have to prove at trial that Odell "acted under circumstances [consisting of] depraved indifference to human life and recklessly created a grave risk of death and cause of death of another human being."

Lungen added, "It's a very high degree of reckless conduct by definition that requires a wanton disregard for human life."

Odell, then, in the eyes of the grand jury, willfully and intentionally murdered her children and knew what she was doing at the time.

The case, however, was a bit different than most cases involving mothers who murder their children.

"In New York, you can't be convicted of both a reckless and intentional crime," Lungen said. "The jury has to make an election whether it's intentional or reckless. In Odell's case, based upon her conduct, it was one of those cases that could have gone either way, because it was my view that by the third baby"—which was actually the fourth baby, taking Baby Doe into account and understanding that Baby Doe wasn't going to be part of the trial—"what started out maybe as unintentional, certainly became intentional by the end. If not, clearly under the circumstances which she became pregnant and birthed these babies—and I'm leaving in the middle of that, all the lack of prenatal care, hiding the pregnancies, staying at home, not divulging to anyone, et cetera, et cetera, et cetera—knowing under those circumstances that one baby died the first time, another baby, and *another* baby. Clearly, if she didn't intentionally kill them, they died by circumstances evincing depraved indifference to human life, or a wanton disregard for those babies' lives."

With a textbook memory of the law, Lungen understood every intricacy regarding trial law and could spurt off legal definitions at will. Thus, in his view, it was clear that Odell, if nothing else, could have made sure those babies lived, no matter what the circumstances were, or whoever else was involved.

Simply put, she was responsible for their lives from the day she became pregnant.

"She never viewed these babies," Lungen said, "to be *babies,* or *people.*"

Lungen believed his case hinged on an important, overlooked point, a taken-for-granted assumption—that the children were people. Because of their age, he was concerned the jury wouldn't see them as babies. After all, he wouldn't be presenting photographs of the children at Christmastime, at the beach, their first Little League game. Those photographs didn't exist. The only pictures the jury would see consisted of bone fragments and X rays of skeletons, not to mention the leathery, mummified remains of one child. It was an honest, sincere question he had to ask himself going into trial: would the jury see the babies as human beings?

"Responsibility for death doesn't change because one is an adult and one is a newborn. It's murder—regardless!"

2

After the indictment, Odell was formally charged with six counts of murder. Stephan Schick went to see her with the bad news, an unfortunate part of being a defense attorney. "I am here to tell you that you're going to be arraigned in court tomorrow," Odell remembered Schick telling her, "and you're being charged with *six* counts of murder."

"Oh shit . . . what, are you crazy?" Odell said.

"No, the district attorney is going for intentional and depraved on each of the three counts."

"Jesus Christ!"

"Well, we'll just have to work with it from here."

Schick's reaction, Odell said, was quite composed, taking into account how serious the charges were. His demeanor struck her, she said, as if he didn't care—that perhaps her life was just one more docket number on a conveyor belt of cases flooding through Legal Aid's offices. It was one of the downsides poor people accused of crimes, who couldn't afford their own attorneys, faced: having to deal with an attorney who was likely overloaded with cases and didn't have the time or the resources to dedicate to what would end up being a complex legal showdown, like Odell's was shaping up to be.

"Schick already knows at this point," Odell said, "that my mother was involved. I had said that to him and his comment was 'It doesn't really matter if your mother was there; it doesn't make you any *less* guilty.'"

Schick, whether Odell agreed, had a valid point. A jury wouldn't care. Odell was there. She could have done something. Questions that jurors might have included: Why didn't she do anything? It had happened three times . . . she had living children in between . . . hadn't she learned anything by the second or third baby?

Odell insisted Schick didn't know then to what extent Mabel was involved, but there were other times when she had said he *did* know, that she had explained it to him the first few times they met in May after her arrest. It was one more incident between Odell and Schick that she would later recall differently.

"I had attempted to tell him several times, you know, initiate the conversation to explain about my mother, and he would go, 'No, no, no!' And he would throw up his hands and be like, 'I don't want to hear it! I don't want to hear it!'"

"In the beginning," Schick said, "she indicated she wanted to tell me more [about Mabel], but needed time to 'be able to tell me things.' We had plenty of time, mind you, for her to tell me things, to prepare for trial. I just didn't write it off. It was *extremely* important."

The problem Schick faced, he said, where Mabel was concerned—and he had discussed the issue several times with his colleague Tim Havas, who was working with him on the case—centered on Odell never telling the police about Mabel's involvement in the babies' deaths. This was the thorn in Odell's current story. Odell had given a statement to the police that only implicated her. Mabel's culpability in the deaths of the children was never broached.

"The police had her words on a tape recorder going into evidence," Schick said. "So, the problem becomes not the Mabel thing, but how do you, with some degree of credibility before a jury, argue what she was saying about the Mabel thing to us, in comparison to what she told the police?"

Odell had never mentioned Mabel in her statements to police. In fact, Schick said, a second problem was that she had told the police the polar opposite: that she had to find a way to keep the pregnancies *hidden* from Mabel. Now, in Odell's opinion, she was teetering on the notion of coming clean about everything. But it presented Schick with a legal dilemma, and at that point in the case, he was looking to win a manslaughter conviction and, with any luck, get her out of prison in a reasonable amount of time.

According to Odell, Schick had been receiving calls from *Good Morning America* and several other national-media outlets, asking if she was willing to appear on air to explain her side of the story.

"I can't even eat a meal," Odell claimed Schick ranted one afternoon, "because the phone is ringing off the hook with people who want to interview you. And I'm *telling* you that you should *keep* quiet."

So, Odell said, she took Schick's advice and didn't say anything to anyone.

"If I had known what was going to happen, I would have spoken to everybody. I would have held a *goddamn* press conference!"

Odell's recollection of those early meetings with Schick, and even later, when the case got close to trial, was again different from what Schick remembered.

"I went to see her more than I would any other client," Schick said. "Mostly because the case was *so* important. The subject matter and the ultimate possible punishment were so important that I would obviously see her more than I would see someone charged with, say, DWI, or grand larceny. However, it's been my overwhelming experience in twenty-seven years, or however long it's been, that clients seldom believe that no matter how much time you spend with them, it's never enough. I can understand. From their standpoint, having a lawyer come to see you is comforting.

"On the other hand," Schick added, "most of the time when we go to see clients is a waste of time."

At some point, there was an offer made. Odell said Schick came to her one day and told her Steve Lungen wanted to forgo trial if she would agree to a sentence of twenty-five years to life.

"What kind of offer is *that*?" Odell said she shot back at Schick after he approached her with the offer.

"No, you're right. I think you should take it to trial."

"Well, that's what I intended to do, anyway."

From the very beginning, Odell claimed, a trial by jury was her only focus. She wanted to sit in front of a jury of her peers and tell *her* side of the story—a story that now involved, of course, Mabel.

"That had been my decision from the beginning. Because, I'm thinking to myself, 'Okay, they got me to sign this goddamn statement, pretty much saying whatever they wanted to say.' But I figured, if they just got up and . . . umm, well, umm, and you see, this is my own naïveté, okay, I'm thinking to myself, 'Well, if they (the police) just get up and tell the truth about what they did . . . then it's going to be okay.' The simple truth. That's all I was expecting."

But what was the "simple truth"? In Odell's opinion, the police were telling a "twisted version" of it, a version that would get even muddier as the fall of 2003 emerged and the first hearings in the *People of the State of New York* v. *Dianne Odell* began.

For his part, Lungen later said he never made Schick a formal offer of twenty-five years to life. Again Schick couldn't recall "an offer" in the same manner as Odell.

One more piece of hindsight Odell remembered differently.

3

With an indictment handed down, the next phase in the *People of the State of New York* v. *Dianne Odell* involved a series of what are called Huntley hearings. In simple terms, the process of a Huntley hearing—which could amount to several court appearances for the accused over a period of weeks—determines what type of evidence the district attorney's office has against the accused, and through a series of motions filed by the defense, there's a fight to try to get the charges dismissed. It was highly unlikely the charges against Odell would be dismissed. Still, Schick wanted to exhaust all of his options and, with a bit of luck, hopefully get a few *key* pieces of evidence omitted from trial. If the jury was allowed to hear testimony regarding the first baby, Baby Doe, it might spoil their capacity to review other evidence objectively. Odell was never prosecuted for the death of Baby Doe. Why should a jury be able to hear about it if it had nothing to do with the charges?

More important, the Huntley hearings were a way for Schick to get certain incriminating statements Odell had made to police suppressed, so they couldn't be used against her during trial. The Huntley process was, essentially, set up for the defense to question police officers involved in the case and determine whether the statements they had taken from the accused were "coerced" or "obtained" involuntarily.

This was Odell's big chance. She had been saying that Thomas Scileppi, Trooper Gerald Williams, and Investigator Robert Lane had forced her to say things about killing her babies she had never said—especially Scileppi. If that was true, the Huntley hearings would bear it out. And if Odell's statements were thrown out—well, what did Lungen have left to prosecute? His case was being built around the premise of Odell saying she had heard the children cry. If he couldn't prove the children were born alive, he couldn't prove Odell had murdered them.

4

For the most part, Monticello, New York, is a tight-knit community of hardworking people who have lived in the region their entire lives. Many who live there believe there is justice and equality for the guilty *and* innocent. Ask someone in town about crime and punishment compared to the scales of justice and you will likely hear, "People get what they deserve."

The Sullivan County Courthouse, where the Huntley hearings were about to get under way, sits perched high atop a sharp incline on the corner of Broadway and Bushnell in downtown Monticello. Looking up at the courthouse from Broadway, tall, Colosseum-like, weather-beaten granite pillars welcome patrons to the Hamilton Odell Library. It is a neoclassic-style building, two stories high, with what looks like an archaic pewter-capped dome on the roof one might be more apt to see on a trip to downtown Rome. In the back of the building, next door to the Sullivan County Jail, is the entrance to the courthouse. Walk in and head downstairs and you're on your way to Steve Lungen's

office, where he has run a flawless operation for nearly
three decades. Walking in on the main floor, after
making it through a series of metal detectors and
rather large, professional wrestler-type men guarding
the building, you head into the hub of justice in Sullivan County: the walnut-dressed courtrooms, as clean
and well-kept as any hospital in the region, where
supreme court justice Anthony T. Kane, county court
judge Burton Ledina, Judge Mark M. Meddaugh, and
the Honorable Judge Frank J. LaBuda, who was chosen
to preside over the Odell matter, could all be found.

On August 19, 2003, a hearing had taken place to
discuss the possibility of Lungen being able to present
evidence during trial regarding Baby Doe. Odell had
never been prosecuted in that case, but Lungen believed the incident showed a "pattern of behavior," not
to mention how the deaths of the three babies later
on could *not* have been accidental. He had to elicit
every potential scenario Stephan Schick might raise.
Baby Doe was going to show jurors that Odell had been
involved in the deaths of *four* babies, not three.

"I tried to make it part of the case," Lungen said,
"but only from a cross-examination point of view."

Little did anyone know, but Lungen *didn't* want evidence of Baby Doe making it into trial. Tactically
speaking, he didn't want to win the motion he had just
filed. Filing it was simply part of a well-thought-out
strategy he had spent months working on.

A week or so before the hearing, Lungen filed a Molineaux motion, and a lengthy argument regarding it
ensued. He believed the information about Baby Doe
should be admissible before the jury because it established motivation on Odell's part. Juries in murder
cases clamor to hear motive; they want to wrap their
arms around why the accused would commit such
horrendous crimes. Doubly important, Lungen wanted
to give the jury an example of Odell holding on to the

corpse of one baby, previous to the three babies she was going to be tried for. It would prove that she had learned a lesson in 1989, because cops had knocked on her door and questioned her, and it would answer any questions jurors might have as to why she went through extensive pains to hide the other three babies in boxes from everyone, including Robert Sauerstein.

It was a respectable argument. Lungen was trying to answer any questions the jury might procure during deliberations. Any clever trial attorney leaves nothing to speculation.

"It establishes a motive," Lungen said, "for her dealing with the other three babies like she did, carrying them with her for all those years and hiding them from everybody. I felt the jury needed to understand why someone would do that—she would do that because she got caught with the first baby."

Legally, Molineaux "permitted the introduction of evidence of previous bad acts committed by [a] defendant toward his [or her] victim[s]."

In the end, the judge decided the information about Baby Doe would be a "clear appellate issue." Based on that, he wasn't going to allow any of it to be introduced. The jury, then, wasn't going to hear about Baby Doe. Of course, one would have to believe many potential jurors were following the case in the newspapers and had heard about the baby, anyway. But formally speaking, Baby Doe wouldn't be part of Odell's trial.

Lungen didn't view the ruling as a loss, however. Because through the judge's ruling, if Odell took the witness stand on her behalf (which was, he assumed, a guarantee), he would be able to cross-examine her about the child.

It was a win-win situation—and his plan from the beginning.

"She and Stevie Schick *knew* that if she didn't take the witness stand, I would *not* be able to talk about

Baby Doe in my case in chief. But if she chose to testify, then that would open the questioning up to my questioning her about Baby Doe."

If Odell planned on taking the stand during trial, it was likely Baby Doe was going to become part of the trial. Lungen couldn't bring the baby up during his case, yet the moment Odell sat in the witness chair, he could walk up to her and begin his questioning with something like this: "Let's talk about 1972 and your first pregnancy: can you tell the jury what happened to *that* child?"

"That ruling," Lungen said, "impacted greatly on Stevie's thinking. He was hoping the judge would allow Baby Doe into the trial, but for an interesting reason."

If the judge had allowed information about Baby Doe into trial, it obviously gave Schick an appellate issue. He could then, if the jury came back with a guilty verdict, argue it had been prejudicial to Odell's guilt or innocence in the other three babies' deaths. More important to Schick's case, however, was if the judge had allowed it in, divulging information during trial about Baby Doe would come from Lungen.

"It would be out there," Lungen said, "because the *prosecutor* put it out there."

As the ruling stood now, if Schick decided to call Odell as a witness, the defense would be, in theory, forced to bring up Baby Doe first, or it would seem like they were hiding something. If Schick didn't, Lungen would surely do it himself when he got a crack at Odell on cross-examination, and thus expose what would seem like another one of Odell's secret babies.

This would weigh heavily on Schick's decision to call Odell as a witness. It was a major part of the defense he and Odell were going to have to discuss under close scrutiny, and a decision that ultimately would be up to Odell. All Schick could do was advise her.

"It was indeed an advantage that the jury wouldn't find out about, you know, a fourth baby," Schick said later. "If the babies in the '80s had been two instead of three, I think it would have been a tremendous advantage. The Baby Doe decision gave an important impetus to make a decision *not* to put Dianne on the stand."

In the end, though, it was Odell's choice—and with Odell, of course, looking to trumpet Mabel's involvement in the deaths of the babies as loud as she could, she was determined to take the stand and tell her story.

CHAPTER 22

1

CONTEMPLATING HER FUTURE, Odell sat in jail as the steamy summer days of August gave way to crisp and chilly nights of September. There were still more Huntley hearings scheduled for the next few weeks, but that's not why Odell was losing sleep these days. She was seriously beginning to question whether she had a competent lawyer. She claimed—later—that Schick was not working with her to build a solid defense. She wanted, and felt she deserved, more from him. Yet, at the same time, despite how clichéd it sounded, she believed in her heart that the "truth would set [her] free.

"If I just get up there," Odell said she kept telling herself, "and tell the truth about what happened, which was more or less adhering to the statement I had given to the Arizona police. Everything that deviated from that statement was done, you know, in conversation with the New York State Police."

Detectives Diane Thomas and Bruce Weddle, however, had never taken a formal statement from Odell.

They had recorded an interview with her, but they had never asked Odell to sign a formal statement.

Further implicating the NYSP in some sort of conspiracy to twist statements she had given them, Odell later said, "If I'm not mistaken, when they began their conversation with me, they said to me, 'We're just going to sit here and have this conversation in lieu of a video camera or a tape recorder.' And there was something else," she added, "but I can't remember what it was."

The cops involved in that interview (Scileppi, Streever, and Lane, along with PSP trooper Gerald Williams) had said, she insisted, that they were just going to talk. They weren't going to record any of it. Just casual conversation among them to try to get to the bottom of the situation.

So, what was the big deal?

"From what I gather," Odell continued, "they turned in notes" from those conversations "that they *supposedly* took. . . ."

Indeed, Lane and Scileppi had jotted down certain sentences from their interviews with Odell. It was part of any good cop's policy. At the time they started interviewing Odell, Scileppi explained later, at least very early on, it was more of a fact-finding undertaking than anything else. They were looking for answers regarding the deaths of three babies. There was no need to shine a spotlight in her face and flip on a video camera. She hadn't admitted to anything. Plus, she was openly giving information and more than willing to talk.

But Odell didn't see it that way.

"Just one page of notes?" she steamed. "For almost twelve hours' worth of interviews? Is that not strange?"

In fact, in the world of law enforcement, it wasn't so strange. As the interviews with Odell wore on through-

out the night and Odell began incriminating herself,
the conversation turned from fact-finding to interrogation. It happened all the time. Cops set out to uncover information from a suspect about a crime and
ended up getting a full confession. From that interrogation, Scileppi and Streever developed a three-page,
single-spaced statement from Odell, which amounted
to a confession—a document Odell had willingly
signed.

"They were doing as much talking to me as—as . . .
they supposedly said I was to them," Odell recalled.
"They were making suggestions to me as to what *could
have* happened, what I *thought* I *might* have heard. . . ."
Furthermore, she said, Scileppi was "the one who came
up with the idea of the blanket, the sheets, the towels.
He's the one who came up with *all* of that."

With the thought of a coerced confession playing
on her mind as the Huntley hearings continued,
Odell said, she was trying to believe in Stephan Schick,
but he wasn't visiting her as frequently as she wanted.
After all, it was a murder case, a multiple-murder case
at that. She had anticipated several brainstorming
sessions with Schick so they could pull together a
solid defense.

For his part, Scileppi was later bowled over by the
notion that he could have "coerced" Odell into confessing. It's a situation, he explained, of Odell wanting to change what she had confessed to after the fact.
She wanted to recant what she had said because she
now knew she was looking at life behind bars. At the
time, she might have figured she would have gotten
out of it somehow; maybe because of the statute of limitations or a lesser manslaughter charge. In theory,
Odell had slit her wrists—and now she was trying to
stitch them back up and claim she had never tried to
commit suicide in the first place.

2

Steve Lungen was rallying his troops, working overtime to secure evidence and develop a point-blank case strategy. The last thing he wanted to be accused of at the conclusion of trial was not turning over every stone. No surprises. No unexpected twists. District attorneys lived and died by evidence and witness testimony they had studied in every possible way. Lungen was confident he had covered every base heading into the witness testimony portion of the Huntley hearings.

Two of the babies' bodies had been in such a decomposed state that Lungen and his team, by mid-September, were able to get only a DNA profile from one of the babies, which was proven to be fathered by David Dandignac.

"It was three months, maybe more," Lungen recalled, "before we found out we couldn't go any further on the DNA testing, and realized this is what we have. We have Dandignac. We were trying to see if we could prove or disprove what was in her statements. Because that's important to credibility matters and to determine [the] reliability of what she was saying, because she lied so often in her statements to us. She had only told us what we *wanted* to hear, essentially."

While Lungen worked to shore up witness availability for trial and how he would proceed with experts, he was still wondering whether Schick was going to present an insanity defense. The option was still open. Under such bizarre circumstances, Lungen was concerned how the jury would react to such strange behavior.

"They were dickering with the insanity defense, back and forth," Lungen said. "It mattered to me. They'd had her examined. I knew that. And if they were going to interplay an insanity defense, I had the right to have her examined by my own qualified psychiatrist."

By order of law, though, Lungen couldn't have Odell examined until Schick and Odell made the first move.

"They were hemming and hawing, and I wasn't privy to the fact, but I can only guess that they were having difficulty getting a psychiatric doctor to definitively say she was, essentially, insane at the time of the crimes. She was intelligent. Articulate. She could say what she did. She certainly didn't present herself as insane."

Lungen said that when a defense attorney doesn't call a psychiatrist it's because they cannot prove insanity. The burden of proof in New York on an insanity defense falls on the shoulders of the defense by a preponderance of the evidence. A defendant, in other words, is presumed "sane" in New York and the defense has to plead and prove insanity under penal law. Lungen didn't have to prove Odell was sane; the defense had to prove she was insane.

Interestingly, Lungen agreed Schick was "meeting with Odell regularly." He knew it, he insisted, because he was constantly pressing Schick, whom he would see in the courthouse, for documents and notes, wondering where they stood on the insanity plea.

"Oh sure," Lungen said, "Stevie was meeting with Odell all the time. I know this because there were continuous conversations about a plea and what she would get and what I would give her. He was trying to talk me into manslaughter charges."

Through these sidebars—legal discussions—there were some interesting legal issues mulled over. The statute of limitations had run, Lungen said, "on any crime with the respect to the babies, but murder."

With the statute of limitations being five years in New York, the only crime Lungen could try Odell for was murder. Manslaughter was not even an option he could legally consider.

"For me to get a conviction that would incarcerate her," which Lungen desperately wanted, "it *had* to be murder."

There was no way Lungen wanted Odell on the street. In his view, she had murdered not one or two of her children, but four. She was going to be tried for three deaths and, with any luck, a jury would convict her based on the statement she had given police—a statement that was going to be at the center of controversy as the Huntley hearings continued.

3

Unlike a trial, where the prosecution opens with its case, calling witnesses and introducing evidence, a Huntley hearing is the defense's game all the way, designed to offer the defense a crack at some of the witnesses the prosecution might call during trial.

The first witness Steve Lungen called on September 15 was Thomas Scileppi. It was time to get to the bottom of the statement Odell had given police on the night she was arrested and booked. Scileppi was the main interviewer. He had gotten Odell to confess to hearing the babies cry and cough. Scileppi and Lungen contended the defense was making an issue out of a statement they had never given a second thought to. For Lungen, the only issue was how much Odell had lied.

Before court got under way, Judge Frank J. LaBuda, along with both parties, discussed Rosario material Lungen was forced by law to hand over to the defense. Under the law, "the prosecution at trial must turn over to the defense all statements of a prosecution witness relating to the witness's trial testimony." In short, Odell was going to get to see those now infamous notes the cops had taken on the nights she was questioned.

Lungen introduced not one page of notes, but ten pages from investigators who had been with Odell at various times throughout the days leading up to her arrest. On top of that, he offered grand jury testimony of Robert Lane and Roy Streever.

Scileppi's credentials spoke of a cop with an iron-clad record: twenty-seven years as a NYSP trooper, ten of which as senior investigator. As Lungen had Scileppi go through the scenario of how he was introduced to the Odell case, Odell could only sit and stare at him.

It was clear from Scileppi's testimony he believed Odell had submitted to questioning voluntarily, and at least at first, she was not under arrest or even under suspicion. He said she initially denied knowing anything about the babies.

"Actually, she was told she was not in custody, she was not under arrest, that we just simply wanted to sit down and talk to her."

Schick had made an appropriate amount of standard objections, but for the most part Scileppi went on and spoke openly about his conversations with Odell and her willingness to talk.

As the interview progressed, Scileppi explained, he began to bounce back questions she had asked him. For example, she kept asking what was going to happen to her.

"What is it that you *think* should happen to you?" Scileppi said he had asked back. Numerous times, Scileppi testified, Odell had said, "I should probably go to jail."

For the next fifteen to twenty minutes, Lungen had Scileppi describe how Odell had talked about the deaths of the three babies. At one point, Scileppi said, Odell had made clear indications that one of the babies had been born alive and, later, how the other two had also made noises that, to him, indicated life.

Lungen then asked, "With respect to the eight children born to Miss Odell, three from Mr. [James] Odell and five from Mr. [Robert] Sauerstein, were you able to get from Odell, for example, dates of birth?"

"Yes."

"Locations of birth?"

"Yes."

"Hospitals and areas of hospitals?"

"Even as far as doctors' names, yes!"

"With respect to the three children, babies that were the focus of the investigation, were you able to get from her dates of birth?"

"No."

"Locations of birth . . . ?"

"Yes."

Obviously, it was a carefully choreographed exchange of evidence depicting how Odell had chosen to conveniently forget certain information. It showed a wanton disregard, in Lungen's view, for hiding certain truths she likely knew.

Schick, as he stood up and approached Scileppi, brought Scileppi's previous testimony into the heart of the matter.

"Sir, you weren't present during any conversations between the Arizona police and Miss Odell, isn't that correct?"

"That's correct."

"And you weren't present during any conversations between the Pennsylvania police and Miss Odell, is that correct?"

"That's correct—other than the interview . . . between Trooper McKee and Miss Odell."

It meant nothing, actually, that Scileppi wasn't there for those interviews Diane Thomas and Bruce Weddle had conducted; there were tapes available of some of those conversations Scileppi had listened to later. But more important, it didn't matter what Odell had said to them; what mattered was what she had admitted to Scileppi.

Schick questioned Scileppi for approximately ten minutes, nearly a third of the time Lungen had questioned him. In the end, it was clear Scileppi wasn't going to stray from his recollection of the events.

Next on the stand were Roy Streever and Robert Lane, who basically backed up what Scileppi had said and further implied Odell had admitted murdering three of her babies, and that the babies were alive when she did it.

In all those conversations, Mabel was never mentioned as someone who possibly could have been involved in the deaths of the children.

Sitting, listening to Scileppi, Lane, and Streever testify, Odell said, she was thinking, *What the hell are these people doing?* At one point, she recalled, she had even turned to Schick and said, "That's not the way it happened."

Schick, she claimed, turned to her and replied, "Don't worry; we'll get them back in trial."

That response, she concluded, "allayed [her] fears a little bit." She began thinking, *This is like a three-ring circus.* "You know, they're getting up on the stand and they're like [here she mimicked the bugle call of the circus] . . . and I am saying to myself, *'Jesus Christ!'*"

CHAPTER 23

1

BY THE TIME the Huntley hearings were nearly over, Odell said, she realized she had been doing things in a "very stupid manner.

"At this point in time, I am very ignorant of what's going on. I don't start to see any of this, however, until after the *trial* is over. Hindsight, you know, it's an excellent teacher!"

On October 8, in what would end up being the last day of testimony in the Huntley hearings, Robert Sauerstein took the stand. The past few months had been rough on Sauerstein. The woman he had shared the past twenty years with was sitting in jail facing a trial by jury, which could put her in prison for the rest of her life. She had given birth to five of his kids and, by all accounts, had been a "great mother," he said, to those children. Now she was being accused of a vicious, callous, and cold-blooded crime.

As Sauerstein sat in the witness chair, a flood of emotion passed through Odell. There was her lover, friend, parenting partner, and confidant, sitting there, forced to talk about their life together. In the end, what could he say to help her cause that wouldn't be viewed as subjective?

Over the course of the first ten minutes, Schick had Sauerstein describe the events of that weekend in May when Odell was first approached by Diane Thomas and Bruce Weddle at Rite Aid. It had been the first time, Sauerstein explained, he had heard about the babies.

As Schick steered Sauerstein into a conversation about Odell's desire to have a lawyer present while she spoke to police, Sauerstein said Odell had not only asked for a lawyer, but demanded one. It was one of the main reasons she had not gone to the Towanda barracks the day after Thomas and Weddle had approached her at Rite Aid. Sauerstein claimed he had spoken to Odell over the phone in the presence of Thomas, who had "persuaded" him to phone her and ask her to "come in" for an interview. Odell had "her mind set. She wants an attorney."

From there, Sauerstein described what type of attorney Odell desired. There was, according to Diane Thomas later, some rather frank discussion over what type of attorney Odell had requested, because Thomas had maintained Odell was concerned about the welfare of one of her children, who didn't get along with Sauerstein.

"Was there any discussions over what kind of attorney she wanted to speak to: civil, criminal? Any identification?" Schick asked.

"No. She just said she wanted to talk to an attorney."

Furthermore, after Sauerstein convinced Odell to return to the barracks to chat with Thomas and Weddle, and agree to be fingerprinted, he claimed she had once again stated that she wanted an attorney after Thomas asked her if she wanted to talk about the babies.

"She said, 'I'd rather talk to an attorney.' And [Weddle] said, 'This case is not going to go away.'"

Time and again, Sauerstein continued to say Odell had never said what type of attorney she wanted. It was a striking piece of evidence to counter the view of four cops who had maintained Odell had asked for a civil attorney, whom she wanted to "take care of some things at home" between Sauerstein and one of her children.

Steve Lungen's first crack at Sauerstein came in the form of "There is no conversation between civil attorney and otherwise that you heard, yes or no?"

"That I heard of?" Sauerstein shot back, leaning forward a bit in his chair, as if he didn't understand the question.

"Yes."

"No. No. I never heard civil."

"What she may have said to the police," Lungen then said, "that you didn't hear, you *don't* know?"

Schick stood up. "Objection, Your Honor. Come on."

Odell sat and looked back and forth—judge, Lungen, Sauerstein—while shaking her head, thinking, *This is unbelievable.*

Lungen asked the question again.

"Objection!"

"Overruled."

"I was present in the other room watching and listening when she spoke."

Sauerstein had explained on direct examination how he had stepped out of the room where Odell was being questioned, but sat, watched (and listened) through a two-way mirror in another room.

"For the entire two hours?" Lungen wanted to know.

"Objection. . . ."

"Let him finish," the judge said.

"I'm trying to answer the question," Sauerstein replied.

"Did you hear the *entire* hour-and-a-half conversation that she had with the police? Yes or no?"

"About thirty-five minutes of it."

"Did you hear the *entire*"—Lungen raised his voice, then slowed his speech pattern down—"hour-and-a-half conversation that she had with police?"

"No."

"You don't *know* everything she said to the police, do you?"

"No."

When it came down to it, Sauerstein may have heard Odell ask for an attorney, but he wasn't there for every minute of the conversation and couldn't testify as to everything she had said.

Ultimately, the judge ruled in Lungen's favor. Odell's statement was going to be one of the prosecution's showcases. Schick's attempt to keep it out had failed. For Odell, she was going to have to explain the statement, along with why, if she didn't agree with it, she had signed it into record.

Sauerstein's version of the events, at trial, would be a crucial part of Odell's defense. When he got a chance to get up in front of a jury and explain things in more detail, Odell was convinced it would at least put doubt in the jury's mind. And reasonable doubt, in the end, was all she and Schick had to prove.

2

As the trial, which was scheduled to begin in December, drew closer, Odell was upset because, she claimed, she still hadn't been briefed by Schick regarding his strategy. He hadn't even, she said, inquired about neighbors, friends, or relatives who could perhaps take the stand on her behalf. She also wondered if he had hired someone to do some sort of investigation.

Most defense attorneys lodge a full-scale investigation into the events to try to counter the prosecution's case. According to Odell, however, Schick hadn't.

"He was being 'cost efficient,'" Odell reflected later in jest. "We didn't have an investigator because it cost too much money."

"Maybe if I was a couple years out of law school," Schick later said with a hint of sarcasm, "I would have considered hiring an investigator. But I've learned a lot over the years. And . . . I had an incredible inkling—a gut feeling you could say—based upon everything she was telling me that I didn't want to find out what she has been telling me is *not* true. You don't want to be in a position of suborning her testimony. So as long as I didn't know anything to the contrary, everything she was telling me, as far as I knew, was the absolute truth."

The other obstacles Schick said he faced became: What positive information would a private investigator find? There was no way for an investigator to determine if Odell had been pimped for prostitution. What john would come forward and admit such a thing? Moreover, how was anyone going to find such a person?

"I didn't want to spend tons of taxpayer money on something that was a wild-goose chase. Plus, an investigator may have found out things that might have been hurtful. I just had an incredible feeling that hiring an investigator was going to hurt us more than help us."

As the days wore on, Schick explained to Odell that it would be in her best interest to admit the babies were hers, so as to save the state the time and trouble of mitochondrial DNA testing, which proves maternal blood typing. It would have nothing to do with proving who the fathers of the children were. In short, if Odell wasn't going to contest the babies were hers—which was never her intention, she said—there was no reason to do mitochondrial DNA testing. It would be a waste of time and money.

"I told Schick I didn't have a problem with that," Odell said. "I had always said they were my children. What I *strongly* disagreed with was their theory. The whole package the prosecution put together."

Lungen had mentioned, Odell recalled, that "money" was a factor in the murders, on top of the fact that she wasn't married or with any one particular man at the time the babies in question were born. His case, she assumed, was being built around those two arguments.

"Well," Odell said, "if those two things were a *factor*, okay . . . how come I didn't kill Doris? I had just gotten divorced. I had been separated from James Odell for a good seven months. I didn't have any money. I was living at the lake. So, why wouldn't I do that to her, too? If I'm this . . . this . . . this *brazen* maniac they think I am, then *why* didn't I do that to her?"

One of Lungen's focal points for trial would be the fact that whenever there wasn't a male figure—a solid male role model: a husband, a longtime boyfriend, or lover—in Odell's life and she became pregnant, she viewed the pregnancy as "illegitimate and unwanted" and murdered the child. It was going to be a key theme, thumping its way through the trial, pushed by Lungen and his growing list of witnesses.

"I am going to blow their main argument right out of the water right now," Odell said. "When I left James, okay, I left him around July or August of 1980." She was pregnant at the time. "I was living by myself and had made arrangements to have someone drive me to the hospital. My mother was not even in the picture at that time; she was taking care of an elderly woman. . . ."

Odell further claimed that the man with whom she had made arrangements, Lou Johnson, a "fifty-something friend" who lived at the lake near her and Mabel, had driven her to the hospital when she went into labor with Doris. So, although she was alone and without a man in her life (she and James Odell had split up months before), she gave birth to Doris at a hospital. A year later, when she had Baby Number One at home, it was her mom, she claimed, who had tricked her into *not* going to the hospital and *made* her have the child at home so her mom could take it from her and kill it.

Beginning with Lou Johnson, though, Odell's theory seems weak at best. Johnson had since passed away. Odell couldn't recall exactly when he had died. But she did remember he'd had an operation "for lung cancer and he was trying to recoup, and he came and stayed down at my house for, I think, a week, week and a half."

Lungen saw Lou Johnson as just one more of Odell's stories, at least from a prosecutorial position, that couldn't be backed up because the person in question had died. But more than that, Lungen said, the reason why Doris lived had nothing to do with whether Odell had a man in her life at the time, or who had driven her to the hospital.

"There were people," Lungen said, "who *knew* she was pregnant with Doris. The baby was James Odell's. She couldn't kill it, had no reason to kill it. It wasn't an *illegitimate* child. Sure, she had separated from Mr. Odell, but he, along with several other people, *knew* she was going to have a baby. That's why she couldn't deny the child life."

Lungen's point, then, centered on the fact that Odell would never kill a child whose father would someday come looking for it. Several people knew she was pregnant with Doris. She couldn't kill her. With the other children—Baby Doe, Babies Number One, Two, and Three—no one save for Mabel knew she was pregnant.

"Sure, she had the baby by herself, but there was a

reason why it lived—and that reason was that James Odell *knew* she was pregnant when he left her."

Lungen was sure this was going be the final nail for Odell. Truth and facts, Lungen liked to say, cannot be denied.

3

To think that Odell had anything good to say about Stephan Schick, her court-appointed attorney, would be grossly inaccurate. Quite to the contrary, as the trial neared, Odell's hatred for Schick grew.

"Between the end of the Huntley hearings, while I'm waiting for trial, I'm in and out of court sporadically, and Stephan Schick is coming to see me the day before. It was a week before trial when he finally started coming around every night trying to prep me for testimony."

From the start, Odell argued, the plan was to put her on the stand. It was openly discussed, she said, between her and Schick the week before trial. When it came down to it, it was her only chance to tell the jury the truth, as far as she knew it. She was going to get up there, she said—as much as it hurt, as much as those memories of Mabel prostituting her like some cheap whore and thoughts of "telling the world what my father had done"—and explain everything in full, shocking detail, step by agonizing step.

Deciding to testify on her own behalf was one thing. It was almost a given she would take the stand. But the bombshell she said she dropped on Schick's lap almost on the eve of trial could possibly—if the witness had any credibility—set her free. It was solid proof, Odell believed, that Mabel was, in fact, the murderer that Dianne had been saying she was all summer.

"I had received a letter from my brother, [*Martin*

Lehane]," Odell recalled. "My brother wrote me a letter that had been mailed on May 31, 2003. At the time, I didn't know he was calling my home and speaking to Robert."

Apparently, Odell was under the belief that her half brother Martin Lehane, who lived in Florida, had been talking to Sauerstein, explaining how he believed Odell's story about their mother and father and that she had nothing to do with the deaths of the babies. To top it off, Martin could possibly prove it to jurors.

How?

By simply walking into court and telling a story he claimed had taken place in 1947, six years before Odell was born.

Early on, it seemed like it could be something that might potentially prove what Odell had been saying all along—that Mabel was the real murderer. Indeed, anecdotal evidence that could, without question, give the jury an image to chew on during deliberations and, possibly, sway one of them into believing Odell had never laid a finger on *any* of the children.

But was Odell hanging on a thread of a story that had little merit?

The truth was about to be unearthed, because Martin was on his way from Florida to New York.

CHAPTER 24

1

SULLIVAN COUNTY DISTRICT attorney Steve Lungen was preparing to take a bifid approach to his case: one-part forensic, one-part witness testimony. Through that simple double-pronged method, Lungen believed he was going to prove Odell had "wantonly and willingly" chosen to end the lives of three of her children in a horrific, unimaginable manner. It didn't make any difference how old the children were, or why Odell had done it. What mattered was that she had taken the lives of three human beings, and for that, she would have to pay with the rest of her life behind bars. It was the only outcome Lungen believed the People of the State of New York deserved.

In early December, the judge ruled that Court TV, which had applied to have its cameras in the courtroom during Odell's trial, could set up inside the courtroom and record the trial for a later broadcast. The media coverage had not let up. Scores of newspaper articles had been written since May and just about every talking head on television had his or her opinion regarding Odell's state of mind at the time of the murders. Some believed Odell was innocent. Every time a baby killer murder case went before a judge and was profiled by the media, it brought up old cases birthed of the same ilk, names synonymous with baby killing: Mary Beth Tinning, Susan Smith, Andrea Yates. These were women who had done the unthinkable: murdered their own flesh and blood in vicious, malevolent fashion. Some more brutal than others, of course, but all with the same result.

Could Odell be placed in that same category? was the question on most everyone's mind heading into trial. Was she the sinister monster the DA's office was propagandizing? Was she competent to do such a thing? What were her eight living children thinking? Were they behind her? Was Odell going to be alone in the courtroom, or was she going to have a chorus of well-wishers and family rallying her cry behind her?

It was anybody's guess. Yet, one could only wonder that Court TV's presence during trial would only add to the allure and high-profile status of the case. Lungen, Schick, Odell, Sauerstein, Scileppi, Lane, Streever—they were all going to be household names inside of a week. Tabloids. Daily newspapers. Tragedy-TV talk shows. Many would be pointing a finger and dissecting every aspect of the case as if it were put before a law class.

Lungen had always spoken very highly of Schick. The two men had known each other for decades. The Odell case, however, put them on opposite sides of the courtroom, where it would become a battle of legal wits. In some ways, Lungen said later, Schick's hands were tied from the beginning of the case.

"Court TV pundits . . . questioned and criticized Stevie Schick during the trial," Lungen said later. "But they didn't have a clue."

Schick's feet would be put to the flame later for not negotiating a manslaughter conviction on Odell's part.

Some felt a more skilled trial attorney could have secured a manslaughter charge for Odell, which would have gotten her out of prison—if not right away, inside of a few years.

"From his point of view," Lungen analyzed, "and I sort of understood it, in order for Odell to be convicted of manslaughter, the defense would've had to waive the statute of limitations question. They had refused to waive it because they took the position of 'If the jury came back and said it's not murder but manslaughter and convicted her of three counts of manslaughter in the first degree, she would still spend the rest of her life in prison.'"

Odell's prison time would run consecutively, potentially for all three babies. The judge could sentence her up to twenty-five years for each child. Even if Odell received ten years for each baby, she'd end up with thirty years. Heading into trial, Odell was in her fifties. She would be in her eighties before she ever felt the sun on her back again as a free woman. Thus, it was murder or nothing. Odell was either going to walk, or she was going to prison for the rest of her life.

Apparently, Odell was willing to take the chance, and in her heart, she said, she felt she could convince a jury Mabel was the true monster.

Schick's goal was to get Odell out of jail. If she was convicted, the plan was to argue for her release. Probation. Whatever. She had children—young children—at home who needed her. She wasn't some lunatic child killer, looking to prey upon children in her community. In all likelihood, she wasn't going to hurt anyone ever again—if, indeed, she had done it in the first place.

Lungen obviously disagreed.

"My position was that it was murder. And I felt she truly killed four babies. The babies' deaths, to me, were no accident. They were *clearly* murdered. And I felt she should be convicted and sentenced as someone who had committed *three* murders."

To Steve Lungen, Dianne Odell was a murderer. No different than anyone else convicted of the same crime.

2

Martin Lehane, Odell's half brother, had come forward with some startling information regarding their mother, Mabel Molina. Odell couldn't believe it. It seemed someone had thrown her a life raft with a confession signed by Mabel inside of it.

In the form of a letter, Martin was about to open up a vein in Mabel's life that might just add a bit of credibility to Odell's contention that she was involved in the deaths of the babies. If nothing else, it would at least give the jury enough to consider reasonable doubt.

Or would it?

"All of a sudden," Odell recalled, "they call me for mail one day at the jail and I see my brother's return address on the envelope. I open it up and I see a little card."

So she started reading.

"I'm sorry you're in jail," Martin had written, she claimed. "I'm sorry for what you're accused of; I know you're not guilty. I know that our mother did it."

It was early June when Odell received the letter. She had just been arrested and arraigned.

"I almost fell over," Odell recalled. "At the time I'm thinking . . . 'I am the only one who knows about this. I am the only one who this happened to. I am the key. I am the secret.'"

Odell then started crying "hysterically," she remembered. There it was: possible evidence in the form of a letter of Mabel's involvement.

When Schick went to see Odell after she received the letter, handing it to him, she explained how important it could be to her case. "He then took it and put it in the file. And I said, 'You have to get in touch with my brother and find out what he's talking about.'"

She wasn't aware then what Martin had meant when he said he knew Mabel had done it. There were no details in the letter. Still, she was sure Martin knew *something*.

When Schick left that day, Odell said, she waited. Months went by. July. August. September. October.

Nothing. Not a word from Schick about Martin or the letter.

Then, in early November, fearing that whatever information Martin knew would never become part of her case, Odell began pressuring Sauerstein to get hold of him. "You have to call him and ask him what he means. What did he mean in that letter? He knows!"

A day or so later, Sauerstein called Martin and asked him about the letter. What had he actually meant when he said Mabel had done it?

When Sauerstein returned to jail the following day and explained to Odell what Martin had told her, she said, for the first time since she'd been arrested, she believed she was going home. It was a story no one could have made up, she insisted. Furthermore, it was proof, perhaps, that Mabel had a track record of killing *other* children.

So, what was the story that would be so compelling to a jury—that might convince jurors Odell was no baby killer and that Mabel was the true murderer?

3

On December 3, the Sullivan County court screened over one hundred potential jurors who had been summoned to the court to participate in the *People of the State of New York* v. *Dianne Odell.* When one receives that dreaded jury duty summons in the mail, the case, in which he or she may become a part, is not mentioned. Most walk into court, sit for a time, and are sent home. For a couple dozen potential jurors on that day, when Odell sat in the courtroom for the first time as the jury selection process of her trial got under way, the horror of the case was too much for her to handle. It was all too real now. Things were happening.

There was a bit of restlessness in the room as Judge Frank LaBuda got himself situated on the bench. By the time LaBuda finished reading the indictment against Odell, however, with the sheer madness and unthinkable nature of her alleged crimes now revealed, the room had gone church silent. Some stared at Odell as she sat there in quiet repose, thinking about what was to come. No doubt, she was already being judged by some.

Lungen was quite calm as he sat and listened to proceedings. This wasn't his show. The judge would have to make some sense out of the crowd and whittle down the pool to fifteen—twelve jurors, three alternates. After the judge asked, "Is there anything about the nature of the charges, about the alleged facts involving infants, newborns, which would make this case hard to follow?" hands shot up as if he had asked who wanted out of jury duty.

Nearly twenty-five men and women wanted to meet privately with the judge. Obviously, there was some concern. People had opinions about babies allegedly murdered by their mother.

After a long process of talking to each potential juror and asking specific questions regarding the nature of the case, some were asked to go sit back in the courtroom with the remainder of the pool, while others were excused from jury duty altogether.

It was obvious the case was going to elicit strong

emotions. Babies. Murder. Mother possibly responsible. It was enough to make some—perhaps more than others—unable to focus on the facts and evidence of the case.

In the face of what appeared to be such a complicated task, nearly everyone in the courtroom was shocked that by 5:00 P.M. on the same day a jury had been chosen. Testimony would begin on schedule, first thing Monday morning, December 8, 2003.

4

When Sauerstein sat down next to Odell and began talking about the conversation he'd had with her half brother the previous night, Odell was both pleased and scared, she remembered, regarding the contents of the conversation.

It was a simple story. But, in Odell's mind, it would explain a lot.

According to Odell, Martin had told Sauerstein that Mabel had "delivered a child in 1947," six years before Odell was born, which in itself wasn't so shocking. It was what happened after the child had been born that could, Odell thought, change everything.

"After my mother had delivered a child in 1947," Odell said, "she gave my brother a package wrapped in brown wrapping paper with a string around it and said, 'Bury this in the backyard.'"

Odell said she understood it was "secondhand information," but the mere circumstances alone were enough to flood her with optimism.

Actually, it was third-party hearsay. Martin had told Sauerstein, who had then told Odell. To believe it was plausible, certainly. Then again, at the end of the day, would a jury not think it was extremely "convenient" information, suffice it to say it would be coming from a family member? That being said, what did it actually prove?

After hearing what could be potentially devastating evidence—if Martin was, of course, willing to share his story with the jury and Schick could get it in—Odell found herself scurrying around, trying to get the information to Schick as the trial approached.

Sauerstein, at Odell's urging, went to Schick and told him. "Schick knew about it," she said, "but he was not doing anything about it."

Schick later said he knew about Martin Lehane's story and how potentially helpful Martin could be. But to say that he hadn't done anything about it was a flat-out lie on Odell's part. Not only did Schick act on it, he called Martin himself in Florida and spoke to him at length several times. Then, after realizing Martin might be able to offer Odell's defense a serious boost, Schick withdrew money from his personal bank account and flew Martin to New York to go over his potential testimony.

"The information about Mr. Lehane," Schick recalled, "didn't become available to us until about a month before trial. I had a number of phone conversations with Martin, and near the beginning of the trial, I flew him up here at my own personal expense."

Martin spent a considerable amount of time in Schick's office going over his story.

"Odell claimed we ignored the information," Schick said. "But we thought the information was *very* important."

Furthermore, Martin's credibility was ironclad. "But, unfortunately, it was *too* good," Schick said. "I think Martin is an honest guy. I believe he was absolutely telling the truth because, in the end, the truth wasn't good enough."

Indeed, what Martin could testify to regarding Mabel's past ultimately wasn't going to help Odell. In fact, it didn't even point a finger at Mabel as possibly being involved in any type of crime against a child. Odell obviously had believed what she wanted to, based on what Martin had said.

Mabel had given Martin a package to bury in the yard, according to Schick. That was true. But it wasn't a child; it was afterbirth, a placenta. Martin was thirteen years old at the time. Mabel had worked as a midwife during the late '40s. She had helped many women give birth to their children at home at a time when it was a fairly common practice. The story Martin told Schick involved Mabel aiding a woman who was giving birth, and then asking Martin to take a package containing the "afterbirth" and bury it in the backyard. Martin knew it was afterbirth, Schick explained, because he had seen the child leave the house with the woman.

What seemed like a beacon of hope, a chilling recollection of Mabel perhaps involving Martin in some sort of plot to get rid of a dead child, turned in the end into a story that added little to Odell's contention that Mabel was responsible for the deaths of her three children. It wouldn't add anything to her defense. Instead, it would only open doors that Odell would have a hard time closing.

What Schick admired so much about Martin, he said, was his honesty. Martin could have embellished the story to support Odell, but he didn't. "If he wanted to color—you see, Martin wanted to obviously very, very much help his half sister, and he felt she was very, very abused as a child—her story, he could have. But he didn't. He could not testify that it was a baby in that package."

Schick and his colleague, Tim Havas, while Martin was in their office, had even pressured him. "*Could* it have been a baby? Could it, Martin?" Schick kept asking him. They were desperate. Maybe Martin was just being naive?

But he stuck to his story. "No, no, no. It wasn't a baby. It was afterbirth."

Regardless of being unable to prove culpability on Mabel's part, Schick believed other information Martin could bring to the trial would still be helpful.

"It at least establishes that the mother was experienced in being a home midwife," Schick recalled. "It wasn't out of the blue that Odell had this idea of 'Have the baby at home and I'll take care of it.'"

So Martin was asked to hang around town, there was a chance he could testify. What role he would play exactly was still an open discussion, however.

Elation soon turned into nervousness, Odell said, as the testimony portion of the trial neared and she felt forced into sitting on what potentially could be her get-out-of-jail-free card, Martin's story. Yet, as the trial neared, the more she thought about spilling family secrets to the world, she intimated, the more it seemed like the wrong thing to do. She was conflicted now about testifying. Wondering whether it would help or hurt her cause.

One would have to imagine that a woman with a four-year-old child at home, along with four teenagers, would jump at the chance to reveal anything she could that might set her free so she could be with her children again. But Odell said she began fighting with herself, debating whether to get up on the stand and tell everyone her father had raped her repeatedly and her mother had turned her into a prostitute. It wasn't what she wanted her family to hear. Her kids, she said, would be ridiculed at school. Called names. "Your mother's a whore! Inbred!" As time moved forward, she began thinking that maybe, "because of the shame and my kids," airing family secrets in open court might not be in her best interest.

The scale of insults the children would endure, however, weighed heavily on the part of being branded a victim, as opposed to a murderer. After all, her children, she said, were already hearing "baby killer" epithets in school and around the neighborhood.

"But you have to understand," Odell continued, "living a lifetime full of derogatory comments, for my own kids to have to deal with the repercussions of that . . . in June, July, and August, I was still ambivalent. But the kids came up to see me and the kids told me, 'Do whatever you have to do to go home.' All of the kids said to me, 'We don't care. Tell them what you need to tell them.'"

That meeting, she insisted, changed her mind. There would be no more debating. She had lived with her secrets, she decided, long enough. She realized now that her children were behind her. Sauerstein. And now her half brother. What, really, did she have to lose? Now all she had to do was convince Schick and Havas, who were beginning to think it wasn't such a good idea after all, that she should take the stand and tell her story.

CHAPTER 25

1

FOR SEVERAL WEEKS before Odell's trial, Stephan Schick and his partner, Tim Havas, visited Odell daily to discuss her case, the possibility of her testifying at trial, and who else would be called to the stand to defend her. "If we were going to put Dianne on the witness stand," Schick said, "we were going to call her half brother."

From the first day Schick met with Odell, he said, she wanted to testify. She needed to tell her story of abuse and prostitution to a jury, and how her mother had drugged her and taken the three babies and killed them. Because Odell was now so adamant about testifying, Schick and Havas spent "days" meticulously going over what she would say once she got on the witness stand.

"Because her testimony would be the crucial part of any defense she would have," Schick added, "we spent hours going over it with her."

A large part of that preparation, Schick insisted, included Havas and him acting out a direct- and cross-examination scenario with Odell. They would drill her with questions Lungen was sure to ask. They would have her tell her story over and over again: Mabel, the deaths of the babies, the abuse, her upbringing, her dad fathering the first child in 1972 and repeatedly raping her, then beating her until the baby died. If she took the stand, the Molineaux decision made it possible for Lungen to introduce Baby Doe. It was a Pandora's box, certainly, but Odell felt she could withstand any attack Lungen might wage.

As Odell went through a mock version of her testimony, telling her stories and answering questions, Schick felt she might be a compelling witness. She could turn on the tears when she needed to, he said, which was what a defense attorney wanted. Although she was uneducated formally, Schick pointed out, she came across as being bright, especially in the articulate way she answered some of the questions.

Part of their thespian undertaking, however, included Schick acting out the role of Lungen, whom he knew to be one of the most experienced—if not the best—cross-examiners he had ever witnessed in a court of law. Lungen knew how to elicit testimony from a witness and get him or her to talk about things they perhaps didn't even realize they were bringing up. He had spent decades mastering his craft. If Odell wanted to testify, she was going to have to survive a grilling by Schick acting as Lungen. If she could get through that, well, it just might be worth putting her on the stand.

"We tried to be as much like a prosecutor as we could," Schick said, "trying to bring as much trial-level skill at cross-examining witnesses as possible, trying to make her look as *bad* as possible."

As Schick and Havas questioned Odell, Schick said, they would try to "shake" her credibility. It wasn't something he and Havas had worked up at the last minute; they had sat with Odell and gone over her testimony no fewer than twenty times, he claimed, over a period of three weeks before trial. Odell had everything to lose by taking the stand. But it was her life, Schick opined—which made it her call.

But as they kept questioning her relentlessly, attacking every possible scenario Lungen might bring up, she broke down.

"After we would decimate her on cross-examination, *she* came to realize it might not be a good idea."

Odell's volatility while undergoing mock questioning wasn't what had bothered Schick the most, however. If it had been just one baby Odell was being accused of killing, he said, he and Havas could have worked with her. It was practical to think that a jury might buy the notion that one baby's death wasn't her fault.

"One baby, okay," Schick recalled, "maybe even two. Maybe we can explain satisfactorily two babies to the jury. But when it's three and then *four,* that's, you know, you know that's . . . even if what she's saying about Mabel is given one hundred percent believability, I think by the time you get to the third baby, you become a coparticipant and you're acting in concert. At what point as an adult when you're pregnant and your mother is saying, 'Okay, I'll take care of it, I'll be the midwife,' when two prior children have died because of her previous negligence or intentional killing, at what point wouldn't a reasonable person know that you can't do this? That it's going to end up in another death?"

Schick was concerned that if Odell began talking about Mabel, the jury would say to themselves, "You should have done something to stop her. You were an adult. You had given birth to healthy children that had survived. If she was this evil, malicious person, you *knew* how to get away from her."

A decision had to be made. Schick's hands were tied,

essentially. Either way, some of the culpability—if not all—would fall on Odell's shoulders. It didn't matter that Mabel was there. There were four babies involved. The repetitious nature of the deaths alone was enough to convince a jury Odell was somehow involved. Bad childhood. Prostitution. Raped by her father. Abused by her mom. None of it gave Odell a license to kill or neglect her children. A bad childhood, in other words, could not have made her do it, simply because she had given birth to so many children that ultimately lived.

"Okay," Schick continued, "let's say I call Martin to the stand and establish that she had been abused, had a bad childhood—emotionally, physically, and sexually—and that the first child was quite possibly her own father's child. But then a long number of years go by and she has living, healthy children and she's leading a fairly normal life. How many more can you keep having and killing because of a bad childhood?"

Still, Schick wasn't going to deny there was a possibility that a strong defense could be built around Odell's alleged abusive upbringing. She could contend, Schick said, that during those pregnancies in which the children had died, she was all alone, which was what she had told the police in her statements, and it was an impossible position for her to be in. Schick's challenge would be to convince the jury to put themselves in a similar position and have them ask themselves, *What would I do?* It was a gamble, of course, but at this stage appeared to be one of Odell's only chances at either escaping life behind bars or getting off on a lesser charge. The argument would be: Odell couldn't make decisions in a proper manner based on the abuse she suffered. Therefore, it wasn't murder; it was manslaughter or criminal negligence.

Convincing Odell it was her best defense, though,

was what stood in Schick's way right up until the first day testimony was set to begin. He and Tim Havas were still teetering on advising her not to testify, even though Odell was now absolutely adamant about telling her story to jurors.

2

"I've lived with the shame, I've lived with the fear," Odell recalled later, reflecting on what she was thinking during that crucial time before trial when she was still trying to decide what to do, "the open anger, the hostility."

It was becoming all too much. But she insisted she had felt like a "doormat" and the "shit on the bottom of somebody's feet" long enough. It was time to take a stand. "I can't do this to my children any longer."

Odell said Schick believed she had "suffered every kind of abuse possible," but that it didn't seem to have anything to do with the case he was preparing. She felt he didn't care, and that he'd already made up his mind regarding the type of defense he wanted to present.

Heading into opening arguments, Odell said thoughts of Martin's possible testimony, Sauerstein's testimony, coupled with her own, fed her strength. Together, she was convinced, they could persuade a jury that, because she had been abused so often, for so many years, she'd had nothing to do with the deaths of the children. In effect, the deaths weren't her fault.

"Now that Martin had agreed to testify," Odell recalled, "all that we have to do is get up on the stand and tell the truth. Word it any way you want to word it, the truth is in the eyes of the beholder. They (the police and Lungen) see their truth one way; I see it another. I mean, you can take moments out of anybody's life and concoct them to make anyone appear as a mass murderer if *that's* what you want to do."

Huh?

But Lungen and his team weren't suggesting Odell was a mass murderer; they were content with the fact that they could prove beyond a reasonable doubt she had killed three of her children. Odell herself had signed a statement indicating as much. Now, it seemed, she wanted to change her mind and blame the police and Lungen for going after her.

Odell believed Scileppi, Streever, and Lane, along with Lungen, were out to get her from day one. She felt they had zeroed in on her and forced the facts to juxtapose with a notion they dreamed up, putting her at the center of some evil plot to kill her own children. She felt strongly that because Lungen couldn't prosecute her in 1989 for the death of Baby Doe, he was fixated on putting her away now. Yet, that being said, she wasn't prepared to call them "liars."

"To be really fair, I am not going to accuse them of lying. I'm accusing them of *omission*. They led people to believe one thing by leaving out a plethora of others. Not one of them—ever—said that I had asked for a lawyer. That goes for all of them."

Even Stephan Schick had a hard time believing Odell had never asked for a lawyer. If one truly believed cops didn't pressure suspects and fool them into thinking they didn't need to speak to a lawyer, Schick said it was an extremely naive position.

Odell maintained that all she had to do was get up on the witness stand and tell the truth. It would save her. But Schick, she said, was "telling [her] that the DA was going to try to twist everything. . . .

"Schick is trying to make me feel," Odell recalled, "like I have to have an answer for everything—and I *don't* have an answer for everything."

Schick had no trouble admitting that he, in fact, did

tell Odell she had to have an answer ready for any question Lungen might ask. It was his job to extend that virtue of courtroom experience to her. After all, Schick had been inside courtrooms for nearly three decades. One of his worries, where Lungen's questioning was concerned, involved the idea that Odell never sought prenatal care while she was pregnant with the three dead babies. Lungen undoubtedly would bring it up on cross-examination. She had to be ready.

"If I did that," Odell said, meaning going out and getting prenatal care like she had with her living children, "I would have had to leave my children with my mother. And she was definitely in control of everyone and everything at that point in time. So I weighed out leaving my children with her for a short amount of time and going to do something I *know* she didn't want me to do, and coming back and maybe finding one of them gone. There was a point in time where I even went to work and I came home from work and I said to my mother, 'Where are the kids?' and she said, 'They should be outside playing.' And they were nowhere around."

Some would later say Odell had a way of explaining away everything that had gone wrong in her life as being someone else's fault, mainly Mabel's. It seemed she had a hard time taking responsibility for anything.

"The problem is," Schick commented, "if you look at her and what she says, it's always everybody else. That's the problem. I mean, I was never accused of killing four people! I couldn't get away from the fact, viewing this thing from a defense standpoint, that *she* had given birth to all these babies. She was there during the births."

Indeed, Odell had an answer for everything—except when it came to certain parts of her obviously troubled life with her mom.

"There are going to be blanks in [my story]," Odell

intimated. "Pieces of time that I can't fill in. No matter how hard I try. My personal opinion is that the things that were going on in my life then, the things that were being done to me, the things that I was trying to do to protect my girls, were so horrific, in my own mind I think I shut them . . . there was a point in time when I just shut them out to save my own sanity."

The abuse Odell suffered—if, in fact, she was abused—was not, in Schick's view, enough to save her from harsh questioning by Lungen, not to mention all the evidence against her. It didn't answer the question of guilt, which was the only initiative weighing on Schick's mind as the first day of opening arguments approached. Would she or wouldn't she testify? That was the question the defense faced.

3

Stephan Schick and Tim Havas sat in Schick's office inside Legal Aid during the first week of December and discussed how they were going to proceed. Time and again, weighing how Odell stood up to pressure during the dozens of times they had cross-examined her, they came to the same conclusion: if she decided she wanted to testify, it was in her best interest, they were going to advise her, not to.

"Another awful decision we were forced to make," Schick said, "regarded manslaughter. If the judge would give her manslaughter as a 'lesser included,' and the jury would find manslaughter, then the charges would have to be dismissed because the statute of limitations had run [out]."

The only way around this option was for Odell to waive the statute of limitations on a possible manslaughter charge. But Odell could still be found guilty of three counts of manslaughter in the second degree, which, in turn, could amount to a life sentence.

Schick said the case, from the get-go, was a tangled web of legalities, many of which Odell (nor anyone in her family) ever understood fully—a dynamic that caused some friction between them. But Schick remained steadfast in doing his job to the best of his ability, and part of it came down to Odell's decision to testify. It was up to her, he said. No one else.

"We were, most of the time, leading up to the trial," Schick recalled, "as she says, under the opinion that we would *have* to put her on the stand. We thought her half brother would have better testimony than he ended up having. We thought there might have been another baby that was buried in the backyard, but it didn't turn out to be his actual testimony. We thought he might be helpful with some other testimony— I think he's the nicest guy in the world and he was absolutely truthful—but, unfortunately, because of that, he was limited to the amount of testimony he could give."

It was an impossible case, Schick insisted. If the judge had ruled in Lungen's favor during the Molineaux hearing, which would have allowed evidence of Baby Doe into trial, then deciding to put her on the stand would have been an easier decision because, at that point, "We wouldn't have anything to lose."

Leading right up to the first day of testimony and opening arguments, Schick and Havas found themselves dealing with the same problem: Odell not being able to answer certain questions that, Schick said, "could not be answered by her in any way that made any sense logically or rationally."

One of the questions Schick had grilled Odell about, on numerous occasions under mock cross-examination, was "Okay, you had the first baby in '72; now it's '82, you have another baby; now it's '83. At that point, you know that your mother is killing these babies. What precaution did you take for the next baby in '85?"

There was, really, no answer Odell could come up with.

"It's hard to come up with an excuse," Schick continued, "as to why you would get no prenatal care if you know your mother, if you *suspect* your mother, might be doing something to ensure these babies die shortly after birth. Would you not go to a doctor or someone else to lay a framework or groundwork to make sure it wouldn't happen again?"

If Odell had done that, other people would have known what Mabel did. There would be a record, a trail of evidence, so to speak.

And then there was another problem, which Lungen was sure to bring up—that Odell had received prenatal care for her eight living children and had gone to the hospital to deliver them. How does one explain that logically? And then there was the fact that Mabel died in 1995. Why didn't Odell run to the police then and explain everything?

Odell said later she was scared Mabel would haunt her after her death and do something to her children. That would be a fine argument for an insanity defense, but Lungen would rip it apart.

"It got to a point," Schick said, "where I believed that on cross-examination we would have ended up worse than without putting her on."

Furthermore, the report Schick had gotten back from the psychiatrist he had hired wasn't supportive.

"After he gave me a report that wasn't helpful, I went back and told him, '*Look,* here's some more facts, go back and see her *again!*' "

In the end, though, there was nothing the psychiatrist could find that would have helped during trial.

Chapter 26

1

STEVE LUNGEN HAD come a long way in thirty years from his days on the battlefields of Vietnam and his ambivalence regarding public speaking. He had given hundreds of opening statements in his nearly three decades of trial lawyering. He felt comfortable standing, talking to a jury, explaining how he was going to prove his case. It wasn't about making false promises and telling a jury things it *wanted* to hear; it came down to presenting facts in an easy-to-understand language a jury could wrap its arms around and comprehend without having to refer to a law book.

If any criticism concerning opening statements could be placed on Lungen, some might say it was a penchant he had for overstating his case and perhaps carrying on a bit too long. But that was Lungen's passion shining through: his nature. He had done his homework, studied the case every possible way and put in the time to devise an opening that hopefully would encourage jurors to pay attention to the case he was going to present.

Before he could start, however, the judge spoke

briefly to the jury, outlining how the day would proceed. One juror had to be replaced with an alternate due to a personal matter, but, for the most part, it was time to ring the bell, butt gloves, and get it on.

After finishing his opening remarks, Judge Frank J. LaBuda underscored the importance of jurors to listen to the lawyers' arguments with a bit of cynicism. "Please bear in mind that when the attorneys speak to you," LaBuda said, ". . . by way of submissions, what the attorneys say to you is *not* evidence. The evidence will come from witnesses that come into this courtroom and are sworn and give testimony. . . ."

With that, LaBuda explained the varying differences between evidence and testimony, and then, kindly, handed the torch to Lungen.

"Good morning, ladies and gentlemen," Lungen began. "This trial will be about a horrible story concerning the death of innocence."

There it was already: *the death of innocence.* It would become one of many references Lungen would make to the victims.

"This trial," he continued, "will be about infant babies that were born alive and that are entitled to the full protection of our laws. Infants, even minutes old," and he lowered his voice a bit to emphasize what he believed to be the true horror of Odell's crimes, "have the same constitutional right as adults, and they have the *right*," and now he raised his voice, "*to live.*"

Lungen next explained the definition of infanticide, and then launched into a discussion regarding Odell's motive. "Each child," he said, pointing at Odell, "in the defendant's mind, she deemed to be illegitimate, they were *murdered.*"

Primarily, Odell sat looking down at the table in front of her, with Schick and Havas by her side, comforting her at times. She looked horrible; the weight of the charges and the trial having had an obvious impact on her physical appearance: dark bags under her eyes, her lip quivering as if she were forever on the verge of crying.

"Most of the time, I *was* crying," Odell recalled. "When I didn't cry, when I listened to the things Lungen was saying, I was thinking to myself, 'My God, this man is taking pieces out of my life, one at a time . . . and he's putting them together and stringing them into a commentary he wants.'"

While Lungen continued, Odell said, she tried to drift away through prayer: *I hope to God that you straighten out this man's tongue. Hail Mary . . . Hail Mary . . . straighten out his tongue.*

It became a mantra she would recite to herself to try to take her mind off the situation.

Like any seasoned prosecutor, Lungen unfolded his case to the jury, piece by piece, explaining exactly what he was going to prove: "How the babies were discovered; what condition they were in; what the defendant initially had to say about those babies; what the defendant *did* say about the babies; what the defendant did *not* say; what [she] did *not* do; how [she] attempted to mislead, falsify, to minimize her conduct; and, ultimately, how and why she is guilty. . . ."

It was a barrage of accusations preceding a chronological dissertation of the events leading up to Odell's arrest: the discovery of the mummified and decomposed remains in Arizona, Detective Diane Thomas and Bruce Weddle's initial investigation, and the Pima, Arizona, medical examiner's early assessment of the bodies.

He warned jurors about the graphic nature of the photographs they were going to see: "You should and you *must* see that . . . it's the evidence of what this case is about, and I can't clean it up," he argued, pumping his fist angrily. "You can't erase certain things and not erase other things."

Again he was trying to keep the focus on what was at stake: infants had been murdered, and it didn't matter what type of childhood or who else was to blame. Odell had given birth to the children and allowed them to die.

"It is what it is. . . ."

Over the next ten minutes or so, Lungen continued with what was, at times, a frightful version of the events leading up to Odell's arrest. On several occasions, he spoke of "full-term" babies, and reminded the jury that the babies weren't stillborn or born prematurely; they were born healthy. He was going to prove it, he promised.

Then he worked his way into Odell's background, as she had explained it to Diane Thomas and Bruce Weddle. Here, he zeroed his argument in on the fact that Odell had given birth to eight "healthy" children, all born in hospitals, and three dead children, all born at home.

From there, he talked about the interviews Odell had agreed to take part in with police, mentioning how she claimed initially to have no idea whose children they were, but under pressure—and more questioning—admitted they were hers.

This part of Lungen's argument carried on, perhaps, for too long, and became quite technical in its step-by-step peeling back of the layers of each interview. Then again, it was a focal point that his case, when it came down to it, hinged on Odell's admission to police. If the jury bought it, she was guilty. If not, she would walk.

There was one thorn that could perhaps cause Lungen some problems during trial. So, like any experienced prosecutor, he attacked it head-on. "The defendant was cooperative," he said, pointing at Odell at times, looking at the jury at others. "She spoke freely, somewhat guarded about information she was going to give." He was talking about the interview Odell had agreed to with Roy Streever and Thomas Scileppi in Waverly, New York, as the media converged on her home and drove her away. The cadence and tone of his voice varied at times, and when he got to certain words and phrases, he called to mind how important certain pieces of evidence would become. "She was *not* under duress or in custody. Like I said, she *drove* herself there. She *expected* the New York police to be there and she *agreed* to talk."

Essentially, Lungen was saying Odell had agreed voluntarily to speak about the case to the police. There would be no question about it.

"Somewhere around eleven o'clock," he continued, getting to the heart of his argument, "the defendant . . . said that the baby moved or gasped, showing signs of life. And *that* simple statement"—he paused a moment for effect—"changed the entire character of everything that was going on. Because not only were these babies now full-term babies, but now we had an indication from the *defendant* herself that the babies were born . . . alive. . . . And, as it turned out, she tells them with respect to each of these three babies, they either cried, coughed, moved, gasped, something."

Lungen needed to clarify how Odell had changed her story several times throughout the three days she was interviewed. One of those stories included who the fathers of the children were.

"Knowing she's under arrest for murder, realizing obviously the story is up, she then tells Investigator Lane with respect to Baby Number One, born in 1982, 'No,' she was not raped! In fact, the father of that

child she believed to be her brother-in-law, her ex-
brother-in-law. She was married to James Odell and it
was *his* brother. She believed that's who the father was.
She was having an affair with him."

After introducing Dr. Baden as a "world-renowned
pathologist," Lungen claimed Baden would walk into
the courtroom and tell the jury the babies had all been
born alive and had all died of "traumatic asphyxia. By
definition, it means an interference with the ability of
the babies to breathe by force. Essentially," he added,
lowering and raising his voice at appropriate times to
bring about the true horror of his case, "it means
that the *defendant* suffocated to *death* each of these
three *babies.*"

The courtroom went silent at that point. It was a
stark reminder, an image, perhaps, of a woman giving
life and taking it back in one quick, constant, evil
moment. Could Dianne Odell—sitting, crying at times,
holding on to a set of rosary beads as though they were
a lifeline, rolling them through her fingers in prayer—
have given life to these children and, by the violent
force of her own hands, taken it away the next? Was
she playing God?

If so, jurors might be asking themselves several
questions: *Why wouldn't Odell just abort the pregnancies?
Why would she go to the trouble of carrying them for nine
months, going through the process of labor pains and having
the children at home, and then murder them? Wouldn't it have
been easier just to abort them? That way, there would be no
evidence left behind. Nothing to explain. Was Odell that evil,
that cold-blooded, to want to give these children life and
then snatch it away?*

Lungen, as he argued his case, certainly thought
so—and was making it clear by hammering his point
home to jurors, who possibly sat in utter shock at the

mere image of what the last moments of life must have been like for the babies.

As he carried on, perhaps getting caught up in the moment, allowing his passion for the case to dictate his argument, Lungen began to talk about the legal aspects of the charges against Odell, one of which being intentional murder.

"Now, intentional murder essentially means that a defendant *intended* to cause the death of that person. It was *that* person's conscious aim and objective to bring about the *death* of another person."

Schick, staring at his colleague and friend, shaking his head in disbelief, stood up after hearing the remark. "Objection, Your Honor. This is not an opening statement anymore."

Lungen stopped, looked toward the judge.

"Objection will be overruled. Ladies and gentlemen, the law will be given to you in tremendous detail at the conclusion of the case. What the attorneys say to you is merely their argument."

With that, Lungen then talked about the six different counts of murder Odell was charged with and, finally, worked his way into a dramatic closing statement.

"Some of you may believe that babies' lives get devalued. The killing of a baby is no different than the killing of an adult. . . . Some of you may say, 'I can't believe this.' Some of you may say it sounds sick. That's not what this is about. This is about whether under the law, the defendant murdered her three babies intentionally or by depravity. And you will find that she committed murders in each one of these three babies and, at the end of this trial, we will ask you to render a verdict that is fair and just, based only upon the evidence and nothing else."

He paused and began walking back to his table. "Thank you very much."

The judge, after what had become a long, emotionally charged opening, decided a break was in order.

Stretch your legs. Take a moment to reflect. This was only one side of the story. Stephan Schick was up next. He would, undoubtedly, have a different story to tell.

2

Stephan Schick knew he couldn't get beyond the fact that his client had given birth to the children and they had died under her care. It wasn't one or two babies; it was three, possibly four, if Baby Doe made it into trial. Schick wasn't naive; he understood a jury wanted answers. He couldn't overlook that Odell—like it or not—had given police a damaging statement. Fundamentally, he had to try to focus on Odell's responsibility for the crimes and maybe point a finger at her without placing her under the same light as a murderer. Tone it all down some. Yes, she had done some things that might constitute wrongdoing. But she was no cold-blooded murderer. Get that out of your head.

First and foremost, he wanted to attack Lungen's argument as a whole. "One would think this case is over," Schick began after introducing himself. "One man can give a speech for an hour and a half and everybody's mind is made up. One man who doesn't know all the facts. Not that I do. You're *not* going to live up to your oath as jurors if you fall prey to and allow yourself to conclude that Dianne Odell is a monster. You're *not* going to live up to your oath as jurors if you permit demonizing a person to influence your ultimate determination."

At first, the Court TV cameras had made some feel a bit uncomfortable, as if everyone were participating in some sort of human lab experiment. It wasn't every day that trials in Sullivan County were videotaped for a national television audience. Nevertheless, Schick had a job to do, regardless of the public eye he now found himself in. He knew his opening was a building block for him to construct a reasonable-doubt defense and maybe persuade one juror that Odell hadn't acted in concert with other, more infamous baby murderers.

Schick spoke with an admirable, articulate nature. He was smart—one could discern it from his choice of words. In the end, though, how far would it get him with a jury of diverse Americans? What hurt him right away was the fact that there were ten females on the jury—some of whom were likely mothers themselves. This was a fragile situation. Women who gave birth would have strong opinions regarding childbirth and death; there was no doubt about it.

"When the jury was picked," Odell said, "it was always my contention to get on the stand, and I knew that if there were mothers on the jury, or any kind of *intelligent* women, that they would hear what I was saying. They would know and they would understand. Even if they didn't ever go through it, they had people and friends they knew who had. They would know the suffering, the anguish, the fear, umm . . . the disbelief in yourself. Ah . . . and all of the other myriad of emotions you go through when you walk around with this kind of hopelessness in your life on a daily basis."

That might have been true. But would that same jury then believe the abuse Odell referred to was, in turn, a license to kill?

Patient, Schick stopped at times to collect his thoughts before continuing in a soft, nonthreatening manner, as if to project: this woman has made mistakes, but haven't we all? It was a gamble to call into question Odell's parenting skills. After all, four of her children were dead and she was being charged with killing three of them. There was a fine line between serendipity and condescension. If he crossed that line, it was likely jurors would feel it and begin to form opinions about Odell immediately. *Presumed Innocent* and *The Burden of Proof* were titles of Scott Turow novels, not to mention clichés among legal observers and pundits. It was okay to imagine Americans were innocent until proven guilty. Yet, for bona fide defense attorneys practicing in the real world, it wasn't prudent to practice law with those same assumptions in mind. Most trials weren't textbook law cases, where the brunt of guilt weighed on the prosecution's shoulders. Most cases came down to the defense proving their client was innocent.

"You see," Schick said, "one would think this case was over already," referring to Lungen's blistering accusations against Odell. "[But] you haven't heard one witness, one iota of evidence; just a filibuster.

"Now, the prosecutor said this case, as all cases, is about accountability, it's about responsibility. My client, Dianne, has things to be accountable for, she has things she's responsible for, but she *did not* kill those babies, and even more so, she *did not* murder those babies."

He continued that there wouldn't be "one iota of evidence" presented to prove the babies were born alive. And with the exception of Odell's statement, he was correct. "Not one bit of scientific evidence. Not one bit of medical evidence."

Part of Schick's case had to confront the undeniable fact that Odell had toted the babies around the country with her for the better part of twenty-two years. He couldn't get around it. The jury would want to know why.

"She wrapped them up and packed them and took them wherever she went because she couldn't bear to part from them."

His argument centered on the prosecution's notion that Odell was some twisted monster, carrying around mementos of her gruesome crimes. She was not anything like that, he insisted. If she was, and she had wanted to conceal evidence and deliberately try to evade being caught, why, he asked, would she keep the babies with her for that long? Why not discard them? Did she keep them in a garbage area of the houses she lived in? No, Schick said. She kept them with her "personal belongings" because they *meant* something to her.

"What was she going to do? She had three infant children living with her. She wasn't going to keep them around the *house!*"

He promised he wasn't going to argue insanity, "but there is more to this case and there is more surrounding facts than the prosecutor gave you. . . . One of the things I want to do, and I won't be as long as the prosecutor, I'll only be a few minutes. . . . I want to be forthright here in the beginning, right at the get-go, with some of the things that are not in dispute. . . ."

That said, Schick explained how Odell had given birth to the babies. "She's the mother! What's not in dispute is that she wrapped them in sheets and blankets and kept them with her as she moved from place to place for employment and other reasons. . . ."

Furthermore, it wasn't in "dispute" that the police contacted Odell, or that "she wasn't truthful. She wasn't accurate." But "there are reasons for that. Doesn't mean she's a murderer. . . . This is a woman who wants to have children."

Successful defense attorneys confront those obvious bad situations for their clients that will come up during trial only one way: head-on. "Did she mislead and falsify?" Schick asked the jury, quite animated. "Yes! It's interesting that the prosecution always wants it all their own way . . . after speaking to police in Pennsylvania for two days, and for twelve and fourteen hours to the New York State Police, and they finally manipulate her into saying something about possibly hearing something," meaning that Scileppi had somehow managed to put words into Odell's mouth regarding hearing the children "gasp" for air. "All of a sudden, that's truth. That's accurate." He threw up his arms in disgust. "See, she's only truthful, inaccurate, and saying things falsely when it serves *their* purposes. But any little tidbit that serves *her* purposes and it's . . . [wrong information.]"

He then launched into a discussion regarding the DNA evidence, which he agreed was "true" evidence. He wasn't going to question any of it. He wanted the jury to understand that "concrete facts" were going to dictate his portion of the case, not assumptions and speculation.

"Don't make her into a monster until you've heard *everything*, heard things the prosecution doesn't even know about as we sit here today. I'm not talking about insanity. I'm talking about *real* evidence of *real* life with *real* situations, all of which should and must be taken into consideration before you make a decision. Please keep that in mind.

"Thank you."

CHAPTER 27

1

SITTING IN A courtroom facing the possibility of spending the rest of her life in prison didn't seem real to Dianne Odell. Yet, as Stephan Schick concluded his opening argument and Odell clutched firmly the rosary beads she held in her right hand, the reality of her life began to settle on her. Was it because she was alone? Sauerstein and the children couldn't sit behind her in the courtroom because there was a possibility they would be called as witnesses. So there Odell sat, wearing a dark blue sweater, white button-up dress shirt, looking like a Sunday-school teacher, tears running down her cheeks, in between two men—Tim Havas and Stephan Schick—she hardly knew. Schick and Havas, like everyone else in the courtroom, would go home later in the day and have dinner with their families. They might turn on the television afterward, relax, think about their day, and get up in the morning and drive to the courthouse for another day of work. But Odell, she was going back across the street to endure another night of screams and fights and strangers, who, for the most part, saw her as a vile person. On the prison food chain, there weren't many inmates lower than a child killer.

Prayer and hope, Odell said later, kept her sane enough during trial to focus on maybe escaping a guilty verdict and going home. Faith in the system. Faith in justice. Faith in the jury.

One juror . . . that's all it took.

2

When Schick finished his opening, the court took a brief break. After that, Lungen called his first witness: Diane Thomas, the Graham County Sheriff's Office detective who had opened the investigation after Safford, Arizona, resident Thomas Bright discovered the first baby.

Thomas explained how, why, when, and where. She described the gruesomeness of the discovery, the sheer horror of finding three dead babies wrapped in plastic and blankets and stuffed into cardboard boxes like trash. It sent a message to the jury Lungen had promised in his opening: the death of innocence. To solidify his theme further, Lungen introduced a host of photographs; deeply disturbing images of the crime scene, quite unlike anything anyone possibly had seen on television. This was the real thing. The babies were dead. And someone—that woman sitting over there, fumbling with rosary beads nervously, praying to herself—murdered them.

For an hour or so, Thomas set the stage for Lungen, explaining how the case had come to her attention and how she and Bruce Weddle ended up in Pennsylvania. Then, a short time later, Lungen had her focus on the initial (recorded) interview she and Weddle had conducted with Odell after she volunteered to drive to the

Towanda state police barracks. Thomas explained how Odell began the interview cooperative and friendly, but then became defensive. Thomas said she learned later that Odell had lied about certain things.

Eventually, Thomas said, Odell had left the barracks and returned to her place of work, at which time Thomas and Weddle drove to her home to speak to Sauerstein.

It had been decided, Thomas told the jury, that on the following morning, Odell would drive herself to the barracks and submit to fingerprinting, but she called Thomas that day and said she wasn't coming in.

"When you asked if she would give you the fingerprints," Lungen asked, "what was her conversation with you?"

"Miss Odell told me that she would not. She was angry with me because we spoke with Mr. Sauerstein before she was able to."

"Did you have any further conversation with her?"

"Yes, sir, we did."

"Can you tell us what happened?"

"I advised Miss Odell that's just part of an investigative process, to try to speak with everyone we can and that's why we did it."

"What did she say, anything?"

"Miss Odell indicated that she wanted to—she did not want to talk to me again until she got an attorney to take care of her home and then she would come in the next day and talk to me and tell me everything."

This would be one of Stephan Schick's opportunities maybe to bring into the record later the fact that Odell had indeed asked for an attorney. The problem, however, was that Odell voluntarily drove to the Towanda barracks that day—without an attorney.

Then Thomas talked about the second day she met with Odell, when Odell finally admitted the babies were hers. One of the points Lungen brought out, again and again, was how clear Odell had made it to Thomas and Weddle that she *didn't* tell her mother she was pregnant. Why? Because she was terrified, Thomas testified, of what Mabel would do or say, and, she added, "Miss Odell was not married, nor did she have a relationship with the father of the babies."

Near the end of Thomas's direct examination, she explained how the case finally ended up in the hands of the NYSP and the Sullivan County District Attorney's Office.

The jury was then allowed five minutes to collect their bearings while Thomas stepped down from the stand for a moment to do the same. When court resumed, Schick would get his first chance to plug holes in Lungen's case.

Schick sat, looking through his notes, conversing quietly with Havas, as Odell listened attentively. For Odell, Thomas's testimony was just one more version of the events she didn't agree with.

"The statement Diane Thomas made on the stand regarding my calling her and demanding an attorney made Stephan Schick jump up out of his chair," Odell said later.

This bothered Odell, she said. Because, "When I had said it to him myself, he told me at the time that it didn't make that much of a difference. But Thomas got up on the stand and she admitted to it . . . and he got very agitated and angry. And I thought to myself, sitting there, 'My God, I've been telling you this for months and it comes out of *her* mouth and you're jumping up out of the chair?'"

For Schick's part, he later agreed there was no doubt in his mind Odell had asked for an attorney, but he categorically denied Odell's "jumping out of his chair" statement.

"From my standpoint, if a person doesn't want to answer questions in that regard," Schick recalled, "why should she say why she wants to speak to an attorney?"

Lungen—and many of the cops involved in the case—had made a point to insist that Odell had asked for a *civil* attorney, not a criminal attorney. Big difference from a legal, investigative standpoint. Yet, should it matter what type of attorney a suspect asks for? When one is being questioned about the deaths of three babies, should the type of attorney requested matter?

"I don't think anybody, rationally, can look at this situation," Schick added with fervor, "and say that if she went to speak to an attorney, she *wasn't* going to bring up the fact that these *cops* were questioning her about dead babies."

It was a good point. Would Odell speak to a civil attorney regarding matters at home and *not* mention anything about three dead babies she was being connected to? One would have to be quite ignorant to think she wouldn't. Odell was manhandled by these cops and, in a way, tricked into talking to them without an attorney, Schick insisted. Does it make her any less guilty? No, of course not. But it does mean she might have been denied a constitutional right any American in her position—guilty or innocent—was entitled to?

Schick didn't begin his cross-examination of Thomas by bringing up the fact that his client had asked for an attorney and what type of attorney she wanted. Instead, he attacked Odell's supposed clandestine approach to first speaking with Thomas and Weddle. By asking the right questions, Schick was able to flesh out a theory that Odell wasn't necessarily hiding those babies in the storage shed, but had put them there to go back later perhaps and retrieve them and go to the police. It might have been a stretch, sure, but through Thomas's testimony, Schick was able to point out to the jury that there was plenty of documentation in the storage shed that clearly proved the boxes were Odell's. If she was hiding the babies, why leave behind evidence of who you are?

After that, Schick got into the attorney dilemma.

"When you called her on a Sunday and you reached her at home, she said before talking to you . . . that she wanted to speak to an attorney, isn't that correct?"

Thomas shuffled a bit, but was certainly not made uncomfortable by the question. It was more of just getting used to the hard seat she found herself once again sitting in.

"Yes, sir," she said without hesitation.

With that out of the way, Schick focused on the interview Thomas and Weddle had recorded. He wanted the jury to understand that the tape recording was not "representative" of everything Odell had said, but was more of a slice of time from what would become three days' worth of interviews.

Thomas agreed.

Then it was on to the question of whether the word "stillborn" was Thomas's idea or Odell's. Who brought it up? It would be important, because Schick was prepared to push the theme that cops had put words in Odell's mouth, beginning with "stillborn."

"Did you specifically use the word 'stillborn' in asking her a question: 'Were these babies stillborn?' Did you specifically use those words?"

"No, sir, I did not."

"Do you even know whether she was aware of the words 'stillborn,' or what it meant? It was never even used in your conversation, was it?"

"I did not ask her that question, no."

"Now, did you—before entering this second conversation with her—did you ascertain from her whether she had been able to speak to an attorney?"

"No, sir, I did not."

Whereas most witnesses were accustomed to answering questions with long, detailed—sometimes too detailed—answers, cops generally know to keep their answers pithy: yes or no. There was no reason to carry on, bringing out things that would be cause for more examination.

Schick asked Thomas a few more inconsequential questions about Sauerstein and then, "Thank you very much."

Lungen had only one point to go over with Thomas on redirect. He had Thomas explain further why Odell wanted an attorney. At one point, Thomas said, "Miss Odell's words to me were 'I need to speak to an attorney to get my house in order before I talk to you again.'"

"Did she ever tell you that she wanted to have an attorney representing her in her contact with you and the police in this investigation?"

"No, sir, she did not."

"At any time?"

"No, sir, she did not."

"And as part of her concern about getting her house in order, is that what prompted the telling her that she'd be able to go home that night . . . to take care of whatever business she had to take care of?"

"Yes, sir."

"And did that satisfy her?"

"Yes, sir, it did."

"And did you, in fact, allow her to do that?"

"Yes, sir. Miss Odell did leave that day with Mr. Sauerstein."

"Thank you."

Schick stood right up and walked toward the witness stand.

"Something else, Mr. Schick?" Judge LaBuda asked.

"Yes, Your Honor."

"So, before she blurted this thing out about the babies, she said to you, 'I'll talk to you tomorrow,' is that correct?"

"Yes, sir."

"You didn't want to wait till tomorrow; you wanted to talk right then, is that correct?"

"That's correct, sir."

"But you knew it was Sunday and she probably wouldn't be able to get in touch with a lawyer until the next day, isn't that correct?" Schick was animated. He was sure he had Thomas on the ropes.

"I object to that," Lungen said.

"Sustained."

"You said she told you she wanted to talk to an attorney," Schick then asked, "she wanted to get her house in order before she talked to you again, is that correct?"

"That's correct, sir."

"But she wasn't able to talk to an attorney and get her house in order before she talked to you again, isn't that correct?"

"Objection!"

"Overruled," the judge said, then, looking at Thomas, "To your knowledge?"

"To my knowledge, that's correct, sir."

"Okay," Judge LaBuda said, "anything else then, Mr. Lungen?"

Apparently, Schick was finished—except he hadn't told anyone.

"No, Your Honor," Lungen said.

"Thank you, Sergeant Thomas," the judge said.

"The next time you visit New York, please bring some sunshine with you."

"I sure hope so," Thomas said. "Thank you, sir."

3

PSP trooper Robert McKee, a criminal investigator, was next. McKee was the liaison between the NYSP and the PSP as the Odell case became a New York investigation. He had met with Thomas and Weddle when they arrived in Rome, Pennsylvania. Beyond that, McKee was there when Weddle and Thomas interviewed Odell that first time. He could give the jury a timeline and explain how Odell had been allowed to go home on that first day.

Schick had little for McKee.

"McKee didn't say much of anything because there wasn't much of anything he *could* say," Odell recalled. "It was just a cock-of-a-walk-strut thing, that's all! Basically, this was a parade of people, paid by the New York State Police, to get up there and say, 'Yes! [She] was cooperating voluntarily. [She] said all of these things. [We] would have no reason to lie.' Even though the fact remained that they were all getting commendations, they were all standing in the back of the vestibule area of the courtroom watching the proceedings inside the courtroom."

PSP trooper Gerald Williams took the stand late in the day. After having Williams go through his impressive list of credentials, Lungen zeroed in on the second day Odell had been interviewed. Williams had fingerprinted Odell. During that process, Williams said, he asked Odell if she would like to talk about the three dead infants found in Arizona.

Odell agreed, Williams said.

"And did she," Lungen asked at one point, "raise any

conversation with you about wanting to have an attorney before she spoke to anybody on this investigation . . . ?"

"Not in reference to this investigation," Williams said. "No."

Moreover, Williams said, Odell talked about "wanting to get her house in order before she really sat down with us and what she had told us is she would have liked to [have] spoken to an attorney in reference to the custody of her son Brendon. She said her young son . . . and his father . . . really didn't get along, and she . . . she described it as rock and water, just really not mixing well. . . ."

Williams next explained that he had told Odell she was free to leave the barracks on that day. She was not going to be held over. She would have time to get her house in order, as she had insisted she wanted.

From there, Williams gave the jury a picture of Odell's demeanor. Important to Lungen's argument, Williams said that after Odell admitted the babies were hers, ". . . it looked as if she was relieved of a burden off her shoulders."

Ending his direct testimony, Williams made a point to say Odell was not under arrest. At least not on that day.

"At some point," Schick said a few questions into his cross-examination, "before she blurted out anything, she indicated to you she wanted to speak to an attorney, is that correct?"

"Yes, to get her affairs in order, her house in order."

"Well," Schick began to say with a bit of sarcasm, "you were concerned because she wanted to speak to an attorney, would that be fair to say?"

"I don't know that would be fair. I asked her what she meant by that."

"Mmm . . . so, you asked her to explain to you, a police officer in a criminal investigation," he added, raising his voice, "what she meant by she 'wanted to speak to an attorney,' you *wanted* to delve into that, is that correct?"

"No, I think I . . . I delved into the part about she wanted to get her house in order and what she meant and she kind of just explained from there what she meant."

"Well," Schick said, again raising his voice, "you were there to protect her rights, *weren't* you?"

"I was there to conduct an investigation!"

"So you weren't there to protect her rights?"

"If she would have asked for an attorney, if that's what you're asking, she would have been offered one."

The problem for Schick—or, for that matter, Odell—was that she hadn't been forthright and direct enough, obviously, in making her demand for an attorney outwardly known. It appeared, from testimony thus far, that she wanted an attorney, yes, but it wasn't a criminal issue and there was no immediacy in her request.

"So, when she said, 'I want to speak to an attorney to get my house in order,' you said, 'Well, no matter what you say today, you can leave the barracks tonight and you're not going to be arrested,' is that correct?"

"Yeah, that's basically—" Williams began to say, but Schick cut him off.

"So if she said to you, 'Listen, I murdered those kids, you know, I wanted to strangle them when they were born,' you would have said, 'Okay'? You wouldn't have been arresting her and she would have been able to leave the barracks that night, is *that* correct?"

"That's correct."

"If she said, 'By the way, I murdered some other kids here in Pennsylvania,' she would have been able to leave the barracks and go home, is that correct?"

"That's hypothetical. I can't answer that question. I really don't know what would have happened then."

Schick argued whether everything said should have been considered hypothetical. Williams said what

Odell had told them was pretty "black and white." There was nothing hypothetical about it.

Schick asked a few more questions regarding the tape-recorded conversation between Thomas and Odell and then released Williams back to Lungen.

For another half hour or so, Lungen poked holes in the points Schick had made and then Schick went back and tried to fill in those gaps on recross. It was a legal battle over whether Odell had asked for an attorney and what type of attorney she was talking about. But the bottom line remained: Odell left the barracks that night, the same as she had the previous night, and never consulted with a lawyer. Those cops might have persuaded her into thinking she didn't need a lawyer, which was certainly a possibility. But the fact was that although Odell had plenty of opportunity to do so, she never consulted with an attorney, even after she had left the barracks.

CHAPTER 28

1

THE ISSUE OF whether Odell had been denied her right to an attorney, after telling Diane Thomas she wanted to speak with one, not only wore on Odell, but her lawyers, Stephan Schick and Tim Havas. How could Schick convince the jury that Odell was not allowed an attorney because, he believed, law enforcement didn't want her to have one? In his view, each witness Steve Lungen had presented thus far had made it perfectly clear that Odell had been treated fairly in the eyes of the law. She had voluntarily gone (driven herself) to the police station each time. She could have taken an attorney with her any one of those times, Lungen said later, or not gone at all.

On the other hand, Odell was sitting in jail awaiting proceedings to begin on the second day of trial. To her, she saw nothing short of a conspiracy taking place—an ambush by Lungen and his goons to secure a conviction.

The buzz around the courthouse was that Dr. Michael Baden was coming into town to present hard evidence the babies had been murdered. Wherever

Baden went to testify, there was always some sort of stir in the air, particularly because he was so well-known. On any given night, one could turn on Fox News Channel and see Baden sitting across from Greta Van Susteren, talking about whichever high-profile crime was news at that moment. Baden had a knack for explaining things in lay terms. There was no doubt his testimony would add a certain amount of credibility to Lungen's case; suffice it to say, Baden had testified in some of the more high-profile trials of the past thirty years, most notably, the O. J. Simpson fiasco in the mid-1990s.

Sitting in the back pew of the courtroom as proceedings began on Tuesday morning, December 9, was a little old man who himself had many of Baden's same credentials. Dr. *Conrad Thurston* was in the courtroom, rumor had it, to listen to Baden and possibly offer rebuttal testimony for Odell's camp, spanking any theories Baden might be bringing up to support the prosecution's case.

More than one person later claimed Dr. Thurston was merely a befuddled old man who would show up at trials where Baden testified to try to besmirch Baden's stellar reputation. Some even went as far as to say Thurston held a vendetta against Baden because Baden had been responsible for getting Thurston thrown out of the medical examiner's office in New York (which was untrue). There was a hearing, Baden admitted later, regarding Thurston, and Baden testified and Thurston was expelled from office, but Baden wouldn't go as far as to say Thurston had been following him around. In fact, Baden spoke highly of Thurston, saying he was a competent, intelligent doctor who had written several articles on sudden infant death syndrome (SIDS) and could have possibly even helped Odell.

"He's always very deferential and polite to me,"

Baden recalled. "I see him rarely. I don't think he's crazy. He's a smart guy."

Thurston was a doctor of osteopathic medicine. More commonly known as DOs, osteopathic physicians are "licensed to perform surgery and prescribe medication." Like a medical doctor, an osteopath completes four years of medical school, but also receives "an additional three hundred to five hundred hours in the study of hands-on manual medicine and the body's musculoskeletal system"—which could be important to Odell's case, at least from a medical, scientific basis. Odell's attorneys needed an expert of their own to counter Baden's testimony. Many were assuming Thurston was that witness.

Schick, however, later denied having anything to do with Thurston's presence at trial. "No, no, no," Schick said, "we never planned on calling him to the stand."

With good reason.

In 1976, Thurston found himself involved in a trial that involved his boss at the time, a man who had been brought up on charges ranging from "taking body parts without permission of next of kin" to "conducting experiments" on those same body parts. During the investigation, Thurston's boss charged him with warehousing body parts of his own. Investigators later uncovered "a large cache of human bones and tissue hidden in several . . . storage rooms" Thurston was renting. Thurston was then charged, according to an article written about the case some years later, with illegally "beheading eleven bodies and stripping the flesh from fourteen others."

The charges against Thurston were later dropped. The judge in the case ruled that Thurston had been "carrying on legitimate research." In turn, Thurston sued his former employer and won a settlement reportedly in the neighborhood of $2 million. But one could argue that his reputation had been destroyed, regardless of the

outcome of the case. More important, Baden had testified against Thurston during the civil lawsuit.

Odell later saw great potential in calling Thurston
to the stand—and she was overwhelmed by the fact
that Schick didn't want to do it.

"The man had offered his services to Schick to refute
everything Dr. Baden was going to say," Odell claimed
later. "Evidently, this guy had some information. . . ."

Schick never consulted with Thurston, he said, and
never considered using him to testify. It was just one
more piece of the puzzle Odell didn't quite understand, or want to see at face value.

Before the jury was brought in at 10:05 A.M. on December 9, Schick stood up before the court and said,
"I have an application before the jury comes in."

"Okay," the judge said.

"Judge, it is my application, my request, that the
court reopen the issue of the Huntley hearing based
upon the testimony of Detective Thomas not available
at the Huntley hearing. That being that Miss Odell,
after being telephoned on Sunday, informed Detective Thomas when requested to come in for purpose
of giving fingerprints, which would not be permitted
absent a warrant unless it was voluntary compliance,
and, at that point, when told the purpose was for the
legal issue of the fingerprints, [Odell said], 'I don't
want to come in. I don't want to say anything any further. I want to consult an attorney.'"

The bottom line, Schick argued, was that if Odell's
rights had been violated—after all, Thomas had admitted on the stand that Odell requested an attorney—
then the tape-recorded interview and statements she
made afterward should be suppressed.

"Mr. Schick," the judge said, "if I were to grant your
relief and require, now based upon testimony that was
unavailable at the Huntley hearing, suppression,
wouldn't that cause a mistrial?"

"Well . . . ," Schick said, "it would require a dismissal of the indictment, not a mistrial." Without the statement by Odell, the state had "insufficient evidence as a matter of law of homicide."

"Okay," the judge said.

"And of asphyxiation!" Schick added.

"What I am going to do now," the judge said calmly, "is we are going to proceed with the trial."

2

Times Herald-Record reporter Heather Yakin had been in court since the start of the trial. She never got that "exclusive" story she was digging for, but she ended up making friends with Sauerstein and potentially could convince him to talk after the trial was over.

"During the trial, I said hello to Bob Sauerstein, but he seemed to need his space during the testimony, especially with some of [his and Dianne's] kids there. He seemed pretty stressed."

On day one of the trial, Yakin filled two steno notebooks. She was busy all day writing, taking down testimony, working up a story. But she was, like nearly everyone else in town, looking forward to Dr. Baden's arrival. Not so much because of the star power Baden's appearance carried, but more for the weight of his testimony. Many assumed Baden was going to present hard evidence that Odell had murdered the children. If he couldn't do that, some suggested, Lungen was in big trouble. It was fine to argue a woman had murdered her babies, but when it came down to it, a jury wanted evidence.

Along with everyone else, Yakin would have to wait for Dr. Baden. Lungen was calling Investigator Bill Maloney first, then Stephen Swinton, the DNA supervisor at the Forensic Investigation Center in Albany, New York.

After Bill Maloney raised his hand and got comfortable in the witness chair, he explained how he had traveled to Arizona with a few investigators to collect the childrens' remains, along with several other key pieces of evidence. Maloney's testimony was chiefly designed to lay the groundwork for Lungen's big gun, Dr. Baden. The jury would want to know how the babies had made it to New York. Maloney was that connection.

Interestingly, when the judge asked Schick if he had any questions for Maloney, Schick said, "No, I do not."

After a short break, Swinton took the stand and talked about his DNA work at the lab, his experience, and how he became acquainted with the Odell case. He said he had attended the autopsies of the babies to collect "biological material from each of the remains for future DNA analysis."

Swinton then clarified, by definition, how the DNA process worked. "You receive half of your DNA from your mother and half from your father," he said at one point. DNA is contained in "every nucleated cell of the body."

The main purpose for DNA analysis was to try to figure out who the fathers of the babies were. Lungen put up a graph on the overhead projector screen reminiscent of those mind-numbing science charts found in any high-school classroom, and had Swinton explain how there wasn't enough DNA available in Baby Number One's body to develop a profile. As for Baby Number Two, Swinton could only manage to get a partial profile, he said. But Baby Number Three, he explained, was a clear match to Odell. Furthermore, there was no doubt in Swinton's mind that David Dandignac had fathered the child.

For the next hour, Swinton talked about the

complexity of DNA as a science, along with how it had been applied in Odell's case.

When Lungen finished, the judge asked Schick if he had any questions.

"No questions."

3

A large man, Dr. Michael Baden, with wiry wisps of whitish gray hair, stood tall at about six feet four inches. He carried an enormous amount of grandeur and authority when he entered a courtroom. If anyone hadn't recognized Baden from his appearances on television, they certainly had heard by the time he arrived who he was and how important his testimony was going to be for Lungen.

"Dr. Baden's testimony was key for me," Heather Yakin recalled, "because I wanted to know how [the prosecution would prove] homicide by smothering mummified newborns. Hey, you've got to know what the evidence really is. And I knew there was definitely a strong emotional component to the case for Lungen, for Baden, and for some of the investigators who'd also been involved in the 1989 case. Baden's argument, I thought, [would] essentially come down to the weight of all the combined facts: three dead babies, hidden for twenty years, moved around before finally being abandoned, left in boxes wrapped in old blankets, sheets, and towels. Plus, Odell's eventual admission to cops that she'd heard a cry."

Yakin was accurate in her assessment. In theory, she spoke for the community. For Lungen, Baden was going to wrap the case up and present the jury with a clear picture of what had happened, how, and why Odell was guilty.

For the first half hour, Baden went through his

long list of credentials, beginning with where he had started as a pathologist and where he now worked. In between, Lungen had him talk about his work and why it was important not only to rely on the forensic evidence but *all* the evidence, which, of course, would be imperative to Lungen's case.

Baden was the chief medical examiner for New York City at one time, he explained. In 1985, he was transferred to the NYSP, "to a new division that was being set up, the Forensic Science Unit, where I am still employed as codirector of the Medical-Legal Investigation Unit."

Not only was Baden one of the nation's most respected and esteemed medical examiners, but he had just returned from Singapore, he said, where, at the request of the Singaporean government, he had helped evaluate the medical examiner system of the entire country. He had also been to Bosnia to examine the remains of mass graves.

"When you work on a case that involves police," Lungen asked, getting more into the reason why Baden was there, "particularly when doing work for the state police, you try to review everything the state police have recovered in their cases?"

"Yes, I do."

"And do you try to make yourself acquainted with what they have learned and what their investigation shows . . . to factor that in, or in your own mind exclude it, however it plays in your ultimate opinion and conclusion?"

"Yes."

"And in this particular case, you were provided, were you not, with various information from the state police that included statements made by the defendant, particularly written statements?"

"Yes."

"And oral statements?"

"Yes."

"Okay. Prior to your doing anything on my case, prior to your doing an autopsy, do you have to make some gross observations? Do you not have to sit and take a look at what you have?"

"Yes. Before doing any autopsy, I try to gather as much information as I can, so I can do an intelligent autopsy."

"And in this case, this information *included* the police investigation?"

"Yes."

"Did you also have the benefit of X rays? And you could take your own X rays concerning this?"

Baden said he had examined X rays that already had been taken by doctors in Arizona and also at the Albany Medical Center. He said he had even spoken to the pathologist in Arizona who had originally examined the remains of the babies. After that, he broke down the technicalities involved in looking at the results of the X rays of the three babies. It was monotonous testimony at times, perhaps too clinical in nature, yet necessary in order to bring into the record a more medical explanation of the evidence. Juries bored easily. Prosecutors and defense attorneys are always aware of that. But juries are not made up of uneducated, uninformed people; they need certain technical and scientific information in order to grasp the larger picture of the evidence they will be looking at and studying during deliberations.

Baden gave long, detailed answers. He wanted to be sure the jury understood exactly what he was saying. They deserved it. It might seem long-winded and procedural, but to get to the truth—at least from a medical perspective—one must be privy to *all* the information, not just sound bites that might make for interesting headlines.

As Lungen handed Baden certain photographs of the

babies, the judge addressed the jury, "Ladies and gentlemen, you will be seeing shortly, as you have saw yesterday, certain photographs which many of you . . . may deem to be unpleasant. . . ."

Within a few moments, the photographs were put up on the overhead projector for everyone to see while Baden began explaining the differences between the mummified remains of one baby and the bone fragments of the other two, on occasion using a laser pointer to direct jurors to certain sections of the photographs.

"If we go more to three o'clock," Baden said, pointing to one of the X rays, ". . . this is the top of the X ray right here. You can go all the way down. See! This obviously is the skull of the baby. The baby's skull was fully developed. These are the jaws," he added, moving the pointer down a bit. "There are no teeth here yet. There are no fractures. This is the spine . . . bones coming down in the arms. The upper arm, the elbows, the shoulder joints . . ."

As Baden spoke in graphic detail—but sounding rather congenial and calm, as if it were all some sort of biology lesson—the full structure of the baby emerged. Odell cried silently. The images were equally disturbing to others as most sat and listened to strangers talk about dead children as if they were mere science experiments.

Perhaps most shocking of all was an X ray of mummified Baby Number Three, whose skeleton was entirely intact. There, before everyone, was a full-term baby, cradled in a fetal position, knees tucked to chest, arms seemingly hugging itself, as if still in the womb. The X ray was clear, a full-figured structure of the baby, every bone and every curve, perfect.

"Baby Number Three," Heather Yakin said later, "that was the one that got the jurors. . . . You could see in that X ray that he had been a perfectly formed little boy."

Little boy . . . exactly what Lungen had been saying all along. Let no one forget these babies, only minutes or hours old, were human beings.

If there was any question in the jury's mind that they hadn't been dealing with fully formed human beings, the X ray Baden was pointing to answered it without question.

It was 12:30 P.M. With the sober images of the X rays playing in the minds of jurors, the judge decided to break for lunch. Everyone was expected back in the courtroom an hour later, at 1:30.

CHAPTER 29

1

AFTER THE LUNCH break, in the span of an hour, Dr. Baden explained the X rays in further detail, telling jurors what the results meant to him as part of his entire investigation. With that, after discussing briefly how he meticulously studied each X ray, on top of conducting an autopsy on each child, Lungen asked, "Could you state, all by itself, that you would know either the manner or the cause of death?"

"No," Baden said, "I could not."

"All by itself?"

"Just by examining the remains, I would not be able to determine each baby by itself the cause or manner of death. I can eliminate a lot of things, but I could not eliminate the cause of death."

Lungen asked him to give an example.

"I could eliminate traumatic injuries to the bone. Most traumas—that is blunt-force trauma, gunshot wound, stab wounds—that cause death cause some injury to bone. So, there was no injury to bone that speaks against a violent death of that nature. I could also eliminate, even without the tissue being present, many kinds of natural diseases that would affect bone. . . ."

Lungen continued asking questions about procedures and what other elements generally aided Baden in finding a cause of death. Was the fact that the babies had been abandoned and stored in boxes important?

Baden said it was.

"Now, you became aware . . . prior to making and formulating any opinions and conclusions, that at some point during the police investigation the defendant had made various statements to law enforcement?"

"Yes."

"And those statements were made available to you for your consideration, were they not, as to how they impacted on what happened to these three babies?"

"Yes."

Lungen then went into a series of questions detailing how Odell had, at first, lied to police. Then he talked about how she had not received any prenatal care while she was pregnant with the three dead babies. Baden agreed it was imperative in his investigation. Additionally, he said, it was also important to him that Odell had given birth to eight living children at hospitals, but the three dead babies had been born at home.

Then Lungen asked, perhaps, the most critical question of the trial thus far.

"With respect to Baby Number One, would it be important to you, as a forensic pathologist, to know that the defendant said to the police in substance, 'I heard the baby's first muffled cry'? And then she said she lost consciousness, and then when she came to, she said there were several inches of one of the towels inside the baby's mouth? Do those two statements, hearing muffled cries and several inches of a towel inside a baby's mouth, have any significance to you, in your opinion, with respect to Baby Number One?"

"Yes."

"Why?"

"The significance is, the baby was born alive to be able to make her cry and that somebody put a towel into the baby's mouth—and that, in itself, would suffocate the baby."

"Why do you say, 'Someone put a towel in the baby's mouth several inches'?"

"Because the baby could not have done that to itself."

Two questions later, Lungen went for it: "What would you determine the cause of death and the manner of death?"

"I would determine the cause of death to be traumatic asphyxia by suffocation by towel in the mouth as the cause of death. And the manner of death would be homicide."

Then Lungen had him tell the jury exactly why he thought Odell had killed the children and how, in his opinion, she had done it.

By the end of Baden's direct examination, Lungen wanted to be sure he had made another point clear to the jury: illegitimate children die at a higher rate.

"Infanticide," Lungen said, "from a pathologist's point of view, essentially means what?"

"Death of an infant."

"Is it a fair statement that in your experience you see infanticide more prevalent with illegitimate children?"

"Yes . . ."

"Right! In this case, all three children were born alive, in your opinion?"

"In my opinion, yes."

"I have no further questions, Doctor."

2

Schick wasn't about to pass on the opportunity to question Baden. After all, as esteemed and renowned as he was, Baden had just called Schick's client a murderer. To *not* cross-examine him would have been detrimental to Odell. Schick needed to try to rebut some of what Baden had said, or least drive home the point that it was his "opinion," which didn't necessarily constitute fact.

Schick wasted little time getting into it with Baden.

"Sir, firstly, you said when a forensic pathologist makes a determination of homicide that that can mean many things, is that correct?"

"Yes, sir."

"That homicide includes many different criminal charges, isn't that correct?"

"And no criminal charges. Criminal and noncriminal charges, yes, sir."

Baden wasn't some callow, just-out-of-med-school doctor, summarizing his first homicide case for a jury. He had been on the stand more times than he could recall. He was a professional, and his "opinions," regardless of how they were perceived by Stephan Schick, would have a major impact on the jury's sense of the case.

"Homicide can be accidental?" Schick asked next.

"We, medical examiners, don't use it in that term. The courts may decide that it could be unintentional, inadvertent."

"Homicide can be negligent homicide?"

"Yes."

"It can be a reckless homicide?"

"Yes."

"It can be manslaughter?"

"Yes."

"Manslaughter first degree and manslaughter in the second degree?"

"Yes."

"And it could be murder?"

"Yes. And can be excusable and justifiable."

Odell sat looking at both Schick and Baden, wondering what was going on, as they volleyed questions and answers back and forth in rapid succession. She wasn't too concerned about courtroom tactics and legal gibberish. She was focused on telling her side of the story to the jury and making each one—or just one—believe it had been Mabel who had killed her children.

"Okay," Schick said, pacing a bit, nodding his head, "now, I think you said in a number of parts of your testimony that it's extremely important to know histories in making these determinations, isn't that correct?"

"I didn't say '*extremely*.' It's important to get as much *information* as possible. Sometimes we don't get history."

"Maybe I've got this wrong? Maybe you can clear this up?"

"Yes."

Baden said he could not make a determination of death "based only upon the medical and scientific facts. . . ." He needed more information.

Schick made a point of saying how important it was that the information—the "outside information," in his words—be accurate.

"To a certain extent," Baden was quick to lash back. "Because I don't adopt the outside information as given. I'll evaluate to see if it makes sense in light of the autopsy or medical findings. But yes, how accurate the information is, is important."

Lungen sat and listened carefully. He wanted to pump his fist in the air and say, "Good job, Doctor. Perfect." But he could only, of course, sit in quiet repose and reflect on how good a witness Dr. Baden was.

"I'm particularly concerned with some of the things the prosecutor just went over with you," Schick said next, quite animated and obviously upset. "He asked you, 'Is that an important part of your determination in this case?' And he started saying things like, 'Reading statements made by the mother of hearing noises and cries'—"

Baden wouldn't allow Schick to finish. "Yes!"

". . . and crying. If that was not true, that could greatly affect your determination here, isn't that correct?"

"It could affect my determination, yes."

What Schick was leading up to, clearly, was that Odell's confession could have been coerced—that maybe she never had said the babies had cried or coughed to begin with, and Baden was basing a major portion of his *opinion* on a situation that actually had never occurred.

Reasonable doubt. It was Schick's job.

Next Schick tried to dismantle Lungen's argument that there had been a towel in one of the babies' mouths.

"For example, in that one baby, if there was never any towel in the mouth at the time of the birth, that's a significant item of information you used and you no longer have, isn't that correct?"

"Yes," Baden answered.

"That wouldn't possibly change your determination of asphyxia?"

"If you were only dealing with the one baby, Baby Number One," Baden replied.

"I'm taking one at a time?"

"One at a time. If I'm told that the mom says, 'There is a towel in the mouth,' given the fact that the baby is full-term and there is no other competing cause of death, that would be sufficient for me, by itself, to make a diagnosis of asphyxia."

For about a half hour, Baden and Schick went back and forth, discussing how Baden had determined cause and manner of death. At one point, Baden agreed that part of his opinion had been based on Odell's confession. After that, Schick attacked how the babies had been stored in boxes for twenty or more years and how the heat might have been responsible for deteriorating their bodies enough to corrupt any forensic investigation. And wasn't it possible, Schick suggested, that being in those boxes all that time, wrapped in towels and blankets, traveling around the country, one of the babies could have ended up with a towel in its mouth?

Baden agreed it was a possibility—but highly unlikely.

"You made assumptions based upon the accuracy and the truthfulness of those statements," Schick asked at one point, "isn't that correct?"

"Yes, based on what was written down, but also based on my interpretation of the findings that these statements were consistent with the findings of the baby."

In other words, Baden went back and tried to corroborate part of what Odell had said in her statement to see if all of the information added up.

"But you weren't present when the statements were being made, is that correct?"

"That's correct."

"You don't know the circumstances under which the statements were made, isn't that correct?" Schick posed.

"That's correct."

Was a medical examiner supposed to be in the same room with a suspect when he or she was interviewed? Was that what Schick was asking the jury to believe? Or, was he merely making a point that for the jury to understand the *entire* case, it had to take into account the mere notion that some of the statements Odell had given to police might have been coerced?

"And you are a colleague of those police personnel, wouldn't that be fair to say?" Schick asked.

"Of some. Yes, yes."

In the end, it was up to each juror to draw a conclusion as to whether the statement Odell had given police had been bullied out of her. The problem, when it came down to it, though, was that Odell had signed the statement, and by doing that, she agreed with every word BCI investigator Roy Streever had typed.

After a series of questions based on Baden's actual role in the investigation process as the case developed, Schick became sarcastic and quite patronizing, perhaps trying to rattle the good doctor.

"Did you want to know at the time of the birth"—he stopped, thought a minute—"Withdrawn. Would you agree with me that childbirth is painful? Is *that* difficult? I know you have to *think* a little!"

Baden didn't crack. Instead, he ignored the insult and remained calm. "It can be painful. However, I've been involved with many situations in which childbirth was concealed and it's amazing how, to me, how a woman, young girls often . . . not wanting the mom in the next room to hear about it, keep quiet and the mom may not know about it. The answer is, childbirth itself *is* painful. But there may be *other* emotional factors that are more significant in giving birth to a child without anybody in the household knowing it."

It was an image, perhaps, Schick didn't want the jury to have. He hadn't followed the one golden rule trial attorneys generally live by: don't ask a question you don't know the answer to. Baden had, with one answer, given the jury a scenario that could have taken place in the Odell-Molina household.

Schick was a bit dismayed. "Then just humor me," he said as if he were playing stupid.

"Sorry?" Baden said. He didn't understand.

"*Humor* me! If I suggest, without all of the things that you said, I suggest the childbirth is painful, I have not done it, okay?"

"You and I would have the same experience, yes."

For the next hour, the two men traded verbal jabs; Schick the aggressor, trying to get Baden to expound on different hypothetical scenarios that could have taken place. Ultimately, the jury sat through a discussion of theory and happenstance. Where were the facts? Where was Schick's smoking gun?

Schick talked about stillbirth for a time, and then launched into a debate regarding how a father's medical history could play a role possibly in a woman having a stillborn child. Could that have happened here?

Interestingly, no mention of Mabel was broached as Schick then worked into a discussion of midwives. He was hoping, maybe, that the jury would at least question the statement Odell had given police. It was, at last, his only real potential loophole in Lungen's case.

After Lungen objected several times to Schick's line of questioning, noting time and again that many of the questions were "hypotheticals" and had no place in the trial, Schick asked Baden, "Is it possible for a baby to be born and never take a breath?"

Lungen stood. "I object to the question—*anything* is possible!"

After the judge allowed him, Baden explained that the term Schick was referring to was "stillborn."

A moment later, after a heated discussion over Baden's determination that a lack of prenatal care would greatly affect the health of a baby at birth, Baden said it was his opinion that, in Odell's case, it was a "minor factor. It's the *concealment* of the pregnancy that's more of significance to me."

"And, of course, concealment *is* an issue," Schick said. "But you don't know 'the why' of the concealment, isn't that correct?"

"I know 'the why' that the mom told police," Baden said firmly.

"Well, you know what the police told you what she said, isn't that correct?"

Lungen bowed his head in disgust. *Come on, don't be ridiculous.*

Baden remained composed. "Yes," he said softly.

"Again, you were not present?"

"Yes. That's correct."

Schick asked the judge if he could have a moment.

"Mr. Schick, do you have any more questions of the doctor?"

"No, sir."

3

On redirect examination, Lungen brought the case back into his world of fact-finding, leaving hypotheticals and theories aside. Baden was a forensic pathologist who had worked in the field for forty-plus years. He had offered his opinion as to how the babies had died, based on all of the evidence he had collected. In the reports Baden read, he never viewed anything, he said, about a midwife or an umbilical cord being wrapped around any of the babies' necks, as Schick had implied near the end of his cross-examination. Furthermore, the medical facts he'd uncovered never pointed to such things.

On recross-examination, Schick once again tried to debunk Baden's way of coming up with a cause and manner of death, but Baden simply stated the facts as he saw them: traumatic asphyxia. That was his opinion. *Traumatic asphyxia.* He was sticking to it. Schick could

say whatever he wanted and speculate and come up
with different theories, but Baden's determination—
and how he came about it—wasn't going to change.

Baden's testimony ended what turned out to be a
long day for everyone. Court TV certainly had some
great footage to air, and Schick thought he had done
a decent job of giving the jury a second scenario to
consider. Yet, if Odell was going to testify, which she
was beginning to think was her only chance at freedom, the case Schick was rebutting on cross-examination had nothing to do with the abuse Odell claimed
to have suffered, or the idea that Mabel murdered the
children.

The following day, December 10, was sure to bring
more heated debate. Thomas Scileppi and Roy
Streever were set to take the stand. Schick promised
he was going to, line by line, dissect the statement
Odell had given to Scileppi and Streever.

But before Scileppi could take the stand, Lungen
called David Dandignac.

Dandignac gave the jury a complete picture of his
rather impressive credentials as a poultry grader for
the Department of Agriculture. He had been working
for the government for sixteen years. He was married,
had two boys from a previous marriage, and his current wife had three children of her own. All five children lived with Dandignac and his wife. Ultimately,
Dandignac could only say he had dated Odell, but
when she got pregnant with his child, the relationship
soured, and he believed when they split, she was going
to get an abortion. He said he offered her money to
support the child, but she refused.

To cover any potential testimony later on from
Odell, regarding her relationship with Mabel, Lungen
was smart to ask Dandignac how he viewed the relationship between Odell and Mabel. After all, he had
lived in the same house with both of them.

"How would you characterize her relationship with her mother?"

"I thought it was . . . I thought it was good," Dandignac said.

"How would you characterize, if you had to describe, her mother, Mabel? How would you describe her?"

"Well, as far as I . . . For me, I thought she was a nice lady."

"Was there any kind of volatile arguments; was it a volatile relationship in the house between mother and daughter . . . ?"

"I don't think it was volatile, but . . . No, I mean, there were days where, you know, something would happen or, you know, something—"

"That would be the kind of stuff you would see normally with people living together?"

"That's what I would say."

"Nothing extraordinary. Is that what you're saying?"

"I don't think so."

"Did Mabel appear to you to be an overbearing kind of woman is what I am really asking you?"

"Not . . . not all the time. I mean, she would have times where she might say something or do something, but overall I don't think so."

After Lungen finished, Schick stood and walked slowly toward Dandignac. For the first few moments, they discussed the relationship Dandignac shared with Odell. Then Schick asked him if it was possible that Odell had tried to hide her pregnancy from anyone.

Dandignac said no, not that he knew of.

From there, they discussed Odell's financial situation at the time and how she was, basically, a struggling single mother.

By the end of Schick's cross-examination, he managed

to get Dandignac to admit he had left Odell when she was pregnant and never returned to inquire how she was doing, or if she'd even had the child.

Lungen had Dandignac explain on redirect examination how, when he left Odell, he never saw any reason to return because he honestly had believed she was going to abort the pregnancy. It was just one more way for Lungen to prove that during each pregnancy there was no man in Odell's life around to question whether she'd had the baby. In effect, she could kill each child because there was no one around to question whether the child had been born—that is, except Mabel.

CHAPTER 30

1

INVESTIGATOR THOMAS SCILEPPI was looking at a grilling from Stephan Schick regarding the statement he took from Odell. According to Scileppi, Odell admitted hearing the babies "cough" and "cry." She'd even said there was a towel in one of the babies' mouths. Yet, if Schick had his way, the jury would understand that the statement was in Scileppi and Roy Streever's words, *not* Odell's.

Lungen, on direct examination, had Scileppi go through the entire investigation and explain how he ended up in Waverly questioning Odell. There were no surprises in Scileppi's testimony, and he came across rather diplomatic and knowledgeable, never hesitating, always sure of his answers. Scileppi had been an investigator, with an untarnished record, for seventeen years.

Eventually Scileppi described a woman who was quite willing to talk about how three of her dead children ended up in boxes in an Arizona self-storage facility. At one point, he even insisted Odell wanted to purge her soul of what was, he believed, a great emotional burden.

He felt she needed to admit to the crimes so she could finally come to terms with what she had done. When asked what should happen to her, Scileppi said, Odell admitted she thought she "should go to jail."

Schick later had some rather strong opinions regarding tactical approach and how law enforcement go about obtaining statements from suspects—especially in Odell's case. There was no question Odell willingly had signed the statement Scileppi and Streever had prepared. The question was: why would she sign a statement she knew to be false?

"The legal answer is, if you ask for a lawyer and don't get one," Schick said, "okay, obviously, if they are going to keep [questioning you] forever until you sign a statement, you're going to sign it eventually. There's a feeling that a lot of this Miranda stuff (meaning, reading a suspect her rights) is a lot of baloney. . . ." Moreover, Schick said, when you have "all these cops marching into a courtroom" and telling a jury how a suspect's rights were not violated, "it makes what the defendant said in her statement all the more harmful.

"From a defense standpoint," Schick continued, "you know, people have guilt. Even if people kill somebody and it's not murder, they can feel guilty. I think you're naive if you think that under all the facts and circumstances of the taking of [Odell's] confession, the police didn't manipulate. She had been questioned for hours and hours, for three days. I mean, there reaches a point where a person becomes very malleable. And they could put words that they'll sign—this particular confession or statement she gave, I mean, a word here or there could change the whole flavor of it. *They* are the ones who are writing it! The New York police know they can manipulate and they do! I'm sure if they recorded everything she had said, it wouldn't have come out like that written statement."

Would a cop, however, suffice it to say with Scileppi's

reputation and standing, hold someone "hostage," until she gave in and signed a statement of guilt? It seemed unlikely. The investigation, at the time Scileppi first met Odell, had just begun. Why would Scileppi (or anyone else working the case) push so hard that early on in the investigation? It didn't seem reasonable.

"Cops don't have to do that. . . . They don't have to beat people or torture people. They are experts at psychologically manipulating people, and I don't put it past them to rub her back and be sympathetic, holding her hand. And to Scileppi's credit, I think if he was the . . . judge, I think he believes [Odell] was pathetic."

The problem Schick faced, however, he explained, was that "you could have all the sympathy in the world for Miss Odell, but four babies are dead and that didn't have to happen. We have to have a society where the birth of children is an extremely important concept and important event. A tragedy is if one or two babies died. Yet, if a person keeps doing something, by repetition, in such an important event that they know that more care has to be taken and they refuse to do it, who is responsible?"

Nevertheless, it was Schick's job to attack Scileppi and possibly get him to admit he had somehow coerced Odell into saying those things in her statement—a statement, incidentally, the jury would be reading during deliberations.

By day's end, Scileppi, along with his partner, Roy Streever, never cracked. They stood firm on what Odell's statement had confirmed. Regardless how hard Schick pushed, he couldn't get either one of them to admit they had coerced Odell or put words in her mouth.

At times, Schick became heated and animated, badgering each witness, but both men, seasoned cops who had taken the stand dozens of times as part of their jobs, spoke with an articulate, intelligent, and calming temperament. Odell had said she heard the babies cry, gasp for air, and cough. She had read the statement and signed it. To Scileppi and Streever, what more was there to discuss?

Next witness.

Near the end of testimony on day three, the jury was able to hear from Odell as a redacted transcript of the tape-recorded interview on May 17, 2003, with Diane Thomas and Bruce Weddle, was read aloud. The following day, December 11, the remainder of the transcript was read before Lungen put his final witness, Investigator Robert Lane, on the stand.

Lane reiterated what Scileppi and Streever had said already, but added one solid bit of information missing from the trial thus far: motive. He testified that Odell had said the children were "bastards" at one point in his conversation with her, and she had kept the pregnancies hidden from Mabel for that reason. It was the first time the jury had been given an explanation as to why Odell would have killed the children— to hide the pregnancies from her overbearing mother, whom she told police she was terrified of.

After Lane testified, the judge ordered the notes Lane had taken during his interview with Odell, where he had specifically written the word "bastards," be redacted to conform to the Huntley ruling that barred the jury from knowing anything about the 1989 case. When that was done, the jury was asked to step out of the room for a time.

Lungen indicated he was prepared to rest his case. With that, the judge asked Schick if he needed any time before calling his first witness.

"Judge, actually," Schick said, "I would like to be able to talk to Miss Odell in the conference room here. Ultimately, it's up to her if I call witnesses and who they might be."

Odell, twirling her rosary beads, looked on and nodded.

The judge said okay.

It was nearing noon, a good time to break for lunch. The jury was brought back into the courtroom and Lungen officially rested his case. Then the judge ordered everyone back at 12:30 P.M., whereby Stephan Schick would begin presenting his case.

According to Odell, after the judge called a recess, she and Schick walked into the conference room and sat down. It was cold, the winter air from outside bleeding underneath a tiny opening in the bottom of the door. Odell took a seat next to Schick, and at first, she said, she just stared at him, waiting for his advice.

"I think I have done a very good job of punching holes in this case," Odell recalled Schick telling her. "I really don't think you need to testify."

"Okay, what happens if I *don't* testify?"

"Well, if you don't testify, we don't have to put the psychologist on the stand." Schick was referring to Janet Hooke, a psychologist who had interviewed Odell several times. Schick was convinced, he said later, that Hooke's testimony wouldn't do anything to help Odell. "Furthermore," he added, "that fourth child doesn't come into play."

Odell said she stared at Schick at that point. "I wasn't even worried about the fourth child coming into the trial," she noted later. "Because Lungen had already put it out in the newspapers, so the jury knew about it, anyway. What the hell was I worried about?"

Schick later said that as an attorney, he had to believe when the jury was questioned during voir dire about the 1989 baby, they were being honest as to their knowledge regarding it. He couldn't "assume" they knew about the baby and shape his case around that theory. It wasn't a professional way to go about trying a case that could have such damning effects on his client.

"Does that mean," Odell said she asked Schick next, "everything I talked about with Janet would be put out on the stand?"

"Yes," she recalled Schick telling her.

"At this time," Odell said later, recalling that day, "even though I was beginning to open up about a lot of things that had happened, there were still very many issues that I had not addressed. And I really didn't want that sitting in black and white in a newspaper before I had a chance to come to terms with it."

When Odell heard Schick's answer regarding Janet Hooke on the witness stand, likely airing all of Odell's past experiences, she said, "Okay, then I don't think I'm going to testify . . . but, can we use the other people?"

"Okay," Schick answered, according to Odell later, "if that's what you want to do."

"Let me go to lunch," Odell said, "and let me think about it."

Odell claimed if she could "do this" without getting on the stand herself, it was something she was interested in pursuing.

Schick was deferential toward Odell's feelings about how to proceed with her defense, but he insisted that putting anyone else on the stand besides Odell would not have helped her case. It would have hurt it, more than anything. Proving Odell was abused as a child was fine, but it still didn't address the main theory of Lungen's case: Dianne Odell had murdered the children.

Odell believed the information her half brother could present to the jury—and she admitted she didn't know the extent of all the information—would have helped her defense raise reasonable doubt. However, Schick still didn't want to use it.

"That's not what Schick said to me," Odell claimed later. "He told me that the information my brother had would ultimately help me."

"I could have put her on the witness stand and we could have argued until the cows came home about her abusive childhood," Schick said later, "but how far does that take you? Does that give you license . . . or does that give you ability to have four dead children and it doesn't mean anything, it doesn't matter?"

When court resumed after lunch, the judge looked at Schick and asked, "Does the defense choose to call any witnesses?"

Odell thought it was odd, she said later, that when she walked into the courtroom, her family was sitting in back of the defense table. She knew something was wrong at that point.

To the amazement of nearly everyone in the courtroom—including Odell, who claimed later she had no idea Schick was going to do it; she said she thought they were going to make a decision together—Schick simply said, "No, Your Honor."

In effect, Schick was resting his case without calling one witness.

"He played both sides against the middle," Odell said. "He told my family I wanted to rest and told me my family wanted *me* to rest."

To his credit, Schick vehemently denied ever doing that.

Nevertheless, the judge then explained to the jury that Schick had chosen not to call any witnesses, which meant "the evidentiary portion of the trial" was over. Closing arguments would follow.

It would be a few days before closing arguments, though. The court had several matters to take care of with Lungen and Schick. Until then, jurors were asked not to discuss the case.

CHAPTER 31

1

STEPHAN SCHICK HAD a job ahead of him. He needed to convince a jury that Odell hadn't killed her children, but was perhaps a victim of abuse by her "ex-husband, parents, and other men in her life," he said. This was one of the reasons why her children ended up dead. He had to do this, however, despite not putting one witness on the stand.

"First, was there proof beyond a reasonable doubt," Schick asked in an unthreatening, soft tone as he began addressing the jury during his closing argument, raising his hand, using three separate fingers to count off his points, "that these babies were born alive? Second, was there proof . . . that Dianne was guilty of *intentional* murder? Third, was there proof . . . Dianne Odell was guilty of *depraved*-indifference murder?"

Principally, Schick focused on the one fact he thought Lungen had failed to prove: that the babies had been born alive. And if the jury believed the children were stillborn, well, there was no chance Odell could have murdered them.

"If they were not born alive, this is not a murder

case—period!" After a pause, Schick then began an attack on Dr. Baden. "He testified that there was no medical or scientific evidence he was aware of that he could say the babies were born alive." Next, in a patronizing, almost angry manner—as if to suggest Baden was some sort of wild-haired, wacky scientist—mocking Baden's own words, Schick said, "'Well, what do I believe? What do I believe from what other people are telling me?' That may be fine," he continued more seriously, "in a classroom or at a university . . . but that's *not* where we are."

He asked the jury to consider the prosecution's supposed "expert" testimony and weigh it thoroughly: fact or opinion?

There was an "alternate" theory, Schick said, for what happened to those babies and why Odell toted them around with her for so long—other than Odell being a murderer.

"She didn't want to part with these babies."

Next he continued berating Baden, calling him "bias[ed]" and "un-independent." He essentially asked the jury to withdraw his testimony and concentrate on the facts.

"It's not a crime to have a baby at home. Does it immediately jump to murder if you have a baby at home and the baby doesn't live?"

It was a good point, made by a competent attorney with decades of experience, who had taken on a case, he knew from the onset, that was nearly impossible to win.

He said Odell carried the babies around with her from state to state, for twenty-plus years, because "she couldn't bear to part with them."

Finally, "Her children are the only thing in her life that ever loved her back," he concluded with an odd sense of contentment in his voice. It was clear he believed wholeheartedly in what he was saying. "I am begging you to send this woman back to her children."

2

In a courtroom, Steve Lungen spoke loudly, with authority. He liked to use his hands to explain things, and was well-known for using graphics and charts to accentuate the underlying themes of the cases he tried.

Thus, on the afternoon of December 15, 2003, as Lungen's closing argument in the *People of the State of New York* v. *Dianne Odell* began, a projection on the screen in the courtroom stared back at jurors. As Lungen began to wrap up a case he firmly believed he had proven beyond a reasonable doubt, there was a sign that, in his view, explained it all:

> A **MOTHER** WHO GIVES BIRTH TO **8** HEALTHY CHILDREN IN HOSPITALS <u>DOES NOT</u> HIDE **3** ADDITIONAL PREGNANCIES; CONCEAL THEIR BIRTHS; REFER TO THEM AS THE "**BASTARD** CHILDREN"; DELIVER THEM ALONE, AT HOME, IN THE **BATHROOM**; PACK THEM IN BOXES (TO PREVENT THEIR DECOMPOSING BODIES FROM LEAKING OUT); **HIDE THEM** AWAY IN CLOSETS AND ATTICS AND SHEDS . . . AND CARRY THEM WITH HER, FROM STATE TO STATE, ACROSS THE COUNTRY *** TO **PREVENT** THEIR DISCOVERY *** FOR **20** YEARS
>
> **UNLESS SHE MURDERED THEM**

The message was there to remind jurors of the facts in the case and the circumstantial evidence that seemed particularly damaging to Odell as it sat there, gnawing at everyone, begging jurors to try to focus on what the "circumstances" surrounding the deaths of the children explained. Lungen knew he couldn't let jurors forget how indicative each set of circumstances in Odell's many pregnancies were to the totality of the case. Nor could he allow himself to fail to make the jury aware of the unadorned fact that the law protected all victims, regardless of age, creed, color, race, ethnicity, or—most important—*relation* to the accused.

"I don't have the luxury, as prosecutor, to talk to you about things that are speculative, things that—by guesswork—were never testified to on the witness stand," Lungen said after introducing himself. ". . . Much of what Mr. Schick told you about this afternoon was fiction-based."

Lungen had a burning desire from the beginning of the case to represent the three babies who, he said, never had a chance at life and, in death, had no one to speak for them.

"The added pressure is that I am here talking for three babies and there is no one—*no one here but me*—to talk to you about these three babies. And I feel that. Make no mistake about it."

As he twisted one of his cuff links and steepled his hands in front of his face, Lungen paused before continuing. Using graphics once again, he put up a second exhibit on the overhead projector introducing jurors to each one of the children.

"I want to introduce you to Baby Number One. . . . Today he would be twenty-one years old. [And] . . . Miss Baby Dandignac [Baby Number Three], she would be eighteen today. And we know Mr. Baby [Number Two], he would be age twenty. There's nothing abstract about these babies. They were real!" Then he hit the podium with his fist: "They were born alive."

From there, Lungen went on to quote one of the nation's most esteemed and noted presidents. Slowly putting on his glasses, looking down at his notes, "Abraham Lincoln said, 'All that I am, of ever hope to be, I owe to my angel mother.'"

Then, later, "Feel sorry for *her*?" he yelled with

energy. "I would . . . if she didn't *kill* three of her babies."

Pointing to the overhead projector screen, then turning and looking at jurors, once again Lungen said that the babies were real people.

"They existed. And they were born alive. . . . Should you cry for the defendant? I leave that to you. She cries for herself. She tells you she cries for these babies. You can fool me once. You can try to fool me twice. But I'm no *damn* fool the third time."

With a commanding presence, he didn't miss a beat, recapping just about every major aspect of his case.

"Fool me once, shame on *you.* Fool me twice, shame on *me.* But I say to you: Fool *us* three times, and shame on all of us. The defendant, by the evidence, is nothing less than a serial killer and murderer of babies."

Further along, "Odell hid the babies to hide her crimes, and carried them with her so no one would find out what she had done.

"She talks about ringing in her ears," he shouted. "The screaming in her ears she's telling you about, that's the screaming of those babies. She's been hearing it for two decades."

Ending what could be called a rather animated, yet at the same time intense and blunt closing argument, Lungen quoted Pulitzer Prize–winning poet Carl Sandburg: "'A baby is God's opinion that the world should go on.' Ladies and gentlemen," he said before pausing a moment and lowering his voice, "do not let this defendant defy God's opinion by ending the lives of three of God's children."

The courtroom was silent. It had been the first time, save for Odell twirling and twisting rosary beads in her hand and mumbling silent prayers to herself, that anyone had looked at the situation through a pious lens.

In the end, Lungen's final argument was everything a closing should have been: terse, direct, emotional.

Judge LaBuda instructed the jury on the law. It was late in the day.

Then, "I will resume tomorrow morning at eight-thirty. You are going to be kept, as we talked about, sequestered. . . ." From there, he warned jurors that they were not entering into deliberations yet. "It would be a disservice to everyone, including yourselves, so please don't discuss this case amongst yourselves this evening. Don't discuss this case with anyone."

After the jury left the courtroom, the judge asked if there was anything else.

"Yes, Your Honor," Schick said, and stood.

"What do you have, Mr. Schick?"

"Judge, I would request a mistrial based upon the impropriety contained in the prosecution's closing statement that included . . . vouching for the police. Identifying the police action as 'we in law enforcement' and 'we were this and we were that, the police did nothing wrong.'"

Schick continued, accusing Lungen of stating numerous inconsistent statements that were simply untrue in his opinion, thus painting a bias portrait of Odell and implying that if she had given birth to the three babies in a hospital, they would have survived.

"Finally," Schick continued, "concluding his statement . . . [Lungen sat down and left] the poster up while the court was giving the instructions to the jury . . . his misleading poster of what the defendant *allegedly* said or meant. For all those reasons, I respectfully request the court declare a mistrial."

When Lungen had his chance to speak, he said he had based his argument on the credibility of police officers. "There is nothing in what Mr. Schick said that is the basis for any mistrial whatsoever."

"Mr. Schick," the judge said kindly, "your application is denied. The main reason Mr. Lungen's comments were in fair response [is that they were] part of the ebb and flow of a summation in a very emotional case."

3

The following afternoon, December 16, Odell walked into the courtroom and, as usual, took a seat next to Schick and Havas. It was time to learn her fate. After five hours of deliberations, the jury had come to a decision. Since the start of trial, which had lasted a total of four days, Odell looked like she'd aged ten years. With her knit sweater, button-up dress shirt, olive skin, penciled-in-looking, thin, dark eyebrows, and salt-and-pepper hair, she resembled actress Bea Arthur during her days on the hit '70s sitcom *Maude*.

As the jury foreperson stood, Odell appeared nervous and shaky as Schick put his arm around her shoulder to comfort her.

"Not guilty."

There was a sigh of relief on Odell's side of the room. On three counts of intentional murder, she had been found not guilty. Could it be? Was Odell going home?

Lungen looked stunned. *What?*

"That first not guilty on the first count, intentional murder, I think that made some butts tighten on the prosecution side," Heather Yakin said later. "Dianne was pretty emotional throughout the trial. . . . [She] actually reacted to things in appropriate ways, crying when the babies were mentioned or shown, stuff like that. Lungen, of course, thought it was all an act. I don't think anything in the case was that simple. I think Odell probably did have a horrible life, and I'm sure she loves all of her living kids. That said, I don't know what really happened during those births. I think deep down, Dianne knows, but I can't decide if she's ever admitted it to herself."

But then the jury finished reading its verdict: "Guilty." On three counts of depraved-indifference murder, the jury had found Odell guilty.

Schick bowed his head and began rubbing his forehead, squeezing Odell tightly as she seemed to be in shock. And as the jury read its official verdict on each count, she broke down as Clarissa, who had stood behind her mother throughout the entire trial, ran out of the courtroom crying.

So it was. Odell had been judged by her peers in a court of law. As she left the courtroom in handcuffs, she turned and stared at Robert Sauerstein and her children and said, "Don't cry, guys. I love you."

4

It would be a little over a month before Odell learned how long she would be spending in prison. Some in town thought the judge might spare her hard time and grant her probation and time served. Several "Letters to the Editor" published in area newspapers supported Odell. Some residents, who had followed every detail of the trial, believed she had been wrongly convicted.

"Odell deserved better," wrote one woman.

"I can't get Odell out of [my] mind," said another.

"Have mercy on Odell," yet another.

The prevailing feeling among the many females who had chimed in after the trial was that prison was no place for a woman who had been abused by her mother and father. What was it that had sparked such support for a convicted baby killer?

On January 8, 2004, Heather Yakin finally got that exclusive interview she had been hoping for throughout the entire ordeal. As it turned out, it wasn't with a long-lost relative who could bring forth startling information that would send the case into a whirlwind, or one of the fathers of the babies—but Odell herself.

It was time, Odell decided while waiting in jail to be sentenced, to tell her side of the story—a side, incidentally, she was now fuming that she had never gotten to tell jurors.

Headlined ODELL'S DARK TALE, the question-and-answer interview detailed, in Odell's words, her "abusive" upbringing by her mom and dad. She spoke of the same horrors she had been telling Schick about all along, sticking to her story that she'd had nothing to do with killing her babies. The article gave the community a clear portrait of Odell's supposed abusive life—something, she had said over and over since her conviction, she had never been given the opportunity to do in court.

After that, Odell spoke to Court TV and gave it an exclusive interview, again detailing her childhood. She shed tear after tear talking to Court TV, which would later run the interview in pieces during its airing of the trial.

Was it all enough to convince the judge to go easy on her? Like Odell, the community was about to find out.

5

January 27, 2004, was a clear, cold day in Monticello, averaging about ten degrees Fahrenheit. Since the close of the trial, Schick had filed a motion to get the verdict thrown out. It was a formality. Lawyers did it because the law said they could.

"By the way of preliminary matters," the judge said,

opening court, "Mr. Schick, your application to set aside the verdict is denied. The court will publish a written decision shortly." The judge then paused, looked down at some paperwork in front of him. Then, "Miss Odell?"

"Yes?"

"You will have the opportunity to say something if you want to. . . ."

"Yes, I do, Your Honor."

". . . after your attorney speaks."

"Thank you."

Proscecutor Lungen then stood and rubbed his chin, thinking deeply about what he wanted to say. "I would normally make a straight-up recommendation to you, or position, with respect to this case," Lungen began, "but since the verdict, there's been some intervening events I think are . . . at least I feel compelled to comment on a little bit."

Above all, Lungen was concerned about the interview Odell had given to Heather Yakin and the *Times Herald-Record*. It had been bothering him.

". . . Of course, *now* she's telling the truth as to what happened with respect to the babies and she claims she was kept off the witness stand by her attorneys because they didn't want [Baby Doe] to be brought out. But I don't think I can allow that to just stand by itself because the real truth is, or part of the truth at least, is that she didn't testify because she knew there would be cross-examination, and cross-examination could very well expose much of what she said in that newspaper article . . . because while it's headlined ODELL'S DARK TALE, it seems to portray throughout that she is the victim and that this represents what really happened."

Talking about the article seemed to open some sort of wound for Lungen he thought he'd closed. Nearly two months now since the Odell trial ended, he was involved in other cases, other trials. With that article, Odell obviously had wanted to do what she had been doing all along: change her story in respect to an outcome she didn't agree with.

Lungen carried on for about fifteen minutes, restating his entire case and how the jury had come to its verdict based on facts, not speculation and hindsight.

After he finished, Schick stood with Odell by his side and asked the court to "sanction that the remains of the babies be turned over to [Sauerstein and the family] for burial."

It was an odd request made at what some might consider to be an inappropriate time, seeing that Odell was about to be sentenced for murdering three of her children. Had she suddenly cared about them now? She'd had two-and-a-half-decades to bury them. Why now?

"The people would like to be heard on that, Your Honor," Lungen said, standing.

The judge tabled the issue for another time.

Schick then argued for a light sentence based on the fact that Odell wasn't a threat to society at large. She should be home with her children. They needed her.

"Thank you," the judge said. "Miss Dianne Odell, do you wish to say anything at this time?"

"Yes."

Odell was upset, she claimed, because the entire process had made her out to be some sort of monster. "Circumstances have been turned around," she said with emotion. ". . . For what I hope is the last time in my life, I will say that I *did not* kill my children. I believe that all the suffering I have gone through, that this is just a continuation of that suffering."

She then went on to talk about being locked up in an emotional jail her entire adult life. She hadn't deserved it. It wasn't her fault. "I would like to know," she asked, "when does my suffering end and when do I finally get out of jail?"

It was a bold statement, made especially more potent by the notion that the judge was going to be sentencing her when she was finished. Judges like to hear convicted murderers take responsibility for their crimes. But Odell was being defiant to the end, stating her disgust in the system.

"I will not apologize for not making conscious, educated decisions," she continued, ending her statement, "but I will say that I hope one day truth and justice will set me free. Thank you."

The judge sat back for a moment. "Thank you, Miss Odell," he said. Then, "Truth and justice was *achieved* during the course of this trial! . . . There *was* a 'dark tale,' Miss Odell, a *dark* tale that you created, a *dark* tale that brought us to the trial into the depth of human indifference, human immorality, human depravity toward life."

The gallery sat back. Eyes opened. Jaws dropped.

The judge further explained how the birth and death of Baby Doe would be "considered for sentencing purposes." Then he talked about the deaths of the three babies she had been tried (and convicted) for, saying, ". . . Your statement, the defendant's statement in the presentence report, alluded to a tale of truth you *now* wish to tell. Miss Odell, it defies common sense and reality. You were given the opportunity by several police officers . . . to tell the truth. You told them what you wanted to tell and it doesn't make *any* difference to me because a jury has spoken. . . ."

Judge LaBuda was obviously taken aback by Odell's bold stance. One might even assume—and rightly so—he felt as if Odell had insulted him.

Ultimately, Judge LaBuda sentenced Odell to life imprisonment with a minimum of fifteen years for Baby Number One, life imprisonment with a minimum of

twenty years for Baby Number Two, and life imprisonment with a minimum of twenty-five years for Baby
Number Three. Clearly, regardless of what Odell
thought, the judge had taken the matters of three dead
babies extremely seriously.

"These sentences are to run concurrently. . . ."

And then, perhaps, the harshest words a judge
could have bestowed on a convicted murderer rang
throughout the courtroom.

"Miss Odell, I know during the course of the trial you
were praying and reciting the rosary. I hope you take
this opportunity to prepare for your final judgment
when you will have to account for the four babies." He
paused, as if to allow the weight of what he had just
said weigh on Odell, but she just stood and cried.

"This matter is concluded."

Gavel.

6

Stephan Schick was never convinced his client had
murdered her children. He fought for her freedom
as best he could and, suffice it to say, in the end was
dissatisfied with the way things had turned out. "Listen
to what she's saying," Schick recalled later, looking back
on the case. "If she intended to murder these children,
number one, she would have had an abortion. I mean,
why go through the pain of childbirth to murder
them at childbirth? What's the point? You can do it
legally! Why risk childbirth at home, risking your *own*
life, because you want to murder them at childbirth—
it doesn't make any sense at all. I tried to argue to the
jury that this person did not obviously want the children to die. That her actions are of a horribly ignorant and misguided person."

In a sense, Schick had won that argument, because

the jury hadn't found Odell guilty of intentional murder.

Toting the babies around for twenty years, Schick concluded, "shows that something is wrong with her mind. But the greatest tragedy of the entire thing is, she doesn't even see it. There's a lot of self-pity there, and she doesn't see it for what it is."

EPILOGUE

AS I SPOKE with Dianne Odell and got to know her better, I sensed that some of the stories she told me had become a version of the facts based on what she *wished* had happened—that is, only if she could go back and change the past. One such scene in the book takes place at the Towanda State Police barracks in Pennsylvania while Odell is being fingerprinted. When we first spoke, Odell told me a version of what happened that day. Later, as we were going back and discussing her story again, she told me a second version that was, basically, the same as the first, but had a few additional memories attached to it that, in my opinion, further promoted her latest version of the truth. To believe Odell, one would have to agree that three investigators with over sixty years of cumulative law experience lied about the same event and then testified in a court of law about it, thus committing perjury.

Is it possible? Sure. Is it probable? No. There was no reason for law enforcement to lie about such an event. This was not an investigation with any time constraints on it. There was no serial killer running loose with the clock ticking. It was, essentially, only the fifth day of the investigation. There was not enough information available for law enforcement even to be certain Odell had done anything.

Stephan Schick posed a question to me when I interviewed him: "Do you think cops don't coerce suspects and put words into their mouths and break them down over a period of days?" he asked.

The thought had crossed my mind. I've interviewed scores of cops over the years and not all of them have been completely truthful. In this case, however, the facts supported Investigators Thomas Scileppi, Roy Streever, and Robert Lane's testimony. The question of whether they badgered Odell and pushed her into a confession only became an issue later, when Odell wanted to take back what she had admitted to.

Odell went to the police station not once or twice, but *three* times, voluntarily, without a lawyer. She obviously wanted to talk about what had happened.

I ended up using all three versions of that interview: the two Odell told me and the one from the record. Furthermore, there are five sources for this scene: three are law enforcement, one who has been convicted of murdering three of her children, and one fathered five of Odell's eight living children.

As I went back and listened to some of Odell's stories on tape, they seemed convincing at first. As I learned more about the case, studying documents, interviewing other people, I began to see her stories under a different light. Holes began to appear in them. Time and again, Odell would call me with an incredible story. But when I tried to contact people who could back up what she was saying, I found they were either dead or wouldn't respond to my letters and/or phone calls. The only person who could corroborate the stories was Odell herself.

Much further into my interviews with Odell, out of nowhere, she said to me one night, "Everybody has made the assumption that when my father hit me, he was drunk." She had told me several stories where her father was drunk and raped her and beat her up. "My father was drunk," she continued that night, "*once*, and beat the shit out of me *once* while he was drunk. The rest of the time when he hit me, he was stone-cold sober."

I have no idea why she told me this. But I suspect it was in response to her learning the previous week that I had interviewed her brother Richard Molina. Moreover, there was an anger in her voice that night I had never heard before. It was a part of Odell I had not experienced inside of our months of conversations. She was seemingly a different person—a much colder, darker person who believed her father was responsible for the life she led.

"When he got drunk, there was a whole different set of rules he lived by," she concluded.

At times, she would call and tell me how much she despised Stephan Schick for not doing his job. Partly because of him, she felt her life was now made up of walls, steel bars, barbed wire, and emptiness. She wanted people to understand that she was abused. She wanted someone to acknowledge that the abuse she suffered did things to her mind. And it was Schick's job, in her view, to get that information to the jury.

I agree—Odell had been abused. There's evidence of it beyond her words. But did that abuse give her a license to kill? This was the question she failed to answer. To me or the jury.

As of this writing, Odell sits in Bedford Hills Correctional Facility for Women in Bedford Hills, New York, awaiting word on her appeal. She claims to have several issues her new appellate lawyers will argue successfully, which will grant her a new trial.

In my view, Odell doesn't belong in prison. She

should be in a hospital, where she can sift through her memories and come to some sort of finality with what has happened. I believe there is still a part of her that wants to claim responsibility for the crimes she was convicted of. I could hear it in her voice when we spoke. I'm convinced she wants to accept part of the blame, yet at the same time ask everyone to believe it wasn't her fault.

At one point, I explained to her that I try to stay neutral and objective while writing my books. She said, "I don't believe that. . . . And I think I have found a new friend."

I cannot be friends with Dianne Odell. I can try to understand what she did and write about it, but I cannot, as a father of three kids, comprehend a parent taking a child's life. Whether Mabel Molina murdered Dianne's children is not an issue for me. What matters is that Dianne could have (and should have) done something to keep her children alive. She had plenty of opportunity to make sure they lived—especially Baby Number Two and Baby Number Three.

A jury of her peers convicted Odell. She had every opportunity to tell her story to police. She chose not to. If she had told police that the children were stillborn, and stuck to that story, she would have likely never been prosecuted for murder. The statement she gave police was the state's only true piece of evidence against her. In the end, Dianne Odell's own words condemned her.

ACKNOWLEDGMENTS

MANY OF THE legal definitions in this book came from the Law.com Dictionary, a wonderful resource.

Sullivan County DA Steve Lungen's confidential secretary Susan Parks was extremely helpful to me in setting up interviews and collecting documents. All those e-mails and phone calls from me that Susan had to manage must have been a nuisance during what are, I'm sure, extremely hectic days in the DA's office. But Susan never once denied a request and was always timely in answering me. I can't thank her enough for everything she did to make this book what it is.

Diane Thomas, Bruce Weddle, DA Steve Lungen, Paul Hans, Robert Rowan, Tom Scileppi, and Roy Streever were all helpful in their own ways. I recall a trip Paul Hans and I took to Wal-Mart one cold winter afternoon in the Catskills to make some digital copies of photographs. I stood there at the machine for what was an hour at least, carefully copying each photograph, as Paul stood right beside me not wincing or complaining once. "Take your time," he kept saying. "Don't worry about it."

It is that simple, yet vital, help that allows me to produce these books. Without people like Paul, or Robert Rowan, who showed me all of the evidence and allowed me to take photographs and search through packet after packet of documentation and photographs, I could not do the work I do. Furthermore, although Robert and Paul don't show up all that much in the narrative, their work in the Odell case behind the scenes was matched by *none*.

Likewise, DA Steve Lungen assisted me in obtaining those documents I needed to make sure I got every aspect of the story—whether it helped his cause or not—correct. He should be commended for the integrity he showed.

The interview I conducted with Robert Sauerstein was extremely helpful for a number of reasons, and I gratefully wish to acknowledge Mr. Sauerstein for being so candid and honest. Odell's lawyer, Stephan Schick, was at first a bit apprehensive regarding granting me an interview. In the end, though, we spoke openly for a few hours one day. I appreciate the trust Mr. Schick put in me. That interview helped this book tremendously.

I need to thank Heather Yakin from the *Times Herald-Record* in Monticello, who was extremely helpful in familiarizing me with Sullivan County and how the case impacted the community. Her detailed answers to my many, many questions were helpful in different areas of the book.

Dr. Michael Baden's wonderfully written book *Dead Reckoning: The New Science of Catching Killers,* cowritten with Marion Roach, an outstanding author in her own right, was helpful to me in understanding the decomposition process. I quoted from it briefly in one section of the book. I thank both Dr. Baden and Marion Roach for writing such an important book.

Special thanks to Kensington editor-in-chief Michaela Hamilton, who helped me choose this story after weeks of e-mails discussing several different ideas. The undisputed queen of true crime, Michaela has been nothing but wonderful throughout my career, and I thank her for that. She was right when she told me, "Yes! That is the book you must do next."

My editor at Kensington, Johnny Crime: thanks for the book's title and support.

I need to acknowledge William Acosta, J.G., A.R., R.K. Also, Peter Miller, Kelly Skillen, and everyone else at PMA Literary & Film Management, Inc., who have helped me along my path in more ways than I can count.

Gregg Olsen, a superb author and journalist, has been a mentor of mine now for several years. Through that relationship, we have developed one of the most meaningful friendships I have ever had in my life. I thank Gregg for a lot of things, but most of all, for truly believing in me perhaps more than I believe in myself.

Of course, I need to thank Dianne Odell. I know she is going to have a problem with some of the material in this book. Although I did repeatedly tell her as we spoke that I was going to report every side of this story, I felt at times she thought I sympathized with her. I came as close as I could to reporting every possible angle. But I need to acknowledge that without the candid, exclusive interviews I conducted with Odell, I would have never written this book.

She spoke from her heart—that much I believe. She told me several times that the horror of what she recalls sometimes comes to her in fragments. I believe that. But I also believe those clusters of darkness she said she experienced during the three births in question were, in some way, the children screaming, and Odell trying to block out those screams.

Dianne Odell is a very intelligent, confident woman, who speaks with a remarkable intellectual sense. I was amazed at times by what she said—and, to be honest, did sympathize with her on occasion. But after we hung up, I had time to go back and listen to the tapes—think about what she had said, apply my better judgment to it all, and begin the process of trying to back up what she said through other interviews and documents. I realized there is a disturbed woman in Odell's head somewhere, struggling with the conscience of a woman with a heart and peaceful soul. I believe Miss Odell's abusive upbringing contributed greatly to her criminal life—and for that I am sorry. But thousands of abuse survivors never commit crimes and learn to deal with their lives.

I failed to thank an old friend, Kerry Williamson, in the acknowledgments of my previous books. It's been ten years since we spoke, but I need to acknowledge that without her direction many years ago, at a time when my soul was destitute and I was deciding what to do with my life—without her guidance, belief, and inspiration, I never would have pursued a career as an author. Thank you, Kerry, for everything you did for me—in many ways, you saved my life. Those virtues you instilled in me (and banged into my head week after week) are still with me today. I need you to know that—although I didn't believe it at the time—you were right about *everything*. The work we did together has had a profound effect on my entire life.

My family is always there to support my efforts: Thomas Phelps, Frank Phelps, Florence and Tom Borelli, Tyler, Markie and Meranda, the Fournier family, the Castellassi family, Mary and Frank Phelps, and, of course, my late brother, Mark Anthony Phelps Sr.

I dedicated this book to my wife. I watch her with our daughter and I feel there is no other mother on this planet who can match her love, parenting skills, tenderness, patience, and will. She is the most incredible mother. My children and I are lucky to have her in our lives.

Mathew Jr. and Jordon—thank you.

BONUS SECTION

Interview excerpts between
Dianne Odell and M. William Phelps,
along with part of Odell's confession to
Detectives Diane Thomas and Bruce Weddle

Please write to M. William Phelps at:
P.O. Box 3215
Vernon, CT 06066
or visit him and send e-mail at
www.mwilliamphelps.com

Exclusive Excerpts from Interviews M. William Phelps Conducted with Dianne Odell

October 7, 2004

Phelps: So what went on in [your] dad's home when you were there? Any type of abuse, emotional abuse, what?

Odell: He would get drunk and the one time that, I would say it was like two months after I moved back into the home (Odell was fifteen years old), he had gotten really, really drunk. What spurred the incident was that my mother came to visit a neighbor across the street. And she couldn't come to visit me. I asked my father if I could go over and see her.

Phelps: Okay. What happened next?

Odell: He told me no, and I had to sit there and literally (Odell begins crying here) watch my mother across the street. I knew she had something she wanted to tell me. And I couldn't leave. I knew if I did, when I came back from across the street, I would probably be picking my teeth up off the floor.

Phelps: So, you're pushing sixteen years old, and you finally go to live with your mother. Are you involved with boys at all by this point, you know, sexually active?

Odell: (Laughing) You have *got* to be kidding me! I couldn't even be involved in life, better yet, boys.

Phelps: Okay, okay, gotcha. So, sex, then, isn't something, you're saying, you are even thinking about at this time?

Odell: Even though it's occurring, it's not something I'm thinking about.

Phelps: "Occurring"? I don't follow. What do you mean "occurring"? You just said—

Odell: It's occurring *to* me.

Phelps: To you?

Odell: Yes.

Phelps: How so? What do you mean by that?

Odell: My father. He's raping me.

Phelps: Did your mother know about this?

Odell: Hell yes.

Phelps: She knew?

Odell: Oh yes. I had told her the first time. I had also told her when my half brother had raped me.

Phelps: How old were you when it started?

Odell: You mean when it started with my half brother, or my father?

Phelps: Dad?

Odell: I was fourteen years old.

Phelps: And with your half brother it was younger?

Odell: Maybe six or seven years old.

November 11, 2004

Phelps: How did you feel, keeping those dead babies in the house, in boxes, for all those years?

Odell: I am going to be totally blunt with you. I knew it was my secret. Okay. But I also knew that at some point or another, it was also my weapon.

Phelps: Meaning?

Odell: Meaning that my mother knew that they were there and I knew that they were there. She was horrified that I had not taken them and thrown them away, because that's what she had wanted done. She knew that at one point they would set me free. Because I would go to the police and I would explain everything to them. You know what I'm saying?

Phelps: Yeah, I guess. . . .

Odell: And they would be my proof. I never expected it to take on the connotation that it took on, where I would have to worry. . . . No one wanted to find out the truth, and that started with the police and went all the way down.

Phelps: So, you're living with [your] mom and you have this "secret" between you. Is it something that you're talking about with her?

Odell: When I tried to broach the subject, she would give me one of those looks as if to say, "We're not discussing that." I kept them, the babies, with me, in my room. I made sure she didn't have access to them because I didn't want them disappearing.

Phelps: Okay, I see, I see. . . .

Odell: I wanted them . . . I wanted people to understand the things that were done to me. I wanted them to see how far it could go. I wanted to let them know that my mother was as crazy as a bedbug and they (the dead children) were my proof. If I let them go, I would never see them again. I would never be able to lay them to rest properly. I would never have a grave site to go to. Because I knew what she had taken away from me. I didn't have the strength or the courage or the tenacity to break away from her. That's my ghost. My monster. The beast that I deal with every day.

Phelps: So, you're saying that was your downfall, then?

Odell: My downfall? I don't know. . . . That is the beast that I live with every day. I could not, for the life of me, break away from her to do what I needed to do.

There was one story Miss Odell told me when we met that first time at the Bedford Hills prison, which I had her repeat

*later on so I could get it on tape. I had originally planned
to include the story in the narrative, but after thinking
about it, I just found it too bizarre, too unbelievable, to include. Thus, I present it here in Odell's words, exactly the way
it was told to me.*

December 29, 2004

Odell: According to my mother, my grandmother was
an heir to a woman by the name of *Betsy Harris.* According to my mother, this woman was a very, very wealthy
woman and she had one-hundred-and-some-odd heirs
listed in the newspaper that they were looking for, because this woman had passed away and all these heirs
were listed in the newspaper. According to my mother,
my grandmother—her mother—was one of them.
Shortly after this was publicized in the newspaper,
there was a fire at City Hall that destroyed the copy of
the will, the deeds to the properties that this woman
owned. Now, the property was supposed to be from the
middle of Manhattan to the Battery . . . that this woman
owned.
Phelps: Okay . . .
Odell: The deeds and everything that was supposedly in her name, and all of the property that she had
owned, was destroyed in the fire. The Rockefellers,
J. P. Morgan, and two other families then bought the
property from the city for next to nothing and became
wealthy from it.
Phelps: Do you think this was one of the reasons why
your mother might have been bitter, or, rather, always
looking for a free ride, as you have told me many
times? And she thought that maybe she deserved
things in her life she didn't get because she got burned
(no pun intended) out of this inheritance?
Odell: Yes, that was the way she viewed things.

Phelps: So, that's a story, you want to make clear, that your *mother* told you? You don't believe it yourself, right?

Odell: You know, if there's any truth to it, it might be that she heard that story but it didn't involve my family at all. It's just a story, that she heard way back when. You know, and she latched on to it. . . . Somebody probably said something and she just kind of put this whole thing together. . . .

One footnote about this story: I had explained it to Richard Molina, Odell's brother, and asked him if he had ever heard it. You know, was it something that had become family lore throughout the years. Maybe a story family members joked about at Thanksgiving and Christmas. A conversation piece, in other words. Richard laughed. "Absolutely not," he said. "That is the most ridiculous thing I have ever heard. But it is typical of Dianne to say something like that—and I would bet she believes it, too. She was just like my mother."

**Excerpts from a Recorded Interview
Graham County Sheriff's Office Detectives
Diane Thomas and Bruce Weddle
conducted with Dianne Odell**

May 17, 2003:

Detective Thomas: When, at what point after a certain amount of time, did you think, I'm never going back [to that self-storage unit in Safford, Arizona, where the babies were found]? What was your thoughts on that? Did you ever think those babies would be found?

Odell: Deep down inside, I hoped they would be found.

Detective Thomas: Why's that?

Odell: Because I couldn't—I couldn't do things the way I wanted to; umm, after we had come back from Texas, my mother had gotten very sick on the ride back up, umm, she was diagnosed with congestive heart failure and because of this condition we pretty much had to stay put. Because she was under doctor's care and she was in and out of the hospital on numerous occasions for fluid buildup on her chest and in her lungs and in her legs and varying degrees of whatever this condition brings along with it and, umm, I could see my hope of getting back to Arizona fade. I didn't believe my mother would die as quickly as she did and pass away as quickly as she did, but it had always been my hope that after she had died, to go back to Arizona because she was gone. I was going to go ahead and bring all this into the open anyway.

Detective Thomas: What were you going to do?

Odell: Go to, gonna go to the police station and tell the police department that . . . to the police station, and tell them exactly what I'm telling you now.

Detective Weddle: (Later during the same interview) Can I ask you a question?

Odell: Sure.

Detective Weddle: You made the statement two or three times, you know, implied the wrongs you've done. What is it exactly in your mind you think you've done wrong?

Odell: Not having enough courage to stand up for those three children.

Detective Weddle: In what way?

Odell: And to . . . and enough to stand up to an overbearing person who was extremely judgmental, and constantly always being afraid of her critical opinion to bring these children into the world because they have—no matter who the father was or is—was always, always my intention to make them part of my family if they had survived.

Detective Weddle: Obviously, you like children.

Odell: Yes, I do.

Detective Weddle: You've got several of them of your own. That was my thought. What is it you think you've done wrong?

Odell: Not having enough courage to stand up for them.

Detective Weddle: Okay . . .

Detective Thomas: Dianne, you don't remember the sex of any of the babies?

Odell: No.

Detective Thomas: Do you remember the first baby's, from your rape, do you remember if that man was white, black or Hispanic?

Odell: No, I don't remember nothing about him.

Detective Thomas: How about the second baby? Do you remember what that man was, his race?

Odell: White.

Detective Thomas: Caucasian. And how about the third baby?

Odell: I believe he was white.

Detective Weddle: (Later) No one has forced you to be here, told you that you have to be here to give this statement?

Odell: Nope.

Detective Weddle: Are you feeling different now after giving the statement prior to, say, two hours ago before you gave it?

Odell: Relief.

Detective Weddle: That's good, I hope so. It's a relief for us, too. We appreciate you talking to us, we really do.

Odell: But I still need to get my affairs in order.

Detective Weddle: Sure you do, sure you do. That's okay. You're going to have time to do that. Like I said, we can't tell you, none of us know what is going to happen at this point.

Odell: Well, I have a good idea.

Detective Weddle: Well, I don't think it's going to be as, I don't know—I don't know, so don't wash yourself away until you find out what is going to happen.

Detective Thomas: What do you think is going to happen, Dianne? What should happen, which is what?

Odell: I think I should go to jail.

Detective Weddle: Why?

Odell: Because I don't, it's hard to live every day,

every day, knowing that you have to look at yourself in the mirror and know that you didn't have the courage or the tenacity to stand up for three little kids that, who needed a mother, and a life because if . . . if my mother hadn't been alive, none of this ever would have occurred.

MORE MUST-READ TRUE CRIME FROM

M. William Phelps